My Teacher is Gay

Peter van Maaren

Published by Peter van Maaren
Publishing partner: Paragon Publishing, Rothersthorpe
First published 2011
© Peter van Maaren

The rights of Peter van Maaren to be identified as the author of this work have been asserted by him in accordance with the Copyright, Designs and Patents Act of 1988.

All rights reserved; no part of this publication may be reproduced, stored in a retrieval system, or transmitted in any form or by any means, electronic, mechanical, photocopying, recording or otherwise without the prior written consent of the publisher or a licence permitting copying in the UK issued by the Copyright Licensing Agency Ltd, www.cla.co.uk

Translated by UvA Talen B.V., Amsterdam

Cover design: Maestro Design & Advertising

ISBN 978-1-907611-57-5

Book design, layout and production management by Into Print
www.intoprint.net

Printed and bound in UK and USA by Lightning Source

Foreword by Ahmed Aboutaleb

"Having two ears and one tongue, we should listen twice as much as we speak" - Turkish proverb.

I think that taking the time to really listen to one another helps us to take a very important step towards cultivating mutual understanding. The author of this book shares the same philosophy. He openly discussed his homosexuality in class with his students because he believed that it would clear a path and help ease suspicion and ignorance. Students today speak their minds; these are young people who refuse to be taken for fools and wish to be taken seriously. Peter van Maaren, former vocational school teacher, respects this and breaks the silence. It takes a lot of courage to do so, especially when you feel like you do not have the support of the school administration. I still hear far too many depressing stories about teachers who remain "in the closet" because management is afraid that talking about homosexuality will prompt a flood of undesirable reactions and encourage aggressive behavior on the part of the students. The way I see it, young people do not share the same view on certain subjects. The real issue is something very fundamental for a society comprising many different cultures, religions and lifestyles. The issue is young people learning at an early age to respect one another.

Obviously, parents, teachers and the individual's immediate surroundings play a significant role for starters. But the schools are part of this, too. Consequently, it is crucial that the learning environment is open and that management takes a firm stand against intolerance within the walls of the school. This book is special because it offers an engaging account of what goes on in extremely mixed classes taught by a homosexual teacher. It teaches us that safety at school also extends to students and teachers having the freedom to discuss topics including sexuality. All young people, not to mention teachers, regardless of their sexual orientation, deserve a safe learning environment in which they are given the utmost attention and support in order to do their very best.

Ideally, schools should be on the front lines in the fight against discrimination. I believe that this book firmly puts the subject back on the agenda.

Ahmed Aboutaleb,
2004 Amsterdam City Council Executive for Education and Diversity Policy
2009 Mayor of Rotterdam

Foreword by José Smits

This book explores the simmering tension between a homosexual teacher and his students, most of whom are ethnic minorities, at a vocational school. Tension already exists when he is initially tasked with bringing a new group of adolescents into line. Misunderstandings rooted in cultural differences arise, not to mention the fact that the school administration feels it would be best if Peter van Maaren kept his mouth shut about his sexual orientation in class.

Each time, the argument is that Turkish and Moroccan students and their parents would not be able to handle it. Why would you want to provoke them? What do other people have to do with it?

Luckily, Peter van Maaren pays little regard to these instructions. Instead, he tells his students about his homosexuality not only because it is relevant to him but also because it is relevant to his students. Actually, they are eager to talk about it; they are curious. He is a teacher who respects his students and wants to educate them and therefore has no use for silence.

In one chapter Van Maaren describes a student pulling a gun on him. The young man is a minority. What happens? Even in the absence of bloodshed the outcome is far from pleasant.

Reading this account, in which many of the anecdotes are upbeat and cheerful, I recognized a great deal. My own adolescence that was fraught with insecurity, being utterly confused about my homosexuality. If only I had had a teacher back then to make it all a little more manageable by broaching the subject. I could also really relate to the stories about people at work, for example; people who are fine with your being gay, no problem--that is, as long as nobody can tell, or runs the risk of being offended by it. The inclination to submit to those types of demands, too, is very familiar. Not wanting to offend anyone needlessly. But it sure is hard to breathe with your head buried in the sand…

In my job as a Member of Parliament I rarely encounter any issues related to gays; the belief is that they rarely crop up anymore. In my personal life I am not even acknowledged as a lesbian. Consequently, very little attention is paid to homosexuality in political policy. We think it is no longer an issue; at most, there is some concern about alleged growing intolerance among young people with Muslim backgrounds. Teachers at the vocational education level are less and less inclined to defend their orientation. Van Maaren worked at a vocational school and refused to accept a spineless attitude, neither from himself nor his coworkers. There is something heroic about that, even though it really should be a perfectly normal, everyday occurrence.

José Smits, Member of the Lower House of Dutch Parliament, Labor Party

Table of contents

Introduction 8
Aunt Trudy 9
Coming-Out : The Internship 10
Tarred and Feathered 14
A World Divided: Gay Versus Straight 15
Hey, Are You Some Kind of Queer? 16
The Mechanics of Being Sensible 18
The Moroccan Touch 20
The Lion's Den (Otherwise Known as the Classroom) 20
Eureka! 22
The Loose Screw (Otherwise Known as the School) 23
A Very Crunchy Christmas 25
Alpine Antics 26
Big Mother is watching me 27
Pearls before Swine 28
Not my Type 29
A Gay on a Mission 31
The Pink Triangle 33
Sexy Peter Pan Briefs 34
Rumors Spread Fast 35
The Staff Party 36
Sex Education 38
The Condom and the Broomstick 40
The Stricter the Better? 42
The School is Not a Prison 44
The Striptease 45
Like the Real Thing 46
The Difference Between an Apple and a Gun? 47
Tick Tock, Tick Tock 49
Punching Bag 50
The Wrong Team 51
Just What is That Man Doing? 54
AIDS? 54
Just One of the Students? 58
Amateur Wrestling 60
Incognito 61
The Creation Story 62
Test Stress 63
Auditing Duty 65
Sexual Assault Awareness 65
Because You Are Black 69
Human Pincushions 70

A Sense of Safety, Bijlmer Style	72
Act Normal	72
The Love Letter	73
The Evidence	76
Hunting Season	77
The Pink Problem	79
Communication problems	81
The Door and the Window	83
Cultural Confusion	86
Russian Roulette	87
The Alarm Gun	88
Turkish Shooting Gallery	89
Raging Hormones	90
Prayer Break	93
Veiled craftiness	95
The Hymen	96
Deadly Candy	100
Haram rolls	101
Racist?	103
Angels and Devils	104
Stifled	106
Do Not Touch	108
Am I An *Ibne*?	110
Locker Room Antics	111
Afghan Nymph	113
The Magic Finger	114
Sewn Up	117
Lactobacillus Acidophilus	119
The New Pink Closet	122
The Sexual Intimidation and Discrimination Committee	124
A 'Sporting' Assault	125
The Inappropriate Trip	127
Those Kinds of People	130
Accountability	130
The Mustache	132
I Buy, You Buy, He Buys	132
The Apology	134
Multicultural Survival	135
Family Ties	138
The Coming-Out Assistance Team	140
Razor Sharp	142
Thrown Out	144
The Attack	146
Banned	148

The Applause 150
Gay = Sex 152
The Islamic Closet 153
The Suicide 155
The Homophobe 157
Multicultural Spitting 159
Roller Coaster Room 161
Broken 162
Epilogue 164
Acknowledgement 167

Introduction

Coming out of the closet. That is the term used when homosexual men or women decide to tell the world that they are gay. Nowadays word has it that it has become much easier to come out; to "officially" announce that one has a different sexual identity than the majority of the population.

As of 1971 homosexuality has not been banned in the Netherlands. This ushered in an Age of Openness. The openness prompted many people to acknowledge their own feelings. They realized that they were not alone. The gay liberation movement played an important role, too. Information was provided in schools, support groups were organized, the government engaged in the dialogue and so forth. The individuals who were "out and proud" served as examples; they openly expressed their feelings. I came out of my personal closet at the age of 23.

The fact that society is continuously evolving and frozen in place is a good thing. Considerable progress was made during the 1980s and 1990s. Today, coming out of the closet seems to have become more difficult again due to the influence of groups that have been brought up differently on account of their personal, cultural and religious backgrounds.

The closeted individuals in these groups have a hard time coming out. This prompts the question whether these ancient, rusted-shut closets need to be broken open with force. Some gays who had already come out are scurrying back in for fear of negative reactions from ethnic minorities and social pressure from coworkers or bosses.

When the government provides a favorable and safe environment using legislation and active implementation, it creates opportunities to once again be who and what you are.

I wrote this book to illustrate what it was like for me, a gay teacher, to work in a vocational school based on my personal experiences with students and fellow faculty members. Some of the stories involve events that took place before I started teaching. I included these to try to show that the situations at work were not isolated events in terms of place let alone time.

The stories about my experiences at school are intended to illustrate how I felt students and coworkers reacted to my homosexual identity and the consequences associated with responding openly and freely to questions about it.

I became an example, not only for homosexual students but also for heterosexual students. Their opinions about gays changed from negative to positive. The events described took place over a period of 13 years, from 1986 until the end of 1999. I want to clearly explain what it was like working at a largely "white" school that transformed into a "black" school during the 1990s.

It should go without saying that this is an account of my way of doing things. This book is in no way intended as a gay teachers' manual or anything else along those lines.

Peter van Maaren

Aunt Trudy

The day is August 26th. The year is 1986. The train from rural Groningen up north was traveling to the urbanized conglomeration of Amsterdam, The Hague, Rotterdam and Utrecht known as the "Randstad" further down south and was moving slightly faster than one of those long American wagon trains heading to the promise of a better life. Me, I was heading to yet another job interview for a job in a vocational school for full-time and part-time students.

The milk run train would not pick up speed until we passed Zwolle and the frequent stops gave me plenty of time to once again consider the major step I was taking. My umbilical cord dragged along the tracks behind the train, still connected to the city where I was born. Groningen is a great college town with a huge party scene, along with a shortage of work, unfortunately.

The unemployment office unwittingly gave me a huge wake-up call when they announced their plan to register me as a factory worker. I believe the term they used was "production assistant." I had already done more than my share of production work in order to avoid long-term unemployment. Now I was being forced to apply for jobs far away from my beloved city. I mean, I had not completed my teacher training in a drunken haze only to end up on an assembly line, right? And if teaching is a calling, then you must heed it, right?

Plus, I had amassed a hefty student debt that I wanted to pay off. Then

Prime Minister Ruud Lubbers had already admonished out of work Holland that we would have to leave Aunt Trudy if we were serious about finding jobs. Aunt Trudy stood for one's hometown or place of residence where jobs were far and few in between. Not that I was the model abiding citizen type, mind you; however, I was 29 and determined to stand in front of a class as a teacher before my 30th birthday.

I kept going over a mock job interview in my head. Each time was different. Compulsively I tried to make sure I had an answer to every confrontational and tricky question. I had already had plenty of interviews that had gotten me nowhere. "What would you do if the students wanted to watch a video; what would you do with a student who was mouthing off; what would you do if the kids refused to work?" And then there was the predictable question: "What exactly is a 'national emancipation' day'?"

I had put that on my resume to show that I had not been sitting around twiddling my thumbs. Actually, it referred to my role in organizing "Roze Zaterdag" or "Pink Saturday" in Groningen; it was a gay pride event, but I left that out. Still, simply by including the item meant that I generally had to mention that I was gay. As it turned out, no school had a problem with my orientation. In fact, in several cases I was the best candidate. This made it all the more frustrating to hear time and time again that the position had been given to an existing faculty member, or that someone with a different type of qualification had been chosen.

And imagine my surprise when in several cases the exact same ad appeared in the classifieds a week later. Of course I called the school in question to demand an explanation. I wanted to know the real reason why, despite being the best candidate, I failed to get the job. Maybe it was a kind of paranoia, but I really started to suspect that the sexual need for male love was a critical factor in the rejection. I could only hope that it was not about to turn out the same way this time. I had to change trains in Amsterdam to reach my final destination. Another 15 minutes in the train to go. My stomach was already starting to churn. Nerves? Or was it the Danish and the accompanying cup of Groningen sludge also referred to as coffee?

It only got worse as soon as I stepped off the train. It was like my entire body was protesting the round of questioning that awaited. I would have preferred to stay cloistered in the train station bathroom, where I had changed into my interview clothes.

"Don't be such a drama queen," I chided myself, and headed off, directions in hand. I did not need them. The school was situated kitty-corner from the station. Anyone who could not find the building was unfit to teach. It was an old, red brick building. Huge and imposing. All of the little windows reminded me of my elementary school. I immediately had a good feeling about it.

I walked in and went to report to the secretary's office. On the way I saw all the students in the halls. The ruckus they made was heartwarming. It got even louder as I made my way up to the second floor. I encountered a group of boys roughhousing on the granite stairs. These were not polite, well-behaved students, but rowdy boys with attitude; the type of kids I had already gotten acquainted with during internships and orientations. I took a seat across from the human resource office at the end of the hall.

I had a view of a row of windows and doors, which concealed tremendous activity.

I sweated out the wait. A young woman dressed in a decidedly alternative style took a seat across from me. We greeted each other with a nod. Suddenly the door opened and I was motioned inside. As soon as I entered the room I was utterly relieved to see right away that my orientation would not stand in the way of landing this job. Seated pontifically at the table was a teacher from the Business department and I immediately suspected that he was gay. Not that he fit any stereotypical criteria; I simply sensed it. Later I would learn that the teacher in question had canvassed the department with my cover letter and photo in hand, announcing "male, 29, unmarried; has to be gay. We have to hire him for our department."

Positive discrimination?

Happily, the initial interview focused solely on my educational background and teaching experience. Okay, I had padded the work experience part of my resume somewhat. Normally, internships do not count as work experience, but I listed them anyway. They asked about it and I explained everything. I was pleased with how the interview went, the school and the faculty present during the interview. Back in Groningen all I could do was wait and see. In the meantime I decided to spruce up the wooden staircase in the house that I had just acquired. And sure enough, no sooner had I applied the last coat of paint, a letter from the school arrived. I tore open the envelope and my heart skipped a beat. I had a real job! And I was due to start the very next Monday.

Coming-Out: The Internship

After the euphoria that accompanied the realization that I now had an honest-to-goodness job came the anxiety. For starters because I had nowhere to live. All it took was a single telephone call to my friend Renze to fix that: he arranged a room in a squat on Conradstraat in Amsterdam. It was one of four enormous warehouses occupied by punks, artists, urban nomads and junkies. For the equivalent of seven euros a month I had a makeshift place all to myself.

The sanitary facilities for business of the number one variety amounted to a rusty tin can. Anything in the number two category had to be dealt with on another floor, which had a toilet. While that poor bathroom had managed to survive the heavy artillery fire of World War II, it was hardly fortified to withstand the relentless intestinal attacks from the dozens of tenants in the building.

But hey, I had a place to stay and from now on I was part of the early morning commuter crush hurrying off to work.

Even before my first day on the job I suddenly began doubting my qualifications and feared I was not adequately prepared to teach. I was also no longer convinced that I had sufficiently accepted my homosexual identity in order to be able to function as a teacher. During my training I had always been urgently cautioned against talking about it in work situations, despite my highly positive experiences with being open during my last internship.

Incidentally, that last internship had been at a school offering short vocational courses in the city of Groningen. The students had a reputation of being extremely difficult, which sounded like a challenge to me. I had an important objective in mind for my final internship: address my homosexuality in some way. It was the last opportunity to see whether I could handle being in a school as an openly gay individual, and how I would handle the reactions of the students with respect to this issue.

I opted for the part-time Mechanics program at the vocational school in question because the students were the least motivated. My aim was to get them interested in school by taking a really involved approach and employing a laid-back style of teaching with lots of humor. My first mistake was thinking that the initials of this type of school (KMBO) meant *katholiek middelbaar beroepsonderwijs* or Catholic secondary vocational education. Wrong. The K stood for *kort* or short. Still, I was pleased to discover that it was a Christian school, making it the ideal place to discuss homosexuality somehow, or so I thought. I figured if it could work here, it could work anywhere.

A door led from the street to the schoolyard. The school itself was a huge, old red brick building. The warm, old fashioned look of the place served to make me even more excited about being there. The kids loitering in the schoolyard wore leather jackets and had chain wallets. Many of them were not actually from the city; they lived in the surrounding villages. I could not have found a better place to pursue my goal. Was I a total masochist, or did I simply love a good challenge?

The first step was to get my supervisor's support. He had to know about my plan. Things got started with a meeting to discuss how we planned to spend the six months. I did not waste much time before announcing: "I am gay and I would really like to be open about it with the students during my appointment here. If it comes up, that is; not something out of the blue."

"Not a good idea," he told me. "The school board would never give me the approval to do that."

"Why not?" I said. "We can just see what happens at school and then tell the board, right?"

That certainly did not go over well with him, but I was young and determined, which meant that all of the ingredients for quietly going ahead with my plan were already in place.

Not that I intended to march into the classroom and announce: "Hi, my name is Peter and I am gay." This was something more suited to bringing up in response to a personal question, similar to the situation in which heterosexual teachers find themselves when asked, "Hey, teach, are you married?"

My initial contact with the boys in the Mechanics department was great. Working with them was a challenge from the very start. Having sat in on the intake interviews I already knew practically all of their names, which got things off to a good start. You should have seen their faces when I addressed the first kid by name. It established the necessary respect to go forward.

I often spent recess with the students outside in the courtyard, where they were more inclined to share personal stories as opposed to the classroom, where the lesson was the focal point. One day, about two months after I started, I was outside in the courtyard again, chatting with my students. Gradually, more kids from some of the other classes joined in and we were having a great time.

Someone asked, "Hey, Mr. Van Maaren, what exactly do you teach?"

"Social Studies," I replied. One of them said that they had a female teacher for this subject. She had talked to them about sex. Plus, it just so happened that they were expecting a visit in the next week from a representative from the COC to provide information about homosexuality. Founded in 1946, the COC is the oldest lesbian, gay, bisexual and transgender organization in the world. The acronym stands for *Cultuur en Ontspannings-Centrum* or Centre for Culture and Leisure. You can imagine the need for such a pseudonym.

The enthusiasm with which the young man shared this news led me to suspect that he might be gay. I took care not to let on, however; I was not about to orchestrate his coming out in front of the other students. "So what do you guys actually think about gay people?" I asked.

"Fine by me, as long as they stay away from my ass," someone called out. A number of the students nodded in agreement. The down-to-earth Groningen folks were far more positive than I had anticipated. Still, I wanted to test the bounds of their tolerance a bit further.

"What would you say if you found out your teacher was gay?" I asked. Everyone looked at me like I was crazy. "This is a Christian school, man! But still, if they were a good teacher, then why should we care, right?"

One of my students shot me a sideways glance and asked, "Why, are you queer yourself?"

After some hesitation, I replied "yes" and nervously awaited their reactions. "No way," they said. "What do you know? We had no clue!"

The boy who had mentioned the upcoming COC info session immediately asked, "Mr. Van Maaren, could you lead the session? I can ask our teacher."

"I will ask her myself when I see her in the teacher's lounge," I told him.

When I approached her about it she agreed instantly. And so the plan was made, the first talk about homosexuality at my own trainee post. But first I had to return to my own students, who had just heard my little courtyard confessional.

They had not seen it coming and now felt somewhat betrayed.

Obviously I blushed eight shades of crimson. It is impossible to feel at ease discussing this subject. You can never be sure how others will react. Hetero people never have to explain that they are married and have children. And chances are they will never have to hear things like: "Man, you are a sick pervert. We are going to beat you to a pulp. Hey guys, from now on we better make sure to put a cork in our ass. Or better yet swallow a fork before we come to class. That way he won't be able to get us."

As a gay man you always run the risk of being verbally attacked with these kinds of comments.

Luckily, this was not the case with my class.

"Why didn't you tell us before?" they asked.

I asked if they would like to know the preferences of the rest of the faculty. "No, man," they told me. They wore wedding rings; no mystery there. They wanted to know why I had not brought it up earlier.

"I was unsure, and I was worried about negative reactions," I said.

This opened the floodgates and I fielded one question after another about homosexuality and it quickly turned into a kind of sex ed class. I was happy that I had already given similar talks at the COC and at teacher's college. My supervisor, who was also part of the group, was amazed that everyone was so enthusiastic once the session ended. In fact, after the bell rang some of the students stayed to ask additional questions.

My supervisor's approval made it possible for me to continue to lead information sessions outside of my regular internship duties. In fact, the school even purchased books about homosexuality, some of which included extremely explicit drawings. The board had given their approval. I felt that the experience taught me that you should do what you think is important--and then wait and see what the consequences will be. So many people shy away from doing something either out of fear of negative reactions or even because they anticipate running into major problems. In college no one supported my openness. The professional didactician who evaluated my teaching style, as well as my sociology professor, both felt that gays should stay in the closet in order to get a teaching job. I was unable to change their minds and do away with their prejudices during my college years. With this final internship I wanted to prove to them that being open and taking care not to give students the idea that you are carrying around some big secret can have a positive effect.

Right before graduation, the two instructors gave me the same speech again.

"Peter, if you want to get a full-time teaching job you are going to have to shut up about your homosexuality. Otherwise you will be unemployed for life."

The internship at the vocational school in Groningen reinforced the idea that I could be myself as a teacher and as a gay individual. For me, it was an extremely significant experience. To hell with those professors, I thought at the time. Now I am truly prepared to really get to work!

Tarred and Feathered

I majored in Social Studies and Drawing at teacher college in Groningen. I am happy to report that I spent those years doing more than just drink heavily, party, draw nude women and try to learn something. We also had to earn bonus points for extra-curricular activities that contributed to the development of one's teaching skills. I chose an activity that I was good at both as a gay person and a storyteller: giving informational talks.

A friend's referral led to a phone call from a social worker in Boertange. She asked if I could give a presentation about homosexuality in the local community center to a group of problem kids. Apparently they were so obsessed with the subject that she felt it would be a good idea to have a "real" queer pay them a visit. I rarely spent time in the rural parts of the province, so I had no idea what I was getting into. Still, I thought it was promising that I had been invited in the first place. After a quick train ride I arrived at a farm, accompanied by my fellow classmate Henk. The building was ancient and there was not much left to destroy or deface. Inside was a group of 15 and 16 year olds. They did not want to go to school anymore, but they did not want to work either. I had already encountered such kids during my internship, so I was familiar with their tendency towards unruly and loud behavior. However, this group was something else. It felt like I was slipping and sliding on this sea of grease oozing from their pores and raging hormones. They were like a pack of hyenas, shouting and screeching. But even more shocking was the physical violence, how they kicked and hit each other. The boys smacked the girls, who gave it right back to them and at full force, too. It was mass chaos; it was like a war zone. I asked the woman in charge why they were so aggressive with each other.

"It's how they show their affection," she said, as if nothing could be more obvious. All I could do was pray they would not like me too much.

It was time to start the session. "Ladies and gentlemen, I have to tell you something: I AM GAY."

To my astonishment the room fell silent. The kids listened closely. After I finished telling my story they eagerly started asking questions. Questions that always come up during these gatherings.

"What did your parents say? Is your twin brother the same way? How do you guys do it? Don't you want to have kids? Who has to be the woman? You can do a woman from behind, too, right? Don't you want boobs? At least that way you would *look* like a chick!" I answered all of their questions like it was the most everyday thing in the world. Afterwards refreshments were served. The group stayed close to me in order to ask additional questions. It was touching to see them this way. And I was happy that they did not kill me as a way of expressing their affection. Henk and I left the building, satisfied and still in one piece.

A month later the same social worker called me to ask about organizing another info session. Kids in a neighboring village had heard about my visit and were also interested in hearing and seeing my presentation. We set a date. But then something unexpected happened. She phoned me again to explain that our plans had led to an outcry in the community. Parents had heard from their children that a couple of queers were planning on visiting their village to give a talk. They were so outraged that they had contacted the mayor, insisting that she put a stop to it. And like any good mayor dedicated to upholding the peace she decided to bar us from visiting the village.

The mayor in question also happened to be a communist: a true advocate of emancipation and freedom! Protector of the oppressed! But not just now.

I almost had the feeling that if I did show my face I would be tarred and feathered, or strapped to a cart and taken to the village square where I would be burned at the stake.

The next day I received another call from the Boertang group leader. The information session was scheduled to take place at the same address as before. Henk was unable to accompany this time and so I arrived all alone. I was completely overwhelmed by the reception. In addition to the kids from the other village, the kids from the original group were also waiting. Several of them had made drawings. While many people would be appalled by their art work, to me it was so sweet and so involved; they had really put a lot of effort into it. Plus, it was clear that the stories had made a considerable impression on them, given the amount of detail in their drawings.

This session, too, was a success. I am not sure whether the leader ended up in trouble for taking the initiative. After all, the kids had been forbidden from attending. It was just that none of them paid any attention to it. And thank goodness for that. This is how exactly teens are supposed to act: in defiance of their parents and authority figures. Personally I have good memories about the experience. It was yet another example of why you should not let these kids' appearance fool you. They may look like savages, but they very well may be sheep in wolves' clothing. The opposite may be true, too, of course, in which case you have to watch your step. These experiences helped reinforce my belief that kids can have a much more positive outlook on homosexuality than many adults think. In many cases the grown ups are far more intolerant. I decided to draw on these experiences in the future, including to defend my right to be who I am in the workplace. I would take a page from the heterosexual employee's book and act like my orientation was completely normal. After all, the less fuss you make about something the less fuss others are likely to make, too. In many cases this would prove to be true, but there also times when I would grossly misjudge people.

A World Divided: Gay Versus Straight

My own coming-out was not exactly what you would call ideal. I was 23 when I approached a good friend and, shaking with fear, told him that I was gay and that I was in love with him. He thanked me "for the compliment" but added that he was not "that way." The next day he scrawled on the chalkboard: "Peter is a big butt pirate." When I explained to the rest of the class (who were almost as shocked as I was) what prompted the message, it turned out that virtually nobody knew anything about homosexuality.

After my coming-out I was caught up in a whirlwind of new experiences. I could not have predicted the consequences that it would have for me personally. You dive into the deep end and everything starts moving at warp speed. Unsurprisingly, there is a risk that you will run into some pretty hefty obstacles. I should first point out that there was a positive side to it all. I no longer had to hide my feelings for another man. Finally I had the chance to re-live my adolescence. During my biological puberty I lived a lie, dating girls as dictated by the prevailing social standards. But I no longer wanted to adapt to those social standards. I could not do it anymore. I was out of the closet. There was no going back. Unfortunately, the social scene at the time was still very much divided into gay and straight. This took a while to sink in. I had to enter a different world in order to meet gays. The world of the COC and the gay bars.

My straight friends refused to go with me to those bars. They were not "that way." After coming out it turned out that no one in my extensive circle of friends was gay. So I divided my social life into time spent with the friends in straight bars and the friends in the queer scene. Obviously, I was living a pretty fragmented existence, even though I did not want to. But back then, dancing with another man in a straight bar was not done. In fact, it is still widely frowned upon. I found out the hard way when my boyfriend and I were thrown out of a club.

Not because of indecent behavior, but for dancing closely. The crowd thought it was great, but the bouncers did not appreciate it. From that moment on I thought that I could change the world for the better by teaching people about homosexuality and confronting them with it. Not through intentionally provocative actions, but simply by saying that you were gay, holding hands with your boyfriend or planting a kiss on him out of pure affection.

The threat of aggressive reactions meant that not all gay couples dared to do the same. Call me naive, but the way I saw it, if I acted like it was an everyday thing then everyone else around me would eventually accept it as an everyday thing, too.

My experiences with my straight friends taught me that social change was possible. At a birthday party I kissed a friend when handing him my gift. Everyone seemed shocked, until someone said, "Oh, he's gay. To him this is normal."

I performed this friendship ritual at every birthday gathering. I kissed the men and I kissed the women. A year later I noticed that everyone was greeting and congratulating each other this way. Sadly, despite the good connection the group eventually drifted apart.

I met more and more gay men, and obviously we preferred to meet in gay bars. My straight friends did not want to go to gay bars, and we gradually lost touch. They had been my friends all throughout college and we had had such great times together. But apparently gay men live one life and straight men live another, and never the twain shall meet.

Hey, Are You Some Kind of Queer?

It was Monday, my first day on the job. I arrived at work out of breath after rushing somewhat needlessly from the train with the rest of the commuter masses.

During my first week at the KMBO vocational school I had the opportunity to meet the other teachers from the various teams and disciplines. The school just so happened to have an entire team of social studies teachers. The group was incredibly close-knit and very much involved with one another. They really took me under their wing and felt totally comfortable talking to almost all of them whenever I had problems in the classroom. However, the team made a point of telling me that I should refrain from telling the students about my sexual orientation. They were worried that it might cause problems. Obviously, my plan was not to market myself as homosexual. The first order of the day was simply to survive and avoid making things more complicated than they already were.

Introducing myself to the technical teams unexpectedly went badly. It started with Wessel, the head of the Road Repairs and Roadworkers department. He informed me: "Social Studies is completely irrelevant to these kids and they are not interested in it. I will be curious to see whether anyone will even turn up for your class."

The importance assigned to the subject was painfully evident when I saw a copy of the schedule. In the Mechanics department the class was given either during the first or last two classes of the day. (I only taught 90-minute classes). You can imagine what the classroom looked like the first time I reported to teach: empty! When I reported to the senior teacher I was informed that I should understand that the kids were not about to come to school for such nonsense. He did not take any disciplinary action to suspend the students for chronic absenteeism. After four weeks I took my problem to the administration.

Pressure from the higher ups finally made the students report to class, but they made it clear that they were not going to make things easy for me. They thought I was a weirdo. I wore yellow suede boots and had a Groningen accent. To them I was a hick. They told the department head that I was a teacher who did not know anything. After all, I asked them questions instead of spoon-feeding them. I tried my best to ignore their rude comments and tried to use humor to get through to them. Despite my peculiar appearance and ways the students eventually started coming to class regularly. Six weeks into the term the Social Studies curriculum turned to the topic of sex. Obviously this was asking for trouble. It was also potentially the perfect moment for my coming out, the very thought of which caused me to break out In a cold sweat. I spent nights thinking about how I should approach the subject. If I should even approach it. How could I not when I had already learned to be open about it?

Plus, the students would immediately call my bluff. They were not stupid. Would I start sweating if I tried to evade the question? Would I turn beet red? The worst case scenario: would I lose all control if I were to choose honesty as the best policy?

But the classes proceeded more or less smoothly; that is if you do not count all the slang terms for sex organs mentioned in the textbook that were shouted out in class. I tried to relate the subject matter to the students' own lives as much as possible by asking lots of personal questions. If you took their word for it, these kids were going at it every day, and had the kind of physical attributes normally seen only in the likes of elephant bulls.

However, in addition to all the posturing and bragging it was possible to engage in a meaningful conversation. Such as what it was like on a first date with a girl, and how to kiss and that kind of thing. At 16 there is no shortage of curiosity, only the experience tends to be lacking. Which makes it nice to be able to talk about this sort of stuff, right? I managed to survive the first four chapters.

At the end of the fourth lesson I announced: "Guys, next week is chapter 5: Homosexuality. Please read it before you come to class."

A week later we were 10 minutes late getting started. I was sweating in places I did not know I even had sweat glands. "All right men, today we will be talking about homosexuality," I started.

This was met by a round of cursing, hollering and the type of comments that were all too familiar to me.

"Eww! Disgusting! Those are fudge packers, ass raiders, butt buddies, faggots!" they called out. I thought: *If I tell them now, they will kill me.*

"Hey, are you some kind of queer?" someone asked suddenly.

"Of course," I answered a little to hastily and without thinking. "Don't you know that this school only hires queers? All of the teachers here are gay. Surely you can tell, right?"

Aghast they stared out the window facing Wessel's office. The department head whose approach to preparing for class included poring over magazines filled with images of scantily clad men and women attempting to sate their carnal desires through a variety of physical acts. You could see the students thinking: *him, too?*

An intelligent boy quickly got the drift of what I was saying: "Hey, be honest, are you or aren't you?" I surrendered. "Yes, guys, I'm as queer as a three-dollar bill." I gazed at them, ready for the attack to commence.

The class fell silent for a moment, absorbing the information. Suddenly they started asking questions, all clamoring to be heard. "When did you know? What did your parents say? How do gays do it? Are you the man or the woman?" The class was abuzz with speculation. The questions went far beyond the information provided in the textbook and it unexpectedly turned out to be a fantastic lesson that covered everything.

I answered all of their questions unashamedly, which is how I always want my students to answer my questions. The cat was out of the bag and I had stopped sweating. I purposely described the bedroom stuff in generic terms; the specifics were nobody's business. And besides, it was better to leave some things to the imagination.

That was the end of that, or so I thought. They acted much more receptive to me, and there were no more rude comments. A week later, however, I arrived in class only to find everyone already seated. All of the boys were leaning back in their chairs with their feet propped against the edge of the table, legs apart. "Hey, guys," I said casually. "Nice view you're giving me there. Unfortunately it's a little too breezy for my liking, so do me a favor and put your legs back together and your feet on the ground."

To my surprise everyone obliged. Nothing seemed out of place. I was able to proceed with the lesson.

The Mechanics of Being Sensible

Two days later I was leading a class with the road repairs group when we were rudely interrupted by the school phone. Irritated, I picked up only to hear Wessel's raspy panting on the other end of the line: "Peter," he wheezed, "I have to speak to you in private right away."

Surprised, I asked: "Why, what's going on?"

"Perversities like queers and stuff!" he barked, perhaps louder than intended. He hung up before I could say anything in response.

It just so happened that the future road repairers I was teaching were the ones who I had just talked to about homosexuality. "Guys," I announced. "That was Wessel. He seems to have a problem with my inclination. Do you have any idea what's going on?"

They said that they had casually talked to Wessel about the lessons and me. They had been surprised by his overly angry reaction. He had told them that he was going to have a talk with the principal to do something about this filthiness.

The students shared this information with a look on their faces that said: *uh-oh, did we get you in trouble?*

Just then I saw Wessel, sweating and pale as a ghost, storm past the window, heading straight for the door to my classroom. Sensing that things were about to get really ugly, I ordered the students to leave.

"Hey!" he said. "You talked to our boys about you being gay. That is way out of line! I will not let a pervert like you teach my boys. What would people say? Before you know it we won't have any students left here."

I tried to explain, but he was not about to give me a chance. Instead, he was dead-set on reporting to the principal to air his grievances about me. "Be my guest," I said, walking out of the classroom.

The next day the principal informed me that the situation in the Mechanics department was untenable for me. Despite admitting that the department head's antics were unacceptable, he indicated that it would be best if I found something else to do at the school. My job was not on the line; instead, I would be transferred to a different department in order to keep the peace. I would still be able to teach in the Business department.

The principal then inquired as to whether I was interested in spending the other half of my day with the SVP groups. SVP stood for *schoolverlaterproject*, or drop-out project. After asking around some I learned that these were kids with serious to severe learning disabilities. Collectively they were classified as the VOS remedial and learning disabled group[1]. These also included kids with behavioral problems.

Classes would be held in the building where the job corps program had previously been stationed. The department had been absorbed by the vocational school as part of a merger. Incidentally, the name of the building was the poetic yet somewhat disturbing *De Klap van de Molenwiek*, which basically translates into The Loose Screw.

Mulling over the proposal, the thought of teaching a completely different type of student sounded like a challenge to me. Plus, the most important thing was that I would be able to continue working at the school. At the time I was genuinely scared that my sexual orientation would eventually get me fired, and that the instructors back in teacher's college would in fact be proven right.

Happily, this was not the case.

---

[1] VOS stood for Vorming, Oriëntatie en Schakelgroepen, or Education, Orientation and Transition Groups

The Moroccan Touch

After my coming-out in the Mechanics department it seemed wise to keep a low profile for a while. My orientation had already caused certain problems, and I did not want any more. I decided that the best course of action was to wait until I was offered a permanent contract.

Still, it turned out that I was not entirely in control. See, I failed to take a Moroccan student in one of my classes into consideration. One day a teacher was out sick and I was asked to sub for one of the Retail groups. No sweat; they were learning about perspective in order to draw store windows, which I had spent hours and hours practicing back in school myself.

Nevertheless, I was shaking in my boots after hearing from the faculty that this was a really difficult group of thoroughly unmotivated 16-year-old boys and girls. All white, too, aside from the one Moroccan boy. Some of the girls were wearing so much makeup you could imagine a tearful outburst would carve trenches down their cheeks. The trendy hairstyle of the time was to tease a ponytail high and spray it with practically an entire can of Aqua-Net to ensure that it would stay plastered vertically in place the entire day.

I quickly explained the assignment and the students got to work. Walking around the classroom, when I got to the Moroccan boy he looked at me sideways and started caressing my wrist with his finger. He continued to gaze at me with a look that said: *I've got your number, mister man.*

The hairs on the back of my neck stood up. *He know, he knows*, I thought, panic-stricken. But how the hell would he know that I might find such an overture appealing? The look in his eyes and his actions left me utterly confused.

If I was going to discuss my orientation with this group, I wanted to orchestrate any coming-out on my terms. Sensing that this kid knew the deal, I was afraid that he would not be able to keep quiet.

I ignored this sensation as best as I could and carried on helping the others. The boy continued to look at me with that same curious, piercing gaze throughout the entire lesson.

Of course, by the next day all of the students had found out. Students were just as good at spreading gossip as faculty.

I was just beginning to find out the hell that is the occupation of teaching. And out of all classes this would be the one to which I was assigned as their permanent Social Studies teacher.

The Lion's Den (Otherwise Known as the Classroom)

Paper airplanes and spitballs whizzed past my ears. The students from the Retail department were trashing the classroom. Nobody listened to what I was trying to teach. At one point I went over and opened the door. From my post I could send the airplanes back. Katrien, a fellow social studies teacher, walked by. "Everything okay with that group?" she asked.

"No problem," I said, and took aim with the next airplane. Katrien walked away, shaking her head. I noticed she was smiling.

Still at a point in my career where I believed that you needed to make friends with your students in order to get through to them, I made a pretty pathetic attempt at asserting my authority. "Stop that; quit it; behave yourselves," and so on. Of course, the big grin on my face effectively cancelled out any alleged authority, and the situation escalated. "That's enough, you guys!" is not what I said, although I came pretty close.

My whole "understanding" attitude and method of using humor to react left me utterly void of any authority. How could this be happening, I thought in desperation, that I had come to the class with such lofty ideals only to have the kids regard this as an act of hostility? I thought I was someone who had the courage to teach them something. Clearly they wanted to teach me a lesson. How could they make it thoroughly impossible for such a friendly, charming young green-eyed man to teach a class? What had I done to deserve this?

Was it only because I was the teacher? The educator as enemy?

At the same time I could not help but take it personally and think that it was <u>me</u> they were against. That is a lousy feeling. Obviously, I had a lot to learn, including how to take action and deal with conflict. And realize that this negative attitude was not personal. That testing was all part of being a student, and not just the multiple choice variety.

One day I reached my limit and I found that I could no longer tolerate this behavior. Once again the worst class had made a mess of the place and as the bell rang I was compelled to stand in front of the door, blocking their exit. It was now time to play cop, parent and janitor.

The group of boys that had made the biggest mess was intent on getting to the cafeteria. I was clearly in the way and, practically shoving his face against mine, one of them shouted, "Move it, asshole! We're on break!"

He did not touch me. It was like there was some unwritten code about this. To touch someone is to cross a certain line from which there is no return. I adhered to the code, too. Considering my less than musclebound build this was a good idea. It very well could have turned into a physical fight.

I said: "First clean up the mess, then everyone can go." The shouting was deafening. The sweat poured down my armpits all the way down between my butt cheeks. I refused to budge. They were not allowed to leave the room until they did as they were told. Wasn't the path of least resistance to simply dismiss the class and clean up everything by myself? Or leave the mess for a fellow faculty member to deal with?

A couple of girls were willing to clean up the mess in order to put an end to the stand-off and get on with their break. I refused to let them. I said that it was only fair that those who made the mess had to clean it up.

The five-minute stalemate ended and finally they tidied up the room. It felt like victory. I could actually set boundaries. The tough guys at the head of the line pushed me aside to get out the door. Three girls stayed behind and said, "Come on, Mr. Van Maaren, just get mad once in a while. You're way too nice to them. They totally walk all over you."

"I guess it isn't bad enough," I said. "I still don't really feel any real rage inside. But you're right. This has to stop. I hope that rage boils over soon." The look they gave me made it clear that they did not expect to see any changes anytime soon.

As I gathered my things while I got ready for a coffee break I thought about what they said. They were right, but I did not have enough experience to deal with this type of situation and to be myself, or to do what I really felt like doing.

Blocking the door was a baby step. But first I would have to figure out this job, gain more confidence. Dealing with aggression is a learning process. I was still convinced that I would somehow ruin everything for good if I would express my anger.

Eureka!

What the girls had said about me needing to get good and mad had a far greater impact on me than I saw at the time. Less than two weeks later the unthinkable happened. Something that a rookie teacher has no way of preparing for.

Once again, the classroom was a madhouse. First I gently tried to settle everyone down. Like always, my wimpy approach had no effect. Suddenly my blood began to boil. The girls' comments echoed in my mind like a repeating gun. *They totally walk all over you.*

"Dammit, that is enough! Henk, out! Get out of this classroom!" I shouted.

"But I didn't do anything!" he wailed in an Oscar-worthy performance.

"I don't care; get the hell out of here. NOW! I will talk to you after class!"

Fuming he stormed out of the room, slamming the door behind him for effect.

Now the entire class let me have it.

"Son of a bitch! He didn't do *nothing*!"

"I don't care. Everyone shut up right now and do your work!" I shouted, a little too loud. The worst of the anger had already subsided. Grumbling they turned to their assignment. Peace. Every now and then someone would give me a dirty look, but they kept quiet.

After the bell rang the students filed out of the class, the air thick with tension. I collected my papers and walked out into the hall. The brunt of my angry outburst was waiting.

"Motherfucker! You kicked me out for no reason! I didn't do nothing! Others made a bigger mess and more noise than me!" he shouted.

The rage I had previously felt flared back up. I shouted back just as loudly, "Listen, you little shit, I had every reason to throw you out! All that non-stop talking of yours, all that roaming around the room, you are constantly disrupting the class and enough is enough. You do it one more time and you can leave this school and forget about coming back!"

We stood there yelling back and forth for a few minutes. Then he turned away and walked off without another word. Now what have I done, I thought. I can forget about that kid. Defeated, I headed home. I lay awake most of the night. Tomorrow I would have to face the class again and the one kid was bound to be completely out of control.

I arrived at school the next day feeling completely shattered after a sleepless night.

The class was already in the cafeteria. All eyes were on me. There was muttering. I just knew they were talking about me. As I drank my coffee I focused all of my attention on my fellow faculty members and their conversations. But it did not help put me at ease.

When the bell rang everyone was already lined up outside the door. I opened it and everyone quietly filed into the room. Including yesterday's target. I calmly explained the situation.

"I was furious yesterday. From now on I expect you guys to just do your work so we do not have a repeat of what happened. Is that clear?"

I took their mumbling as a yes.

From that moment onwards I was able to go about my work without any further ado. Finally, after five months. The girls who had given me the pep talk about being more strict gave me a satisfied look.

The Loose Screw (Otherwise Known as the School)

It was November when I began teaching at the school. As I mentioned earlier, the school's name basically means The Loose Screw. Which is kind of funny. I mean, there were certainly many times when I felt like I had a screw loose, not to mention what I thought about my fellow faculty members or the administration. And the students, too, could act pretty screwed up sometimes.

Anyway, the trip by bus to my new workplace took only 10 minutes but it was a world away. Not only in terms of students but also in terms of faculty. Never before had I been greeted by such enthusiasm and involvement. My new coworkers all had this zaniness that apparently was required for working with kids with learning disabilities.

The school building provided the appropriate backdrop. Approaching the school, you could not help but think that it should have been razed years ago. It was a squat building, surrounded by grassy fields littered with dog crap. Around the back, by the entrance there was a schoolyard, the concrete squares cracked and upended by the tree roots underneath. Of course there was no money to fix this, but for some of the students with physical disabilities the tumbledown schoolyard was highly dangerous. If this was where they were supposed to have recess then the school might as well hire a dentist full-time to attend to all of the broken teeth. Of course, a lot of the students' teeth were already beyond disrepair, which had nothing to do with the jagged carpet of pavement outside the school.

To the left of the entrance was the shop room, where students were taught how to make functional and artistic products. Most of the finished items did not exactly match the teacher's example in terms of form or function, but at least it kept them busy and off the streets.

Directly across from the entrance was the door to the teacher's lounge, where Frits the janitor brewed the best coffee I had ever tasted in a public school or pretty much anywhere else for that matter. He was everyone's rock. Always willing to listen to all sorts of problems. A man who, in addition to his busy job, took the time to counsel faculty in the dimly lit lounge, and even do some odd-jobs on the side like custom building a surfboard.

The liberal atmosphere of the school made it perfectly acceptable for him to do so. His work did not suffer, although some teachers may have argued otherwise.

The teacher's lounge was where the faculty gathered. Four permanent teachers and four who also taught at the main building. The permanent staff comprised Harry, a slightly older, father figure type of man who patiently taught the kids how to repair and service bicycles; Jeanette, a young, energetic and cheerful teacher with the gift of gab who also taught one of the drop-out groups; Harmen, a calm mustachioed man who dealt with his drop-out group as if he were a social worker (later he would become our department head); Frieda, an arts and crafts teacher who put tremendous effort into getting the kids to produce the most amazing textile products; Wouter, a confident, blonde gym teacher with a good sense of humor; Arjan, a boyish, flirty gym teacher; and Hans, a quiet, timid young man who was also in charge of a drop-out group.

The team was led by Boukje, a fiery, responsible, energetic, driven and sometimes chaotic mother hen with a loud laugh and who really set the tone for the team and constantly came up with new work. She demanded 200% from herself and everyone on her team.

The gym teachers and I were the ones who bounced back and forth between the school's main building and our building, The Loose Screw.

The teacher's lounge was the place where we could sit and talk, sometimes with the students, and where we could vent, if necessary (in a respectful and responsible way, of course). Sometimes you just needed to get a break from the whining, which was like a broken record.

The lounge and the classrooms were furnished with stuff that had been retired years ago. The lounge had these low couches and tables painted brown, and everything was made of indestructible heavy wood. The classrooms had high, long tables of the same sturdy quality. The chairs had probably been taken down from the attic of the main building where they had been stored away on the off chance that some ragtag department may need them one day.

Due to a lack of funds or perhaps the faculty's lack of computer skills, all written material was produced on a typewriter. One typewriter, that is.

Agnes, our secretary, was in charge of the only computer in the entire building. In the late Eighties, computers were still a long way off from being introduced across the board in schools, and therefore not every teacher let alone student had access to one. Basically, everything still had that fun old-fashioned feel to it. The kind of place where it felt like anything was possible.

My job was to teach one of the drop-out groups. These were kids with a considerable number of learning and physical disabilities who actually had a chance here to acquire some skills. The idea was that this would make it easier for them to function in society. Even though the classes resembled occupational therapy more than anything else, I would soon discover that these kids were capable of doing so much. The job demanded an entirely different attitude and skills than dealing with the students in the main building required. Although I had not been trained to teach this type of group, I quickly learned to adapt my lessons to their workpace. They would prove to be patient and curious students.

The faculty had no problem whatsoever with expressing their frustrations with one another. Everyone pretty much spoke their mind, sometimes by poking fun and sometimes in a sarcastic way, but I appreciated the directness and sharp-wittedness.

Gossiping and backbiting, too, were all part of the exchanges. The gossip mostly concerned how well or poorly certain teachers were doing, how well or badly dressed someone was, and who was sleeping with whom. Like so many other workplaces, romances were inevitable in this type of environment where everyone was working so closely with one another, and little was done to keep these couplings a secret.

My training period lasted all of about an hour. That was how long it took to find out where the teaching materials were kept. I also received a list of the classes I was supposed to teach. Other than that, it was up to me to decide how I wanted to teach them.

"What is expected of me here in terms of teaching style?" I asked.

"Whatever you want. That's how everyone else does it. Find out which way works best for getting the students to understand something. There isn't a fixed way of doing things. A lot of times they can't remember what you told them five minutes ago," I was told.

The message was clear: figure it out yourself.

A Very Crunchy Christmas

At The Loose Screw I would learn to never think of anything as normal. Because things here simply were never normal. Take the preparations for the big annual Christmas party. We spent the entire day in the kitchen with the students making the food. It did not take long before everything was total chaos.

We could not turn our attention away for one minute. Not so much that we were worried about the place burning down, but more because we had to make sure that good hygiene was observed. Otherwise we were looking at mass food poisoning.

The cake was the first lesson in the importance of paying attention: we provided the students with the flour, sugar, butter and eggs. All they had to do was blend it into a smooth batter. However, I neglected to mention that you have to crack the eggs first and empty the contents into the mixing bowl. Before I knew it several of the students had mixed in the eggs--shells and all. The result was very crunchy to say the least.

This clearly taught me that you could not simply assume that these students understood something. This lesson would come in handy, also when dealing with other groups at our school. I warned the faculty in advance not to eat the cake unless they wanted to get their daily calcium requirement in an unorthodox manner.

The meal itself was not exactly entirely festive, either. Some students collapsed in epileptic fits while others vomited on the table, their brains having neglected to send a sort of "that's enough" warning signal to their bodies.

In the midst of all the activity an appropriate Christmas story was read aloud to get everyone in the holiday spirit. We had actually managed to find a well-known Dutch actor who was willing to do this for free. Sure enough, the experience would still pay off, providing him with enough material for some kind of bizarre performance piece.

Filled with cheer and covered with glitter, the students headed home with their

Christmas decorations. We were left with hours of clean-up.

It was also important to make sure that nobody had passed out during an epileptic fit and ended up covered in party detritus. It was quite a school, and quite a team.

Alpine Antics

After Christmas break everyone at school was running around all excited about the big annual snow camp outing. Just my luck. Ten fun-filled days on the slopes of Innsbruck. I was allowed to come along because of the skiing I had done during my internship in Switzerland. The plan was for me to supervise the skiing part of the trip.

The chosen chaperones were announced during a team meeting. However, it turned out that everyone had already selected their roommates in advance. As the new kid on the block I had no clue about the various "relationship processes" involved in these arrangements.

After a long and exhausting bus ride and a night's sleep it was time for me to demonstrate my skiing prowess. There I was, all bundled up, gathered at the top of the slope with a male coworker, a female skiing instructor, six boys and one girl.

Despite their mental limitations the kids were eager to learn how to ski. My coworker Wouter, who had full confidence in my abilities, called: "You go first, Peter!"

Off I went down the beginner hill with what ostensibly was an expert synergy of body, ski poles and skis. I managed to stay upright for about six feet before skidding on my stomach for the remaining 40 feet. It wasn't merely my skis and poles scattered on the hillside; more than anything, I'd been losing face there. Obviously, the kids were not the only ones in need of lessons!

Of course now Wouter had the opportunity to show the busty blonde ski instructor that he, mister jock, could do a much better job. From where I lay all I could do was watch in admiration as he gracefully zigzagged down the slope. Still, the kids skiing alongside him were more inclined to follow my example. Nearly every one of them disappeared in a flurry of snow, skis, poles, bodies and limbs. But I have to say, my opinion of them soon changed. As mixed-up as they could be sometimes they sure picked up skiing quickly. Utterly fearless, some of them were even zooming down the slopes already without falling. I was impressed.

After a few days of lessons I was able to chaperone by myself. Wouter and Frits were in charge of teaching the more intermediate students.

One night I wanted to take a short break from all the heavy-duty athletic activities and went back to the room, where I collapsed onto the bed, with my clothes on and all. I had the bottom bunk. Suddenly I was awakened by violent shaking that I could not immediately identify in my somnolent state.

For a moment I thought I was on a ship being tossed by raging waves. Then I realized that the noise was coming from two coworkers, who were pursuing their own after hours social agenda in the bed above me. This was accompanied by the kind of involuntary epileptic convulsions normally observed in our students.

Obviously the pair was unconcerned about the presence of someone else in the room. They must have been either highly intoxicated or highly aroused. I have to say, this is the last thing I would have expected from them. I fought the rising nausea, cringing in vicarious shame. I tunneled into my sleeping bag, trying to get away from this amplified display of primal urges as best as I could. I felt suffocated not only by the lack of oxygen in my sleeping bag but also by the loud asthmatic noises bombarding my ears from above.

To me, reading about heterosexual mating rituals or seeing them on TV had always been a big turn-off. But being exposed to it all against my will in this school trip bedroom setting was downright embarrassing.

I mentioned my unusual experience to Frits, the janitor. He shrugged it off, assuring me that this kind of thing was perfectly normal during these field trips. In fact, it was why the field trips had been organized in the first place, to give coworkers a chance to finally take care of business they couldn't get around to under other circumstances.

I could not help but think: what would one of my coworkers say if I was the one knocking boots with a man right next to another coworker who was presumably fast asleep? Pass the barf bag, I would guess.

I never brought up the event to the team for discussion. After all, how could I be the one to end this long-standing tradition?

Big Mother is Watching Me

The whole ski trip ended on an unpleasant note that would have certain repercussions back at The Loose Screw. At the outset of the homeward journey, a couple of loudmouths on the bus asked to be dropped off in Amsterdam once we got back to the Netherlands. "Then we can pick up some chicks!"

When I indicated that going to Amsterdam was not a problem but that I did not feel any particular need to "pick up some chicks," one of them shot me an accusatory look and demanded to know: "You aren't queer or something?" "Yes," I answered. "As a matter of fact I am gay."

When I arrived at school a week later, I saw the loudmouths from the bus sitting at the wooden tables under the coat hooks. As soon as they saw me they started chanting: "Fag-got, fag-got, fag-got!" Everyone could hear them.

I turned to face them, raised my arms, put on a brave face and announced, "So what?"

The silence was deafening. Several jaws dropped in astonishment. And that was that, or so I thought.

I made my way to Frits' coffee corner, where a couple of faculty members were already seated.

A curious hush fell over the room. Nobody mentioned the incident, and conversation resumed as if nothing had happened. With the ski trip shenanigans still fresh in my memory, I was not exactly eager to hear what they might have to say. It was only a matter of days until I was greeted one early morning upon arrival at school with the request from Wilma, who was the principal of the school at the time, to come see her for an important meeting. She had been put in charge of checking up on things at The Loose Screw.

I reported to her office at the end of the school day. She seemed nervous, and I sensed that she was not looking forward to our meeting. I suspected Boukje had told her to give me a talking to.

"Peter," she said. "Your coworkers are keeping tabs on you. You are new here, and you are not behaving as you are expected to. Your openness about your sexual orientation is not appreciated. Several faculty members have been eavesdropping outside your class to find out whether you are discussing your sexuality in class, too."

I knew that they did not have anything on me, because I did not find it necessary to discuss my homosexuality with my group and thus had not said anything "incriminating" to them.

After she finished her little speech I asked, "I would very much like to know how I am expected to act in certain situations. Upon returning from a field trip, during which the various members of faculty have enjoyed the opportunity to once again reinforce their intercollegiate relations to the optimum state, to find their partners waiting for them, then in the future will my partner be allowed to join the happy welcoming committee, or must he wait outside until we can discreetly leave together? As my fellow faculty members swap saliva with their reunited partners during a passionate kiss and warmly greet one another warmly with cries of "Oh darling, how I missed you so!" am I supposed to offer my partner my hand to shake, or may I, too, engage in a kiss?"

"Big Mother" was dumbfounded. She said, "I did not even think about that."

"Well, you should think about it," I said. "Let me know when you have figured it out. And please, if you have any questions, just ask me."

She never raised the subject again. I figured that that said more about my fellow faculty members than me. Still, this little "meeting" had an impact on me. No sooner had I left the building I ran into one of the students with Down syndrome. He was crying. Apparently he had just been punched by his dearest friend, a girl with Down syndrome. I put my arms around the shaking and blubbering boy. Suddenly I let go of him. Not because I cared about all of the saliva and snot ruining my clothes, but because I was keenly aware of my actions.

I was afraid that Big Mother and the rest of the faculty might misinterpret the situation. Of course my students had no reason whatsoever to worry about me, but what about the probing eyes of others? That could very well be justifiable cause for alarm.

Pearls before Swine

By now my first school year had come to an end. Completely exhausted, I was looking forward to summer vacation. You experience so much in such a year that your mind cannot even fully process it all. `

Out of my three part-time classes for retail assistants and sales personnel, about 25 students qualified to take the final exam. The results were cringe-worthy. Nobody passed.

This was not entirely due to their lack of motivation. It may also have had something to do with a teacher simply forgetting to assign them a certain project or paper. Then when one of the examiners asked them about it, the students looked like deer caught in headlights. Oops. This is why these students were doomed to faiAfter all, if the teachers are not motivated, what can you expect from the students?

Unsurprisingly, it was a tearful scene when the remedial teacher threw the exam results in the air in the middle of the Chinese restaurant and announced, "Okay, everyone failed. Let's eat."

Many students would not return; instead, they would enter the work world without any type of diploma. For most, the best they could hope for was a job as a cashier or a stock clerk in a grocery store.

I had never felt so frustrated in my life. What had become of my ideals? Why had I not managed to motivate everyone to earn their diploma? It could not solely be ascribed to the fact that the department had adopted the attitude that this part of the student body was not worth the effort. Some parents and teachers had already abandoned all hope. The parents practically never responded when I wanted to talk to them. Some of the faculty, too, said that it was not necessary to put too much energy into these students. They were written off as a lost cause.

The message was clear: education for this group was like pearls before swine. Of course they gave off the very same message. Was it a case of self-fulfilling prophecy? I took it personally. I had not done my best. Maybe I should have been tougher. Gotten on their case more. Tried to reach their parents more, even if the parents were not interested. It was right then and there that I swore to myself that I would do things differently - much differently - when the new term started in the fall.

Not My Type

Right before everyone left for the summer the Social Studies team had a faculty meeting. Like always there was way too much yakking and not enough actually being said. Like always I was overwhelmed by the amount of abbreviations used; it was like listening to people speaking in tongues. Even with a list of definitions in front of me it was impossible to follow these meetings. By the time you located the abbreviation on the list, read the definition and actually grasped what it meant, the speaker was already off on another cryptic tangent.

Therefore I decided to use the time more productively by writing a note to Wouter, my jock coworker who I had gotten to know a little better during the ski trip. He was seated at the other end of the table so I asked the teacher next to me to pass the note to him. The contents were faculty-related; specifically, who was hooking up with whom - and where. Just some good old fashioned philosophizing about the things that really matter in life.

He wrote back and passed the note back down the same line of teachers. I had to bite my tongue to keep from laughing out loud when I read the answer. I quickly wrote back. After four or so rounds of note-passing, our fellow staff members snapped. They had figured out that we were not discussing the matter at hand and we were promptly thrown out of the meeting for disruptive and subversive behavior. Great! It was a beautiful day outside and much too sunny to spend it sitting inside droning on about nothing important.

When we got outside Wouter announced, "Peter, I think you are a great guy. I really like you. But not in a sexual way!"

"Well, you know, Wouter," I intoned. "You aren't my type at all. You are way too white."

That was all it took. From that moment on I was no longer any type of threat. We were now free to have all the fun in the world together without fear of any misunderstandings about any possible perceived sexual tension.

I was used to this kind of reaction. I had already experienced something similar during a field trip to Kassel back when I was at teacher college. I was supposed to share a tent with two other students. During the drive to Kassel one of them casually informed me that plans had changed. There simply was not enough room in the tent for me. It was nice of them to wait until the last minute to figure that out.

Luckily I was able to make other arrangements. However, during the trip I found out that their tent was big enough to accommodate the two girls who spent every night with them. Of course, sleeping on top of one another certainly conserves space. A little bit of extra room to change positions was all they needed. Clearly, this would not have been possible or desirable with me around.

The same problem came up again during a later trip to Berlin. We were staying with a friend of one of the students in my class. Originally five of us were going to crash in a room that was only big enough to hold four mattresses. The two guys decided that there was not enough room for five people on four mattresses, and they wanted to put the fifth mattress (mine) in front of the door.

I had my own solution in mind. After a wild night in the gay bars of Berlin I arrived back at the room early one morning. My classmates were already fast asleep.

Silently I crept over to the guy in the middle and quickly patted down his legs, butt and torso. He stirred and moaned in a drowsy haze, "Peter, what the hell are you doing?"

"I'm looking for my pajamas, I think you're on top of them," I said.

He moved over a little and promptly fell back asleep. While this could be construed as a form of sexual harassment instead of a joke, it really was just a minor act of revenge without any ulterior motives. At least now I had enough room to lie down between them and I quickly fell asleep.

Several hours later the two guys in question awoke with a start, realizing that I had spent half the night wedged between them. My presence prompted them to hide in the bathroom to change.

Back in the Netherlands that night we had a huge party that everyone was expected to attend. After a few beers one of the homophobes came over to me.

"You know, Peter," he said. "That was really a great time in Kassel and
Berlin. You're a really cool guy. I like you! But not in a sexual way, of course!"

"Please. You're not my type at all," I answered.

He immediately hugged me and planted a kiss on my cheek. Then he linked his arm in mine and started reminiscing about our trip.

I refrained from mentioning their hurtful behavior and how they had rejected me. He had come around and that was enough. At the time it seemed like an isolated incident, but here I was seeing the same thing all over again with the PE teacher.

Do heterosexual men actually believe that they are so attractive to gay men that we have this tremendous need to jump their bones?

Apparently there is this widespread belief that all gays are programmed to want to rectally penetrate every single man out there. Regardless of each individual's personal appearance, sexual orientation, cultural background, and so on.

I wonder: are all of these heterosexual men intent on catching every single woman that passes within spitting distance of them? Regardless her looks like or her interests, as long as she qualifies as a potential lay?

Whatever the case may be, Wouter was sufficiently reassured, so much so that we would be roommates on future ski trips. He would undress in front of me, curl up in bed and close his eyes, all in my presence. I had never felt so respected and safe as I did around him.

A Gay on a Mission

The school year was now officially at an end. One of my fellow teachers simply swept everything on his desk into the trash. Another neatly filed all of the various papers and documents in binders, ready to start the summer vacation in an orderly fashion. Meanwhile, intake interviews were being conducted with the newly registered students for next year. To me, the end of the term felt like victory. I had actually survived. It had been a year of figuring out how to teach and how to relate to the students and faculty, and a year to learn that angry outbursts do not necessarily have to lead to ongoing aggression.

My coming-out played an important role in these developments. There was no going back now. The entire school was now aware that I was gay. It was like I had a huge scarlet G on my forehead. I was Peter, the gay one.

That was the consequence of the ease with which I shared my sexual preference. It was definitely not some kind of political statement. The same way that saying you are married or that you have a child is not some kind of political statement. I was not trying to be some missionary out to convert others, and I certainly was not trying to wage some Jehovah's Witness-type of campaign for the gay movement by putting my foot in the door and proselytizing.

Unfortunately, that was how certain faculty members saw it. I had been transferred to a different department on account of my threatening orientation, and my classes were being spied on under orders of a supervisor.

Still, I was not a pariah. I had not been cast out. In fact, I had lots of fun with everyone and had lots of stories about my experiences so far that had nothing to do with homosexuality. Stories that spiced up many a dull break, although some felt that my vocabulary, enriched with all manner of crude sayings and expletives, could use a little toning down.

You would think that the kids would take serious offense to having a gay teacher, but nothing could be further from the truth. They were open to receiving information about things that they knew little if anything about. This goes for more than just homosexuality, incidentally. They wanted to know everything about the things that they encountered in their daily lives. Of course they had been raised to believe that gays were disgusting perverts who you had to watch out for. However, getting to know me better and having the freedom to ask questions about this subject helped make it less threatening. By addressing these sorts of topics I was able to lengthen their attention span. It never lasted more than 15 minutes, and then I would simply resume the lesson at hand, which was a smart tactic in these double classes.

The adults turned out to be a little trickier. With them, the foreign and often negative association with homosexuality was often very much internalized. Some still regarded it as an unnatural form of sexuality. Not only that it was between men or between women, but that it was also constantly associated with sexual acts such as anal intercourse.

During this first year, I failed to convince anyone of the fact that it was an identity, just like heterosexuality. Likewise I failed to get them to see that gays are people just like them; we, too, need appreciation, love, relationships, trust, security and affection. It was unnatural, remember? So you did not talk about stuff like that. Well, maybe for a moment, but not too long, and not too often.

To some, a lot of what I said automatically had some homosexual connotation. "I went to a bar last weekend" meant: I went to a gay bar, where all sorts of disgusting things happen.

"I met a nice guy in my neighborhood" might provoke the response: "But he isn't like that." I did not use the word gay, and I did not say anything about what I might want to do with him. In fact, the guy was not gay, and I was not sexually attracted to him. But to say that I liked a man or a guy was interpreted as something sexual, even when I did not mean it that way. This was simply the way a lot of people thought.

Still, I was determined to provide information. Solicited or not, and in what I felt was a natural, unforced way. A lot of people thought that I was laying it on too thick, and some even regarded me as an agitator, but I did not see it that way. Actually, a lot of the time I did not really have any control over it. I simply talked about things that were going on in my personal life without having some elaborately prepared plan of attack in mind. It was not like I was out on the warpath armed with a briefcase stuffed with props and brochures and who knows what.

"You are still hung up on it, aren't you?" I was told from time to time.

"Hung up on what?" I would ask.

Inevitably the response would be: "Well, with the way you are."

"You are still hung up on the way you are," I would counter.

"What?"

"I mean, you keep talking about your wife, and your kids. You make a point of advertising your heterosexuality. So maybe you are still 'hung up on it'?"

This would effectively put an end to further discussion on the matter. Apparently you are no longer hung up on something when you no longer talk about it, when you stop bothering straight people about it, or making them uncomfortable with stories about your homosexual identity.

The Pink Triangle

The second school year had started. I still felt like it was a huge privilege to be a part of the VOS remedial and learning disabled group because it allowed me to carry out so many projects on my own. We produced the teaching materials ourselves. We had a fixed schedule in terms of hours, but during the actual lessons we could copy material or come up with what we felt was best suited to the individual student. As a result, it was not unusual to have five different methods being used in a class of 15 students.

After each of these intensive lessons I was able to catch my breath over a cup of coffee with Frits and my coworkers in the lounge. We had so much fun together that I was able to recharge and face the next round of classes.

To make the lessons even more appealing and varied, faculty members could sign up for courses at the start of every new school year. These were extracurricular sessions during which attention was paid to your shortcomings as a teacher. Those without the necessary teaching credentials could earn their social studies certificate this way and join the faculty. For the "real teachers" there were macramé, video production, airbrush, woodworking and origami classes. I took a week-long course in working with acrylic glass.

Like me, the rest of the faculty preferred to sign up for classes that lasted at least a week. Most of these classes were held far from school and home, so you would stay there for the duration. In other words, it was basically a paid vacation, room and board included. Plus, it was an opportunity to meet other teachers from schools all over the country. The perfect way to share useful information and gossip, all in an informal type of setting.

Of course, you were supposed to come back and apply what you learned. Unfortunately this was often a problem, since there was hardly ever any money in the school budget to buy the required machines or materials. Or only enough for cheap equipment, the use of which meant risking your life. Sometimes you would hear stories about other schools that had access to ample budgets and could buy top quality materials. It was maddening. For us, these courses were a waste of money sometimes. But at least we had a certificate to show for it.

In fact I was able to make good use of my acrylic glass skills. The plan was to spend a day working with it with the disabled students. We were going to make jewelry. The great thing about arts classes with the disabled kids was how they always came up with the weirdest things that in no way matched what I had in mind when originally drawing up the lesson plan. A fellow teacher who had taken the same course had already led an acrylic glass session and had enough materials left over for another class: all sorts of different colored acrylic glass, pins, hooks, glue and everything else needed to produce junk--albeit well-meaning junk, of course.

It was important for me to keep a close eye on everything in order to avoid ending up with students glued to each other, not to mention sawed-off limbs or other extremities. It was necessary to finish every lesson with a full inventory of both the supplies and the physical condition of the participants.

When it was time to start I heard the familiar cry of, "But what am I supposed to make, teacher?"

After I had provided a lengthy explanation as well as dozens of examples, they finally got to work. For my own personal project, I thought it would be fun to make a pink triangle pin to wear during the upcoming Gay Pride Week. However, I neglected to remember how students love copying everything the teacher does. Before I knew it, the entire class was busy making pink triangles. Once the fastener was attached, they could pin their handiwork to their shirts (or in some cases chests). They proudly walked around the school, showing off their artistry to everyone. It was a veritable junior gay and lesbian parade!

The normally understanding and fun-loving faculty members were not amused. They assumed that I had pulled this stunt on purpose to shake things up. The nerve of that guy!

I struggled to explain what had happened, but my attempts were in vain.

Still, it was pretty cool to see how proudly the students showed off their self-made brooches.

Sexy Peter Pan Briefs

Little was said about my homosexuality among the students in my drop-out project. They knew I was gay and that was enough. They did not have any problems with it, or perhaps they did not understand what it meant. One of them was Lucas, a boy who was tough and at times out of control. During one break I sat down at the table in the smoking room with a couple of kids from his group. All of the chairs were occupied when he showed up, which prompted Lucas to say, "Scoot back a little, teach. Then I can sit on your lap. I need to talk to Jolanda for a minute." I pushed my chair back a little and he sat down on my legs. Now he could talk freely to Jolanda, who was sitting across from me, without bumping me out of my seat. For him it was a completely logical and familiar move. After 10 minutes I was ready to go. I still needed to copy a few assignments for my next class. When I arrived at the office there were five or so teachers inside talking - until I walked in. The silence was deafening.

"Were you guys talking about me?" I asked, giving them my best Alice in Wonderland impression. No one said a word or looked up. I felt it was better to simply do an about-face and return to my classroom. Agnes, the secretary, chased after me and I was forced to stop.

"Listen, Peter, Lucas sitting on your lap? That's not okay. You mustn't allow it," she said.

"Why, there wasn't anything wrong with it, was there?" I asked. "He was casually sitting on my lap, talking to the other kids. Considering what a tough guy he is, it's good to see how familiar and non-threatening I am to him, right?" She disagreed and said that it was grist for the gossip mill. Imagine hearing something like that from the very same team of teachers who had already done so much hugging and cuddling not only with the students but also with each other. As a way of comforting someone, or calming them down in the event of a temper tantrum. It was as if I had lured Lucas onto my lap and sexually molested him. That whole "Big Mother is watching me" feeling came over me again. And it was downright ridiculous that they had ordered the secretary to tell me this. They did not have the guts to do it themselves. I went to my class and discussed the situation with the students. They did not understand what the fuss was all about.

A couple of months later, Lucas arrived late to class. Upon entering he tossed a present onto my desk without saying a word. I opened it and found, as promised by the writing on the box, a pair of "sexy Peter Pan briefs." He had bought them in Amsterdam just for me. "A late birthday present," he said.

The class stared at him in surprise, but nobody said anything. I thanked him and carried on with the lesson, without paying any further attention to the present.

After class, I showed the item, which was so miniscule it was practically invisible, to Frits the janitor. He thought it was hilarious but advised me to keep it a secret from the rest of the faculty. There had been more than enough gossip already. His motto was that there was no need to add any fuel to the fire.

I made it clear to the class that this type of gift giving was inappropriate. I did so simply to avoid the situation from escalating. They did not ask any questions about this.

Rumors Spread Fast

One of the surprises during the new school year was the hiring of an actual printer. Or to be more specific, "the repro man". His name was Freek and he was a fun-loving queer, and we got along great right from the start. The nice thing about Freek was that he plastered the walls of his printing room with posters of men. I do not know exactly why, but I usually have the best time when I am around other gay men. I guess it is like a group of women hanging out together: you get to catch up on the latest gossip, or listen to everyone talking about their love life.

I wanted to test Freek to see just how well he could keep a secret. The "secret" that I confided was entirely fabricated.

"Listen, Freek," I said in a semi-serious tone. "You won't believe what happened to me last night! Ron, the principal, called me at home to see if I could come over. He had something important to tell me. He said he couldn't tell me over the phone. I rushed to his house in Amsterdam-Zuid and rang the bell, utterly clueless about what I was in store for. Ron opened the door. There he stood, proud as could be, in a short robe, which was half open. You could totally see that he wasn't wearing anything underneath it. He grabbed my arm and pulled me inside, dragged me into the kitchen, ripped my clothes off, threw me face down onto the kitchen table, and had his way with me, so rough and clumsy. I couldn't help but think during his wild fit of passion that he had a rather unorthodox way of conducting an employee review. When he breathlessly indicated that the review was over, he grabbed a full tumbler of vodka and disappeared into the living room. I gathered up my torn clothes and tried to put them back on as best as I could. Without saying anything I left and went home. On the way I thought, 'Hmm, I bet I'll get that permanent contract now…'"

After I finished my story I cautioned him, "Listen, Freek, you can't tell this to anyone, okay?"

"No, of course not," he said, still in shock after what he had just heard. I left the print room to go teach my class. On the way I nearly collided with Wouter, the PE teacher. We said hi and I continued to class. I was curious to find out how fast my non-sensical story would make the rounds.

The next day I had to go to "The Loose Screw." My talkative coworker Jeanette made a beeline towards me. "Peter," she said. "Don't you have something to tell me?" I had already forgotten about my story from the day before and said, "No, I can't imagine what that might be."

"Of course you can," she said. "Didn't something unusual happen during the past few days?"

"No," I repeated. "I have no idea what you are talking about. And enough is enough; I have to get to work." Jeanette dropped it and left me alone.

At the end of the school day I left the building and walked to the bus stop. Suddenly I felt a hand on my shoulder. It was Wouter's.

"Hey, Peter," he said. "Do you have a second to walk with me to my car?"

I did. At the car he asked, "Did anything unusual happen?"

"What, now you, too?" I said. "Jeanette already asked me."

"Well, you can tell me anything, confidentially. I won't tell anyone. See, I talked to Freek yesterday and I heard the whole story." I burst into laughter and said, "Wouter, it was a made-up story. I wanted to test Freek to see whether he could keep his mouth shut. Apparently he can't."

"Well," said Wouter, "they already suspect that Ron is bisexual, so your story isn't entirely unbelievable. And he drinks like a fish. So it would be plausible for him, being permanently drunk, to pull something like this."

"Wouter, believe me," I said. "The story is fictional. Now you see just how fast this kind of nonsense gets spread around the school. Let's leave it at this." He accepted my explanation. And now I was sure that you could not tell anyone at this school anything "in confidence."

The Staff Party

A staff party was organized for all of the departments in October. The administrative employees decorated everything nicely with tables and chairs, umbrellas, candles and of course the indispensable cocktail peanuts. There was enough alcohol to float a cruise ship. And "true to tradition" it was no party for the administrative employees. Their job was to run around filling the thirsty faculty members' glasses, as if they were not part of the staff. To add insult to injury, they were also expected to clean up the mess after the party was over.

The nice thing about these parties was that it finally gave you a chance to get to know everyone better. Every day I saw plenty of colleagues in the main building, but we had numerous establishments scattered around various neighboring towns, too.

The party was a success, with lot of dancing and drinking. About halfway through the night they played a nice slow song and I enthusiastically grabbed Freek the "repro man" and we hit the dance floor. Of course we danced close, not to provoke anyone but simply because we liked it. We danced with female staff members all night, too. We had been dancing for a while when we noticed that we were the only ones left on the dance floor. Either nobody was in the mood to slow dance or maybe they were just too embarrassed.

Clearly, it was a case of the latter. I saw a few coworkers elbow their partners or each other, exchanging looks that said, "What is this?" or "Would you look at those two!"

As naive as I was, I really did not expect this to cause such a scene. Suddenly the vice-principal appeared out of nowhere and started dancing next to us. He said, "It's so great that you guys have the guts to do this! Good job!" As he sashayed away Boukje approached us.

"I'm going to dance next to you guys to show everyone that I completely support this," she whispered with a giggle. To emphasize her show of solidarity she stayed there for a little while, dancing along.

Freek and I looked at each other like "Since when did we ask our supervisors for approval and permission to dance together?" Nobody said anything to us about this during the party. Still, I can imagine that there was plenty of talk at the various school buildings the next day.

An unexpected advantage to all of this was that Freek and I would be able to dance together during subsequent staff parties without raising any eyebrows. We could not get any of the other male employees to join the fun; they preferred to stick to the ladies. And actually it also seemed like the whole controversy surrounding my openness was over. I was no longer openly criticized. I now felt like emancipation had been achieved.

I decided that with respect to future parties I would help the administrative employees with the decorations. I was already accustomed to making the decorations for the VOS remedial and learning disabled student parties, so why not the staff parties, too?

I did this in the evening at "The Loose Screw" because the rooms were bigger and thus better for painting my oversized props, which ranged from 9 to 12 square feet. I worked better at night, too. Frits would always stop by to check on my progress, and I would take coffee breaks with the Turkish cleaning crew, too. On rare occasions a student would come by to talk or discuss a personal problem. Those were always really special moments.

Sometimes the Construction & Woodwork department would provide the wooden frame, but usually it was Frits. My creative efforts produced an Egyptian backdrop with pyramids and the administrators as pharaohs; Hawaii; St. Peter's Square; and leafy *alberi debili,* a name I made up to describe highly unusual trees. The disabled students helped stick the leaves on.

The result was pretty wacky. It was thrown together quickly and the kids were high as kites on the glue fumes. They could not work without a protective mask for more than an hour and the leaf gluing was getting sloppier by the minute. But it was all about creativity, right?

Sex Education

Despite warnings from my fellow teachers about the dangers of giving sex education at your own school they still sent their students to the sessions.

The part-time groups were probably the worst. Generally speaking these students were extremely blunt. They were also quick to run their mouths without thinking first, which is something that really bothered a lot of teachers as well as the outreach representatives from the COC.

Given a choice, teachers would avoid these students like the plague. Luckily, however, there were enough who could get along with them. Obviously it is unpleasant and in fact downright insulting to have someone call out during a presentation, "Hey, dyke! Maybe you just need a big fat sausage! That'll cure ya!"

Getting angry would only give them the satisfaction of seeing you lose your cool. Their goal was to try to intimidate you.

They were also prone to shouting things like, "Hey you filthy faggot! We'll get you outside in the schoolyard!"

If they could see your fear, they would take things even further, and things could really get out of hand. On top of that, if the teacher was unable to get them in line, then you would have to take matters into your own hands. By the time I started teaching sex education at my school I had already been confronted by these students' behavior on many occasions. I tried to engage them by sharing exciting stories that related to their world. This aroused their interest and curiosity. Anyway, by then I was confident enough about my identity and exercising my authority. My first group was 20 or so 17-year-old masonry students. Rowdy and awkward in that oh so adolescent way. Great! I arrived in class wearing my leather jacket. I took it off and sat on the table.

"Guys," I said. "I'm hear talk about homosexuality."

"Hey, queer! You've got some nerve coming in here alone. We'll be waiting outside for you when you leave the school. And we'll beat you to a pulp."

"Well, as long as you do it nice and hard," I said. "That's the way I like it."

Everyone in the classroom started laughing and the tension evaporated. I could get on with my talk.

I always began with a personal anecdote about how it all started. Predictably, everyone was shocked when I mentioned that I started dreaming about guys at the age of seven. I remember the exact age because I always fantasized about St. Nicholas' helper, Black Peter, taking me to Spain.

But when I asked the students when they started thinking or fantasizing about girls, it was pretty much the same. I was not talking about sexual experiences, merely dreams and crushes. These came earlier in life for some and later for others. By consciously drawing a connection to their own sexuality they were able to relate to my story.

Nothing was taboo. Because they did not feel like they had to be embarrassed about anything the whole hush-hush vibe vanished. Now they finally had the chance to ask the questions that they never could at home.

We discussed more than just the mechanics of oral, vaginal and anal penetration and the meaning of passive versus active, but also the emotional aspects. What kind of feelings crop up? How do you relate to the other person? How do you deal with your insecurities? As a girl, how do you react when you are suddenly confronted with a glistening protruding object seeking, sometimes in a less than skillful way, an opening to enter? How quickly you have to determine whether your opening can accommodate that enlarged male object, your knowledge of which is most likely limited to stories, pictures and your brothers when they are asleep.

Boys, too, must learn what goes through a girl's mind. Be considerate of their feelings. And know what homosexuals experience and feel. Like all groups this one listened closely.

At one point I leaned forward a little and asked with a whisper, "You know what I like?" As if on cue everyone leaned forward in order to hear.

"My earlobe," I said after waiting a few seconds.

"Huh?! What do you mean, your earlobe?!" someone hollered.

"What is your most sensitive spot? Where do you get goose bumps when your girlfriend kisses you somewhere?" I asked.

Everyone volunteered an answer. They looked so tough and manly, but they were in fact quite sensitive.

During the first sex ed class a big burly kid parked himself on the windowsill, stretching out as casual as you please. I decided not to say anything. It would be a useless waste of time to try to get him to sit up and take a seat in a chair. Besides, my fellow teacher obviously did not regard his behavior as unusual. I had moved on to a new topic when all of a sudden he called out, "My neck. I get goose bumps when my girlfriend kisses me in my neck."

The entire class fell silent. The kid never said anything in class. He was chronically apathetic. They said he was simply counting the days until he would no longer be required by law to attend school.

I was proud of this moment. Everyone stuck around after class. They were not interested in the break. Long after I was done with my presentation they would come and sit with me in school, even though I was not their teacher. Obviously I was not a threat to this group. They liked me. Of course this encouraged me to keep being open.

At some point I was asked to give a presentation to the electrician group. I started out with the same story as during my previous presentations to the other groups. Suddenly one of the boys stood up and made a show of leaving.

"Why are you leaving?" I asked him.

"You aren't a real gay. You are just telling us some story. A real gay doesn't talk that openly about being gay. And besides, my religion is against gays."

It turned out that he belonged to a strict Dutch reformed church. The teacher tried to get him to stay but to no avail.

A year later I was about to give a talk to another group of future electricians. To my complete surprise the Dutch reformed kid walked in. The teacher explained that the boy had graduated in the meantime and had asked whether he could attend the talk. He had heard from friends that I would be giving the presentation again. I was delighted to hear it. I also felt proud that, despite his religious convictions, he wanted to hear my story. After class he said that he thought it was a good story and that he was pleased he could attend.

See, that is why you are there. If I had heeded the warnings from my coworkers and refrained from teaching sex ed I would have missed out on this experience.

The Condom and the Broomstick

Sex ed was never just about homosexuality. That would have been terribly one-dimensional and not very interesting to the heterosexual students, who I also wanted to be able to relate to my story. I regularly brought up safe sex, for example. Time and time again it turned out that students knew very little about sex and safe sex practices. I cannot count the times that I heard that you could not get pregnant the first time you had sex, and that "early withdrawal" (the Dutch expression translates to "leaving church before the choir sings") was an effective method of birth control.

Some parents feel that they are capable of teaching their kids about the birds and the bees and therefore the school does not need to cover the subject. In my experience, however, students are pretty much in the dark. At 16 their hormones are raging and it is imperative that they find the answers to their questions.

I made it clear that safe sex is for preventing not only pregnancy but also STDs: sexually transmitted diseases. The students were familiar mostly with gonorrhea and syphilis, but only the names; they did not know how to recognize the symptoms, or that these diseases could cause infertility or, if left untreated, actually prove fatal.

They knew nothing about Chlamydia or even AIDS. In their perception, only gays were susceptible to HIV and AIDS, not them. There was a tremendous amount of confusion about these diseases among the students at the end of the '80s and in the early '90s. I gathered data from the Dutch HIV Association in order to provide the students with the most reliable and accurate information possible. I received brochures and posters, and the area health authority (the GG&GD) provided information about STDs in various languages. An important part of the presentation was the difference between having AIDS and being HIV or seropositive.

Chlamydia was a venereal disease that actually caused them more distress because the symptoms were all but impossible to discern. They were also shocked by the fact that it was so easy to contract simply by having sex without a condom. To them, the worst part about it was that it could cause infertility in women. Even though they were currently concerned with not getting anyone pregnant, all of the students hoped to have children some day. Durex kindly supplied a huge stock of condoms for me to use in a demonstration during my talk and distribute afterwards.

One student asked if there was a difference between a gay and a straight condom. I went to my office and retrieved one of the condoms in my jacket for assessment.

I also often asked the students to show their condoms. In most cases, they looked pretty old and tattered. "Hmm, I guess you haven't had much sex during the past few months," I would say. "Or have you been having unsafe sex?" Usually they would fess up to the latter.

Back in those days I was dealing primarily with Dutch students. There were very few Muslim students. The Dutch viewed the condom as time-consuming and awkward. So why would you use one if you were all worked up and ready to go?

The Turkish and Moroccan students considered the condom an insult to their masculinity, even though they usually could not exactly say why. Apparently they had adopted this attitude based on comments made by other men. They also complained that condoms took away too much of the sensation, which is why you were better off not using them.

"So you don't want your girlfriend or your future wife to be able to have children?" I would ask.

"Oh, come on, teacher," they would respond. "I always do it with a clean girl."

"A Dutch girl or a Muslim girl?" I would ask.

"Teacher, please. A Dutch girl, of course. Doing it with a Muslim girl is *haram* [sinful]. A Dutch girl doesn't have to stay a virgin until she's married."

"Oh, so you're going to marry them?" I would ask.

"No way, teacher. They're whores. We aren't going to marry whores."

Most of the Retail students were girls. These types of comments usually caused the girls to lash out, and effectively shut the two or three Muslim boys up. Still, these boys were perennially popular with the girls. This is mostly due to the fact that they are extremely good-looking, with their shining brown eyes and black hair. They also happen to have an especially charming way with girls. Born Don Juans. Unsurprisingly, a lot of girls had a weakness for them.

Whenever I pulled out a condom from my personal stash, inevitably someone would ask: "Teacher, why do you always carry a condom?"

"Well, because I never know when I'm going to have sex with someone," I would explain.

"You don't just jump into bed with anyone, do you, teacher?" they would ask, somewhat taken aback.

"No, that's not my style," I said. "But I never know what might happen. And I want to be prepared for the unexpected. I don't want to have to try to find a drugstore at the last minute just to get condoms. Oh and by the way, gay condoms aren't available everywhere. So I always have to make sure I have a couple on me."

"A couple, teach? You only come once, right?" someone asked.

"And if you want to twice then you have to go back to the drugstore to buy a new one!" I replied. It did not matter whether there were Muslim girls present during a presentation or demonstration. I let one of the Muslim girls open the package, too. The key words were "with care." The most important thing to remember was not to use your teeth, which could end up damaging the condom and leave you up the creek. I did not ask the girl to help out of disrespect, but to allow her to feel a sense of equality. She did not have a problem with it. I had someone else remove the condom.

The entire class was invited to feel the difference in the structure of two types of condoms: the straight condom was thinner than the gay condom. I was obliged to point out that one was intended for vaginal and the other for anal intercourse. The next step was to example these "difficult" words, of course. Finally, I grabbed a broom and had someone unroll the condom over the broomstick.

If there were no further questions, we would proceed with our regular lesson. The entire talk did not have to take up more than 10 minutes. At our school the classes were 90 minutes, so it worked fine to have this kind of a little break. After one of these sex ed sessions everyone was wide awake and paying attention in class.

I never received any complaints from the Muslim students. The mood was always very relaxed, and there was no tittering. I could not help but notice how a Muslim girl was regarded with respect and looked at differently after one of these sessions.

Also, my talk usually left a couple of students worried, mostly about Chlamydia. I would simply give them the address for the GG&GD on the Groenburgwal in Amsterdam. The clinic offered free and anonymous testing for STDs, which was more appealing to the students than going to their family doctor. That was usually too big of a step, since their parents went to the same doctor.

I told the students that I got tested at the clinic every year, reminding them that men feel very little if any sign of Chlamydia. And because it is easy to catch, even if you practice safe sex. You can never be entirely risk-free.

One time I went to the GG&GD to get tested. I took a number, walked down the hall and took a seat in the waiting room, only to find myself next to one of my students, a young man from Ghana. His eyes widened in shock.

"Teacher! I'm only here because I wore gym shorts that were too tight," he stammered.

I set his mind at ease, telling him, "Listen, son, we're both here for the same reason. It's not a problem, and there's nothing to be ashamed of. Actually, it's a really good thing to get yourself tested. I wish more people would do what you are doing."

I was teaching the students in my own classes about STDs but I really wanted to reach the other departments, too. I decided to put up posters about STDs on bulletin boards in the cafeterias and in the halls. I left brochures in various languages on tables. Looking back, maybe I should have asked for permission first, because the posters and the brochures were gone by the next day. Initially I thought that the students had taken them, until one of the janitors informed me that the administrators had ordered the removal. When I asked about it, management denied it. Supposedly they were not even aware of the materials in the first place. I tried again a second and a third time, but by then I had run out of posters and brochures.

Obviously there is no place for sex education in our modern schools. Perhaps some members of the administration, board and faculty believe that 16 and 17 year olds do not have sex. And that the only thing kids do in their free time is homework.

When it came to sexuality, nothing had changed in Calvinist ethics over the past 50 years. Apparently I was a maverick, a libertine, or at least too far ahead of my time. And yet I was rarely criticized publicly.

The Stricter the Better?

The Retail students had acquired a bad reputation over the years. The girls (and several boys) went to school only one day a week, spending the rest of the time working in a store. Most of the girls were cashiers and the boys stocked shelves.

The law required them to go to school, but they were not happy about it. For them, it was an obligation that they could not get out of. Sometimes the full-time students sort of looked down on these kids. But their bad reputation had more to do with school attendance. Allegedly, not much was done in the way of dealing with bad behavior and absenteeism.

The parents, too, knew by now that very few of the students managed to finish the program, let alone pass. This was brought up several times during open house evenings designed to attract students. I was mortified. How could the faculty simply stand back and do nothing about this problem? Maybe it was due to the fact that most of them taught full-time and part-time students, and the latter were not a priority.

Now that I was able to be more strict in class, I felt that it was time to make the rules stricter, too. I was sick of the constant changes in attendance. This was not education, it was occupational therapy. Wasn't I being paid to motivate students and to help them earn a diploma? Given the total lack of rules, I could knock myself out doing my best but the results would always be non-existent or minimum at best. This is not how I wanted to spend the time leading up to my retirement.

After my first year I made an agreement with my fellow team members, most of whom were teaching full-time students, to draw up school rules for our groups. The teachers who worked with both groups did not see the point. They were opposed to the extra work: filling out classroom attendance books, calling parents, that sort of thing.

Actually it was also kind of stupid of me to ask them to do that. Twelve long months I had sat there twiddling my thumbs in one meeting after another. Not once did we talk about "my" students. When I did say anything about them I was met with surprised or mocking looks. Sometimes it seemed like I was the only one who ever taught these groups. Eventually, the first item on the meeting agenda would be the part-time program. This never took very long, so I could get out of there early.

In the end my coworkers agreed with the initiative to set rules. I think this was mainly due to the fact that the full-time students were going to be transferred to a different building anyway. So I did not have much interaction with them anymore.

To be honest, the forced separation worked out well for me. It allowed me to work with the remaining teachers on the part-time curriculum.

Ultimately, I decided to go ahead and draft some department rules for the students. Iris, who was older and was a veteran of the school, took the time to go over everything that I had written and make quite a few contributions of her own. The plan was to allow students only five absences a year, which was reasonable considering that they only attended school one day a week.

Every time they skipped school or acted out, a letter would be sent to their parents. After the first letter, the next offense would prompt a meeting with the parents. Not by phone, but in person, at the school. The direct contact was important to me, even though I would be forced to sacrifice my time in the evening for these parent-teacher meetings. In most cases, both parents worked.

In response to a third offense, a meeting would be called with the "vice-principal." Actually, I asked a department head to assume this role. The students did not know who it was; they would not have had any reason to. So basically we had a straw man, acting and dressing as a vice-principal. Suit and tie, rain or shine. My co-conspirator got a kick out of it.

The fourth offense meant a meeting with the alleged principal of the school. This time, I recruited the sector head of the Retail department. Her office was located near the cafeteria, and she seemed very important.

A fifth letter meant getting expelled. There would be no more meetings. Instead, the message was: thank you for your tuition fees and your brief participation in the program. We wish you all the best in finding either a new program in which to enroll or a job elsewhere. Yours truly, bla bla bla.

We not only expected the students to behave and to arrive on time, but we also expected them to start passing their tests from now on. If they failed, they would keep retaking them until they passed.

For us teachers, this meant that we would have to come up with multiple choice questions for every chapter. Plus, we would be obliged to keep an accurate attendance record for every class. I would check it at the end of the day, make calls to parents and write letters.

The first year was tough. Some faculty members refused to fill out the attendance books correctly. Their excuse was that it was too much work and did not make any difference anyway. "Screw them. I'm not getting paid to be a cop or a social worker. I'm a teacher," was one commonly heard statement.

Once the full-time students had been transferred to a separate building, however, the only teachers left were the ones working with part-time students. From then on, attendance records were kept more accurately, and I took care of the letters and meetings.

Usually I was on the phone as soon as someone was absent. And damned if it didn't work. Not right away, of course; the students still had the idea that the new zero tolerance policy would disintegrate sooner or later. But when the first student was on the verge of getting expelled, the mood shifted. They understood that we were serious.

Not one student received a fifth letter. In the past, they could skip school as much as they liked, with no repercussions. Now they were coming to school and on time for the most part. Their behavior had vastly improved, too. They were never going to be angels, but there was a huge, palpable difference compared to the old lawless days.

As a nice side effect the more intensive contact with students and parents resulted in more respect for the program and the faculty. This was also undeniably due to the fact that we showed our respect for the students.

I enjoyed putting my energy into a specific goal. And when things got too much I could let off steam by shouting, in fun or in all seriousness. The students were there to support me a little, too, right?

The School is Not a Prison

One day a student announced, "Mr. Van Maaren, I don't feel like doing any work today." I said, "I understand completely that you aren't in the mood. You may, if you feel it's necessary, be excused from class. The school is not a prison. It's up to you to decide what you do. Stay or go. It doesn't matter one bit to me. But just remember that your choice will have consequences. If you stay, I expect you to get to work. If you leave, I will write your parents a letter informing them of your absence."

"I don't want a letter," the girl exclaimed.

"Too bad," I said, "but your parents need to know that you weren't at school."

She looked at me with fearful eyes. "I'll get in big trouble at home."

"That's something you'll have to figure out with your parents," I told her.

Eventually she took her seat, unpacked her books and got to work. My point is that students should take responsibility for their actions. Earning their trust was always something that I thought was important. The prerequisites to do so were openness, honesty and clarity.

At the start of a new school year I was assigned a class with an entirely new group of students. I would start by saying, "Hi kids, I'm Peter, your new homeroom teacher. You know, right before I walked into class I suddenly got all nervous. I had butterflies in my stomach, and I could feel myself breaking into a light sweat. Do you guys feel like that too right now?"

"But how can that be?" someone called. "I mean, you're a teacher. You don't get nervous anymore!"

"Well, all of you are new to me. I don't know what I'm getting into. And it's all new to you guys, too, right? Not everybody here knows each other, right? Aren't you guys nervous?"

Several nodded. I added, "I'm always nervous whenever I have to stand up in front of a group, students or parents. It's some kind of stage fright, I think. It never goes away, I'm pretty sure."

It was important to show the students this vulnerability. They could see that you, the teacher, were also a mortal human being. There was some muttering among the students. Everything was fine. Class could start.

The Striptease

I tried to avoid using the word "must" around the students as much as possible. That verb seemed to activate the "big mouth" lobe of the brain. Sometimes it would prompt them to start talking back and do exactly the opposite of what you wanted them to do. Especially if you said it with a little too much authority and aggression. Their oh so delicate and sensitive souls simply could not handle that. However, I was convinced that I had to find a way to set clear boundaries. I wanted to instill values in a friendly rather than authoritarian way.

When the new students sat down at their desks I announced, "Welcome, ladies and gentlemen. I have a special tradition in my class. We start each class with a striptease. Each student can choose an article of clothing to remove. And some students can even choose two." I then shot a look at anyone sitting there with a jacket or hat on. This inevitably caused the students to exchange surprised looks. And they always managed to quickly get my drift.

But there was one time that someone did not quite grasp that I was talking about hats. I said to the guy slumped back in his chair, "I would like to kindly request that you remove your hat."

He stared at me angrily and announced, pointing at a Muslim girl, "If I have to take off my hat, then she has to take off her headscarf." I could feel my blood pressure sky-rocket and I informed him, "If you can bring me proof in writing that you are obliged to wear a hat on account of your religious convictions, and then you will be allowed to wear it. Until then, lose the hat."

He refused to budge. I was really on the verge of losing it. "Do you want to ruin this school year for both of us already, punk? Take off that hat and sit up straight!"

Grumbling he shifted in his seat and took off the hat. You could hear a pin drop in the room. When class ended I stopped him for a moment. I calmly explained my outburst. He accepted my explanation and left. I did not have any further trouble with him during the rest of the year. Or from anyone else for that matter. And I loved to be able to vent my aggression that way. Incidentally, sometimes you had to remind certain students about the dress code.

Another class rule was that no one was allowed to leave to use the bathroom. "This isn't a community center, is it?" I asked. "The breaks are long enough for you to take a long, leisurely visit to the bathroom. It's all about priorities, folks."

Sometimes a student faced an urgent bladder problem. I could tell by the pale face and panicky look that it could not wait. In that case I would make an exception. Of course you would then have to explain to the protesting class why one person was allowed to go when another had to wait. The kids loved to turn everything into a discussion.

Over the course of a school year you were tempted to stop enforcing a rule like that as strictly. But when you let one person go to the restroom, suddenly the entire class had to go, of course. And then you would have to immediately revoke the privilege. You gave these kids an inch and they would take a mile.

A lot of times it was the parents who would storm in, demanding an explanation.

"My son (or daughter) has the right to go to the bathroom. If he has to go, he has to go. And you cannot stop him!" they would say imperiously, knowing that I was not about to give in. Sometimes they would tell me stuff like, "My daughter suffers from chronic bladder infections." I heard this so many times you would think that I was teaching a class of incontinent 16-year olds. What, was I supposed to start changing diapers, too?

Calmly I would tell them, "Would you like to take over the class for me? I would love to see how you like it if everyone is constantly going in and out of the classroom. You want your kids to get an education, right? The break gives them more than enough time to attend to business."

Usually this speech would shut them up. And no one ever volunteered to take over a class.

Like the Real Thing

I wanted to instate a report in order to make the students with learning disabilities at the school feel like they were being taken seriously. These students were being trained for various tasks, but nothing was ever put on paper. It seemed important to me for them to receive something at the end of the school year to take home to show their parents and relatives. They took a lot of subjects during a given school year, and they were better at some than others. There were also subjects in which they could be tested, such as math, language and social studies. The tests were the same level administered to the Retail students. Of course it was difficult for them in the beginning. They were not accustomed to being expected to do anything. I recorded their test results in my daily planner. The report indicated whether the work was good, fair or poor. The report also included a written assessment of the student's motivation. In order to make everything look official, the finishing touch was a stamp bearing the principal's signature. Did the students take it seriously? They sure did! They worked like crazy. Some of them lost sleep over it. And the results were on par with the students at the lowest level in the Retail program.

My official presentation of the reports, complete with plastic sleeve, included a speech to the class. Each student was called forward to accept their report, and some even dressed up for the occasion. They accepted their official report looking as presentable as could be. Of course I had been making a huge deal about how important these reports were for weeks.

The report was later introduced for all of the groups. It was a lot of work, but it was definitely worth the effort, for students and faculty alike. This gave us a way to brief a teacher on a student in the event of a transfer, and we could also provide other institutions progress updates.

For example, one time a couple and a psychologist came to the school to discuss one of my students. The foster parents felt that the girl in question should be institutionalized because she was functioning at an unacceptably low level and could not retain anything. At home apparently she was a disaster. Everything had to be explained to her dozens of times, and even then she never managed to do anything right. This struck me as odd; she was the best student when it came to test results, and now I had a way to prove it.

The psychologist and the parents were astonished by her test results. Happily, the girl was not sent to an institution; she was moved to a different foster home. At this point you might be thinking to yourself, "But aren't reports a perfectly normal part of school?" Yes, but apparently different standards and methods applied to disabled students. Consequently, their efforts were never recorded in any standardized way in the past. Now they were. Upon hearing the result, Boukje was pleased that my record-keeping was now paying off.

The Difference Between an Apple and a Gun?

Even though you might think you have everything under control for the students, someone may go astray from time to time. One situation proved very telling in terms of how the school dealt with certain issues.

There were several boys in the Salesclerk group. Boys were in the minority in the Retail program. Two of them, Mike and Raymond, worked in the same supermarket. One night before closing, Mike stole the key to the warehouse. He had cooked up a plan to go back to the warehouse later that night to steal a huge amount of cigarettes. However, the teenager's plan had some serious flaws.

His classmate and fellow employee Raymond had seen him steal the key and went to stakeout the warehouse. Mike was too clueless and convinced of his plan to notice. He tiptoed to the door, used the stolen key to open the warehouse, and stole a ton of cigarettes.

Once he was back outside, he realized that although he had planned the robbery, he had made no arrangements for transporting the haul. The only solution he could come up with was to first dump all of the cartons in the shrubs and high tail it home or find some friends to help with the transport.

Meanwhile, Raymond observed Mike's bumbling heist. He was mobile, and as soon as Mike was gone he loaded up everything and took off. The next day when the manager discovered the theft, Raymond had no problem ratting out Mike to his boss, fingering him for the pilfered key and the stolen cigarettes. He wisely neglected to mention his role in the caper.

The police arrested Mike the same day. The poor kid must have really had a shock when he came back to the scene and found his entire stash gone. Who could have done it? Unable to keep from bragging to his friends, Raymond talked and Mike found out a few days later. It was also painfully obvious who was standing around handing out free cigarettes to win friends.

The police were forced to let the thief, Mike, go due to lack of evidence. There were no witnesses to the robbery. To the key theft, yes, but that did not prove anything.

Mike returned to school. Filled with rage towards Raymond, who had ratted him out, Mike treated him to a royal ass-kicking in the schoolyard. Stupid. Very stupid. He should have attacked Raymond outside of school. After all, we had a no fighting rule. And thus he was suspended indefinitely from school. No cigarettes, no education. Two strikes and you are out. And of course the "victim" Raymond was allowed to stay in school. With cigarettes and education. Did the faculty understand what was going on here? Well, Raymond certainly did.

After Mike was suspended, the key thief and his friends unleashed a campaign of terror against Raymond, who even claimed being shot with air guns on the train.

One day someone called out in class that Raymond was carrying a gun. I asked him, "Raymond, I heard you have a gun on you. Is that true?"

"Yes, Mr. Van Maaren. A real nice one," he answered.

"Let me take a look at that gun."

He took it out of his bag and handed it to me. I thought it looked very real, and I said, "You know that this is not allowed at school. I am going to confiscate it."

He protested angrily and cried, "Give it back, it's mine!"

Of course I did not give him the gun back, but it was really bothering me during the break. The cartridge in the gun was empty, and therefore not suitable to fire. But it was still a weapon that could be used for threatening someone, and basically you could put bullets in it. So what was I supposed to do about this?

I hoped that central management would know the protocol for dealing with students or faculty in possession of a weapon. I called the head office and Edwin, one of the administrators, answered. He was just as unsure about what to do. "This has never happened before," he said. "I have to ask the other administrators. It just so happens we're in a meeting right now. I'll call you back in 10 minutes."

After 15 or so minutes I received the astonishing news that I was to return the gun to the student. According to the school rules, teachers were obliged to return any confiscated property to students at the end of the school day. The rules did not specify the type of items to which this policy applied.

Obviously the pencil-pushers in Zoetermeer naively assumed that confiscated articles would be limited to apples, candy, Walkman players or hats. To our management, a gun fell into the same category. They were not the ones in front of the class. Not that I was afraid to work with these kids, but I did know that something had to change at school. This was the late Eighties. Violence and the use of weapons had not become commonplace.

Management wanted to keep the incident quiet for fear of giving parents the wrong impression. I called Raymond's father and asked if he was aware that his son was walking around with a gun. He knew nothing about it. However, he was aware of the problems that Raymond was having with the boys from the city. He did not know what exactly, but he agreed that this type of self protection was taking it to an extreme.

I asked him to search Raymond's room to see if he could find any bullets. He called back an hour later. "No bullets," he said, "but I wonder if the school is missing three top of the line portable cash registers with register tape?"

I had no idea what that was all about, and I promised to get back to him. I asked a fellow teacher whether we were supposed to have that kind of high tech equipment.

Sure enough, we were. He searched the closet where the machines were supposed to be kept and came up empty. The sign up sheet for borrowing them to use in class, too, was blank. The little jerk had decided to express his thanks for not being expelled by stealing from us.

That was it. I called the father back and asked him to tell his son to report to me, and to bring the registers. And sure enough, at the end of the day Raymond appeared with the stolen property. I chewed him out and suspended him indefinitely. The faculty decided that he should be expelled. The father understood our decision. However, it meant that both Raymond and Mike would have a hard time finding another school to accept them.

Nowadays these types of expulsions no longer happen. You have to bend over backwards to get a student transferred. Students are not allowed to just leave school without a diploma. Unfortunately, things were different back in those days.

Tick Tock, Tick Tock

As a teacher you have to be constantly aware of what the students are doing. At my school you often had a group of 15 to 25 students ranging in age from 16 to 25, each with his or her specific personality. Generally speaking, this was not a problem. A lot of problems were resolved without any special intervention. But there are times when you have to completely trust your gut or intuition.

During one class this heavyset kid would not stop talking to his neighbor. Finally, I got sick of it and I said, "Nick, turn around and be quiet. I would like to continue with today's lesson." Within 10 minutes he was turned around again, talking to the guy behind him.

"Okay, Nick, that's it. Pack up your stuff and get out of here. I've had it!" I fumed.

"I'm not leaving," he said. "I didn't do anything."

"I want you out of here--now!" I spat.

"I'm not leaving."

"Fine. If you won't leave the class, then I'm not going to teach," I said, somewhat more calmly. "I want everyone to keep quiet now. I'm not going to continue with the lesson until he leaves."

I leaned against my desk and surveyed the class, clicking my tongue to imitate the sound of a loudly ticking clock.

Deathly silence.

"Get your ass outta here," one of the other students said to the boy. "We want to have class."

After this sentiment was repeated several times, a couple of students stood up and started walking towards the obstinate Nick. He could see what was coming. He quickly got up, packed his things and left.

"Report to me after class," I called after him, speaking to his broad back.

He looked over his shoulder and growled something that I took as a yes.

"How come you didn't throw him out?" a couple of students wanted to know.

"As a teacher I'm not allowed to grab a student to throw him out of the classroom," I replied. "If I do that, I'll get in trouble. So I'm not about to try that."

The class was confounded. Surely you should be able to grab a student by their collar?

Punching Bag

I arrived our building at 12:30, unaware of anything out of the ordinary. To my surprise there was no fabulous coffee, and the faculty was in an uproar. Not because of the lack of coffee, but on account of a violent incident at the school.

A teacher had banned two troublemakers from class for the rest of the day. As a teacher, that really is a last resort when nothing else works. The boys went to Frits and demanded coffee. He refused, pointing out that break time was over, and therefore they could not have any. He told them that they would have to wait until the next break at 12:15. He was not aware that the teacher had ordered them to leave the premises.

The boys stormed over to the smoking lounge, at the back of the building. At some point Frits' keen janitor ears heard a ruckus going on. He quickly went to see where the noise was coming from. He was shocked to find the two fellows passing time by throwing chairs around. What did they care; the chairs did not belong to them, and they had a lot of energy to burn off. And of course none of the teachers in the adjacent classrooms heard anything. Could it be that the din in their own classes drowned out the commotion in the smoking lounge?

"That's it, you two are out of here," Frits said. Like any totally unmotivated young men worth their salt, they ignored him and continued what they were doing. Frits had now had enough and grabbed one of the boys by his arm to use slight force to remove him from the school, hoping that the other would follow him.

But his actions prompted an unexpected response.

The other grabbed Frits from behind, pinning Frits' elbow to his back and leaving him unable to defend himself. The first kid, who Frits had grabbed by the arm, was now free to attack him. After delivering several blows to his stomach and face, the other kid let him go and Frits collapsed on the floor.

You would think that seeing their victim on the ground, defenseless and bleeding, would be enough for them to leave him there and exit the school but no. First they had to kick Frits until it appeared that the very life had been beaten out of him. Not one single teacher left their class to intervene.

Eventually the attackers left. It was only after the noise had died down with the exception of Frits' agonized groans that the faculty came to his aid. His face was entirely unrecognizable. Even though the swelling was so bad that his head had swollen to twice the normal size he refused to go to the hospital.

Boukje was concerned and stayed with him. After several nerve-wracking hours, it was obvious that he needed to go to the emergency room. He was diagnosed with a severe concussion. It was crucial to keep Frits awake. If he fell asleep, there was the risk that he might slip into a coma. The doctors would be able to tell if there were additional complications after 24 hours.

Of course the kids were expelled. Frits was advised not to take any legal action against them. In fact, management felt that Frits was partially to blame for the entire incident. After all, he was the one who first laid hands on the one boy. That could be seen as provocation.

Consequently, management also did not feel the need to see how Frits was doing. Frits did not pursue the matter. He simply decided from that point on never to take action again, and to let the teachers clean up their own mess. Even if the school was under siege, he had learned his lesson.

I do not know what hurt more, the violence inflicted by the boys, or the lack of solidarity and support from the faculty and administrators. After he had recovered, Frits got the former janitor's baseball bat out of storage. Not to attack anyone, but to be able to defend himself the next time any of the kids lashed out violently.

The cafeteria was where you learned the most.

The Wrong Team

During my third year, the decision was made that it was time to integrate the student body; that is, the students with learning and mental disabilities would be confronted with the "normal" students in the main building and vice versa.

The Loose Screw underwent an extreme makeover to accommodate the change. It was a resounding failure. The retarded children were bullied, even to the point where a student from the Retail class pulled down the pants of a girl with Down syndrome. Lovely boys.

Eric was one of the new teachers and they ripped the curtains down in his classroom, along with a piece of the ceiling. "It just happened." I recognized these gentlemen from the main building. I had already had a run-in with them after they put dog feces in the lunchbox belonging to another one of the new teachers. Their stunts also included barricading their classroom with all of the chairs and tables. After I had reprimanded for the curtain stuff, one of them asked, "Hey, we heard that you're gay. Is that true?"

"Why do you want to know?" I asked. "Well, we heard it from your students, and we were just curious, that's all," the kid said.

"Okay, I'm gay," I said.

"Great," a different kid spoke up. "Will you come to our class and give a talk? It'll be a riot."

"First I will have to ask Arjan, your homeroom teacher. If he says it's okay, then I'll do it," I answered.

Arjan and his team gave me the green light. It actually went really well. We already had established a rapport, and it only got better. Plus, I found out that they had already known about it for ages from friends who were in my class.

A week passed and the mood at school was good. That is, until I walked into the building and ran into the boys from the curtain incident.

"Hey, Mr. Gay!" they said. "What's up?" They walked past without waiting for my answer. The next day, same thing: "Hey, Mr. Gay, what's up?"

What the hell, I thought. I felt my blood pressure rising. "Hey, guys! Get back here!" I yelled angrily. "My name is Peter, and I'm more than just gay. You will address me as 'sir' or 'Peter', got it?"

"But we thought you'd like it," they said, surprised. "We aren't trying to make fun of you, man! We'll drop it. See ya, Peter!"

Once again, I assumed that the matter had been settled. That is the fun thing about teaching 16 and 17 year-olds. Every day is different, and you must always be prepared for the most unlikely and outrageous situations.

It was a sunny, crisp day. The kind of day when you feel like a million bucks. The kind of day when all of that sunshine makes you forget where you are headed as you approach the school building. The place where *they* await. The little darlings, the little angels, who have been dumped here in order to give their parents a desperately needed respite, thanks to the mandatory education act. The place that the students need in order to escape the dull routine of the real world by constantly coming up with something new to wreak havoc and bring chaos to order.

Innocently and without a care, I rounded the corner to head for the entrance to my source of income. I was passing by the arts and crafts class when I heard someone call my name. "Peter!" someone cried. "Look!"

The four gifted and talented curtain hangers were standing about seven feet away in the schoolyard, near the dumpsters. No sooner had I turned my head towards them when the most charming and cutest one of the four boys made a great show of dropping his pants, bending over and spreading his boyish butt cheeks. I could practically see his tonsils. The other three stood there, staring at me expectantly.

The flasher stared awkwardly through his legs, waiting to see how I would react.

"Ooooh, nice!" I called out. "I would love to get my hands on those cheeks!"

I threw my bag down and moved to rush towards him, gesturing with my arms wildly in a lewd back and forth motion.

The three boys stared at me in horror, along with the streaker kid. His butt still in the air and his head hanging upside down, he saw me rapidly approaching and freaked out so badly that he managed to fall on the concrete, hobbled by his pants and tripped up by the uneven pavement. He went down face first just before I reached him, landing without any charm and with a great deal of pain, squarely on his privates.

I screeched to a halt and did an about face, smirking with satisfaction. I picked up my bag and left them there, beside themselves. I made a beeline for Frits' coffee corner and announced in pseudo-shock to the teachers who were parked there: "Oh my gosh, you will never guess what just happened to me!"

As everyone had come to expect from me, I gave a no-holds-barred report of the event, sparing no gory detail. "That's scandalous!" a couple of the teachers declared after I finished my account. "That kid should be suspended!"

"Nah, I don't think so," I said. "Don't you think falling bare-assed on his face was punishment enough? He made a complete fool of himself in front of his gang."

Not everyone agreed with me, but they figured that it was up to me. After the incident our rapport was even better. I refrained from teasing the student in question about his performance that had left so much to be desired.

Days passed and I found myself drinking coffee with Frits during a break. As we sat there talking we realized that we were being watched by four familiar pairs of eyes. The curtain molesters stood there grinning at us from the other side of the coffee counter.

"Hey, Peter, don't you think we're good looking guys?" one asked. All four gave me their best tough guy looks, while swiveling their heads, fixing their hair.

I was not accustomed to seeing this type of behavior from anyone besides my fellow gays at the COC and out on the town in the Regulierdwarsstraat, one of the gay hotspots of Amsterdam.

"Sure, sure, you're all very handsome specimens," I affirmed, "but what's the use? You guys are on the wrong team!"

They exchanged shocked looks. "No, you're the one on the wrong team," sniffed one of them. "Not us!"

"Well, it's all in your perspective," I said. "You guys like girls, right? So to me you are on the wrong team. I like men, which to you is the wrong team!"

It took a few moments but once their brains kicked into action and managed to process this information, they agreed, "Yeah, you're right!"

"But what are you guys doing here, anyway?" I asked

"We're supposed to be in Eric's class," one of them explained. "We told him that we had to go to the bathroom. He was like, whatever. He'd had enough of us for awhile."

"Well, it's time for you to go back. Now we've had enough of you for awhile, too," I said.

Just What is That Man Doing?

At the end of that second school year I could look back on a year filled with extremes. More students, more levels in each program and the accompanying behavior and problems, extreme confrontations with myself with regard to that behavior, reacting from my gut more quickly, lots of new employees on the team, and an increasingly less complicated feeling about my homosexuality.

I felt like a victor having achieved my goal of becoming a teacher. You could become an exception to the rule. You could change student attitudes and outlooks. Motivate them to learn and earn a diploma. They likewise had adopted a more tolerant and accepting stance after receiving information and on account of my openness.

Humor and stories helped put the students at ease and made them want to come to school. Classes were a treat for them--and for me, too. Better learning results and low absenteeism clearly showed that success was finally being achieved.

The fact that this could also be attributed to tougher school rules and more strict enforcement was especially surprising in the beginning. Now we understood why all of us were here. The department's reputation grew among the parents, the students and their employers. This school year was when I finally received my permanent contract.

Jeanette, ever impulsive and decisive, had discovered that there was room for the school to offer a number of permanent positions. First she managed to get one for herself, and then she immediately let me in on the secret. If I acted fast, I would be eligible, too. And so the sword of Damocles hanging over my head disappeared.

The knowledge that I could no longer be fired at the drop of a hat gave me a tremendous sense of freedom. I had now staked out my claim in both teams and I got along well with everyone. It took my fellow faculty members quite a bit of getting used to the ease with which I touched people. It took some of them a while to realize that I did no have any ulterior motives.

While students had fewer problems with it than the faculty, they did have to get used to other aspects of my behavior, which included moving around a lot in class. I waved my arms constantly whenever I was explaining something. I bet there were times that they ended up terrifically dizzy trying to follow my hands. As if they were the very source of the explanation.

For me, teaching was a theatrical performance. The students thought that all the hand and arm waving suited someone gay.

Visitors came to the school from time to time. Parents, yes, but also teachers from other schools. They saw me teaching animatedly, as if I were an actor in a play. Usually it drew a lot of laughs from the students. Someone who peered in the window of my class later asked one of the other teachers, "Exactly what subject does that guy teach?"

"That's almost anyone's guess," my coworker answered.

AIDS?

Entering the third school year, the school was once again getting ready to open after the long summer vacation. The first to return were the teachers and all of their stories.

All too quickly, however, we had to turn our attention to welcoming the hordes of youngsters in desperate need of education.

I had planned my vacation so that I would be back on Sunday and able to report back to work faithfully on Monday morning. Looking back I can see that this was not exactly one of my brightest ideas. See, I had contracted food poisoning in Italy and spent more time in the bathroom than anywhere else but now I did not have any time to see a doctor before I had to be back at work. I decided that it was not necessary anyway; a stomach bug eventually goes away. I carried on teaching for a week and a half, running to the bathroom both during and in between classes to relieve my cramped bowels. The pain in my stomach and intestines was so bad that I really should have been more concerned. Work was too busy for a quick visit to the Bijlmer doctor's office, which only took walk-ins at a certain time of day, and of course it was impossible to make an appointment in the weekend.

It got to the point where the pain was so bad that I could no longer walk upright. Of course my coworkers could no longer stand seeing --let alone hearing--me like this. I was no longer able to finish a conversation normally; instead, I ended up dashing to the bathroom.

"Enough is enough, Peter," Jeanette said. "You are going home now and you will make an appointment with your doctor."

It was Wednesday by the time I finally followed her instructions.

I tried to get an appointment as soon as I got home, but despite my cramps the doctor could not see me until the next Monday.

Getting some rest helped and I started to feel a little better. I was fine as long as I did not move. And provided I held everything in.

Jeanette phoned me in the evening, terribly worried. "How are you, Peter?"

"Not good," I said. "The diarrhea isn't as bad, but my stomach is killing me and incredibly bloated."

"What do you think is causing it?" she asked with interest.

Or so I thought.

"Oh, just an intestinal virus, that's all. I've got a doctor's appointment on Monday and they'll give me some medicine," I answered.

"You know what's going on, but you're afraid to say so, right?" Jeannette asked.

"What?" I asked, completely mystified.

"Aren't you thinking…. AIDS?"

"Of course not," I said. "Why would I? I always practice safe sex. So AIDS is not the first thing I would be worried about. It's just diarrhea, end of story."

"Whatever you say. Anyway, get well soon," she said, and hung up.

That night the cramps were so extreme that I thought I was dying. I called the doctor and explained the situation, in amidst the groans of pain.

"I already know what the problem is," he said. "I'm writing a prescription. Take the medicine and it will be over quickly."

I did not have much faith in a telephone consultation but doctors in the Bijlmer area preferred not to make house calls. I picked up the medicine and after one dosage the problem was more or less resolved. I left for work Monday, well rested and in good spirits.

The long weekend had done me good. I went up the stairs in the main building and saw Winfried, one of our administrators, walking down the hall on the second floor. As soon as he caught sight of me he asked, "Peter, what are you doing here at school? Aren't you extremely sick?"

"No. Where did you hear that? I'm totally fine now," I answered.

"You don't have to be at work, honestly. You should stay home. It's really no problem," he said.

The thought crossed my mind that he was acting unusually concerned. And completely out of order. I added, "There really isn't anything more to it. I'm fully recovered and can go back to work."

"Whatever you say. You can also cut your hours back and work part-time," he said, looking over his shoulder as he descended the stairs. I turned around and went to our office. On the way I passed a couple of faculty members, but nobody even looked at me.

I gathered my things from the office and headed for The Loose Screw. I would find out over there why my presence was causing such strange reactions. I was taking it personally, but maybe it was just my imagination. When I arrived in the building I was greeted by an unpleasant surprise: immediately a hush fell over the teacher's lounge. Before I could even ask what was going on Jan Pieter, the head of my department, walked in. He looked at me in amazement and asked, "What on earth are you doing here? Don't you have AIDS? I heard that you were dying, and I was supposed to quick hire a replacement to teach the business classes!"

"AIDS?!" I shouted. "Dying?! I had acid reflux and an intestinal virus! That's all!

Dammit, I can feel it flaring up again. Who started this rumor?"

Jeanette looked at me sheepishly and said, "Well, I mean, you had such terrible diarrhea and stomach pain…we thought that it might be AIDS. But how Jan Pieter caught wind of it…I have no idea."

"I heard it from the Human Resources department!" Jan Pieter said. "That's why I had to find a replacement as fast as possible. Now I'm obliged to keep him on for six weeks! So until then you'll have the evenings off."

"How did this story reach the Human Resources department?" I asked.

"I shared my suspicions with Boukje," Jeanette said. "You know she's really tight with Ron, right? She probably told him. And she probably blew it all way out of proportion so that he assumed the situation was so grave that he had to inform Human Resources. I mean, you know how Boukje loves to be the first with a juicy rumor, right? It's not like you can tune these things out."

"Well, this is utterly scandalous," I said. "I'm out sick a few days and the whole school is grieving my demise. Now I see why everyone was ignoring me. Dead man walking! Clearly you don't look someone who is apparently dead in the eye. Let alone say anything to him."

"Peter, we were very concerned about you," Jeanette said.

"Wow, you have a really nice way of showing it," I spat. "Nobody bothered to call me or send me a card to express their concern, let alone find out if there was any truth to the rumor."

Silence fell over the room and everyone stared at the plastic cups filled with coffee growing colder by the minute.

"You know what else is great?" I continued. "Normally we have to wait six weeks for a substitute when someone is out sick. But apparently when it's a presumed AIDS patient they send one in right away. The job must go on!"

Frits handed me a fresh cup of his elixir-like coffee to help me settle down a little. I had just enough time to gulp the scalding hot liquid anti-depressant before class started. Class gave me more time to try to come to terms with this ridiculous turn of events. I sat there asking myself how in god's name these people, these well-educated teachers, could possibly subscribe to the theory: A STRAIGHT PERSON WITH DIARRHEA HAS THE STOMACH FLU. A GAY PERSON WITH DIARRHEA HAS AIDS.

After this happened, I raised the subject several times during break, both in the main building and in The Loose Screw.

Perhaps it was a type of self defense, but I felt it was important to explain what AIDS was all about to others. That it was not a disease that affected gay people only. I knew that everyone assumed that was the case. But it was no excuse for these intellectuals. It also seemed like a good idea to me to make sure everyone knew that gay people can get sick just like anyone else, without it being a dead giveaway of having AIDS.

Something that slowly dawned on me during those coffee break conversations was that many of my heterosexual coworkers did not consider using condoms as an everyday activity. Instead, they believed that the Pill provided sufficient protection against unwanted pregnancy, and since only gay people caught AIDS, then why should they be concerned with that? It never crossed their minds that they were at risk of contracting other sexually transmitted diseases. That was exactly what the 16 and 17-year-old students thought!

I began wondering how the other social studies teachers discussed the sex education material, considering how limited their own knowledge was about the subject. Or worse, their unsafe sexual practices.

By talking about it I was breaking a taboo. However, I think that made people see me even more as a sexual creature; someone whose entire life is defined by sex. I assumed that these discussions led to more clarity, and that people now understood that I did not have AIDS. I did not die, I did not develop any Kaposi's sarcoma or any other outwardly visible signs of this serious disease, and life at school returned to normal.

People started looking me in the eye again and smiling. Peace had been restored, I thought. Still, I would later provide plenty more grist for the AIDS rumor mill. You see, my vacation preferences for third world countries and visiting places that were hardly beneficial to my health meant that I regularly returned home with one kind of bug or another: malaria, blood poisoning, intestinal parasites, and a severe ear infection. And every single time my coworkers would start speculating about the dreaded disease again. I did not know about this at the time, however; Frits told me about it long after the fact.

Just One of the Students?

As a teacher you are more than just the bearer of the information required for tests and exams. In most cases you find yourself playing many roles. You will be an *actor and entertainer* to lighten up the serious lessons with anecdotes and jokes. Or a *police officer* trying to maintain order in and outside of the class by doing everything from intervening when things turn violent, putting a stop to drug dealing, checking for weapons and stolen goods belonging to students or the school, to dealing with misconduct, bullying and so forth. You can be a *parent*, instilling certain values in the students and comforting them in times of sorrow or distress; a *social worker*, to help them cope with problems at home or in daily life, including run-ins with the law, registering for welfare benefits and so on; a *mediator* between students and their parents, their fellow students, various institutions or other social workers in case of problems or conflicts; a *job counselor* to help those who cannot find employment on their own; a *psychologist* who talks with the students and in doing so helps them figure out why they act a certain way and how to change it; a *confidant*, providing a confidential outlet for the students to air their personal problems and grievances without their parents or anyone else finding out. And of course you are the *janitor*, cleaning up all the mess in the classroom, making coffee when the real janitor is out sick or on vacation and mopping up the vomit from sick students.

When you look at it that way, the government should be grateful that teachers only get paid for a single profession.

Personally I considered it a privilege to be involved with the students in all of these different aspects. It helped me get to know the students and their environment better. Plus, over time I established the considerable trust that young people need. Trust that cannot be betrayed, of course. This does not mean putting on kid gloves to deal with them. The key word is transparency. Transparency in taking disciplinary actions and transparency in paying compliments.

When this trust and sense of safety was established, many personal stories would be shared in class. The stories were often heartwarming. The students knew that they would not be ridiculed. Of course, if anyone did try to laugh at them or otherwise poke fun, I would immediately make it clear that I did not appreciate it. Sometimes I felt that my openness and honesty regarding my homosexuality helped create an additional tie with the class, that it made me that much more human in their eyes. It encouraged them to share their personal lives with me. Plus, none of them interpreted a physical gesture on my part as threatening. Sometimes outside the classroom we would walk arm in arm, with both boys and girls, and we would take smoke breaks together outside, too. Our conversations on these occasions were very different from what we normally discussed in class. In many cases students from other departments would join in. Usually these were friends of my students.

Sometimes they would ask me questions about being gay. I was always willing to talk to them. The conversation would often turn to the religious aspect whenever some of the Muslim students joined. There was something so familiar and safe about these discussions. I do not know what others observing us might have to say about our behavior, but to me and my students it was completely innocent and safe. We broke the code that teachers and students are not supposed to touch each other, but we had clear-cut, unspoken boundaries. Boundaries that were not violated.

A friend's brother expressed interest in making a short film about the way I taught and interacted with the students. He was in film school and after listening to my enthusiastic stories he thought it would be worthwhile to visit our school. Break had just ended when I received a call from the office saying that he was waiting to see me. I quickly went to meet him.

"Winnie, I'm afraid I don't really have time to talk right now," I said. "Class is starting. Come with me to get an idea of what goes on here."

As soon as we reached the wing with the classrooms I was surrounded by the students who were already waiting to go inside.

"Hey, teach," one girl cried, as she linked her arm through mine, "I gotta talk to you, it's really important."

"Sure, sure," I said. "Nice timing, class is about to start. Go on, get to class. I'll talk to you afterwards."

She let go of my arm and followed the others into the room. Some went quietly, others in a tangle of shoving and yelling.

Suddenly a girl behind me threw her arms around my neck.

"What do you want?" I asked.

"Nothing," she said.

"Then get your butt to class and make it snappy!" I said, pretending to be upset.

She walked off towards her class, laughing all the way.

"Where is our teacher?" a student asked.

"He'll be here soon," I said. "Go to your room and wait for him there," I told him, pushing him in the direction of his classroom. Using the same deft move I herded another pair of students into their class. They protested loudly, opposed to the idea that it was time to go to class. Their teacher had not arrived yet, so there was no need for them to be there. Or so they felt. After a bit of pushing and hollering all of the students from the three different classes were in their rooms. I quickly made the rounds, poking my head into each room and ordering, "Everyone sit down and open your books. Hurry up. Class is starting now!"

Some of the students were still standing around. They looked at me and answered, "The teacher isn't here yet."

"I know, I'm not blind," I told them. "But you know what you are supposed to do. Go on and get started on your work. That's enough bitching."

I closed the door and finally could turn to say goodbye to Winnie, who was standing there in the hall, speechless. Now it was time to start teaching. I knew that it would be another five minutes before everyone had taken off their coats and gotten out their books.

In the evening Winnie called. "Was that a typical day?" he asked.

"Yep, every 90 minute segment of the day, every single day," I said.

"How on earth do you do it?" he asked.

"Oh, after a while you don't even notice. This chaos becomes the most everyday thing in the world. And in the midst of it you can actually talk about quite a few things with the students."

Amateur Wrestling

Sometimes at the end of class it was not unusual to find this one guy blocking the doorway. In a way that was more provocative than hostile he would stand there and try to make it hard for me to leave the room. I would have to come in physical contact with him if I wanted to exit the class; the doorway was too small for two people to fit through. I was up for the challenge, so I would throw my arm around his neck and try to wrestle him to the floor. He in turn would grab my waist and within seconds we were rolling around on the floor. But if I said "stop" it was all over immediately. One time during class I brought up our latest amateur wrestling session.

"So, Vincent," I asked. "Who was stronger, you or me?"

"You're gay, teach, so I'm stronger."

"But I still managed to get you down on the floor like a sissy, right?" I asked.

"Yes, but only because I let you," he replied.

"But doesn't it bother you that a gay man like me would wrestle you like that?" I asked.

"No, sir," he said. "I mean, what could happen to me? I'm the one who is stronger. I'm cool with everything as long as you don't touch me here," he said, pointing to his crotch.

"But teachers aren't supposed to fight with their students, are they?" I asked the class.

"Oh come on, Mr. Van Maaren," someone said. "You gotta be able to have fun with each other, right? I mean, if you can't do that…"

We resumed the lesson. While the students were busy working I surveyed the class. Just look at these boys and girls, I thought to myself. They were considered unmotivated and stupid, but they were plenty tolerant and perfectly able to put things into perspective. Society should be happy that these kids exist. I realized that I loved them dearly.

Time and time again it was these brief moments that made the job completely worth it all. A quick, powerful shove from a boy to show that he liked you. A visit from a former student, regardless of whether they had actually graduated or left school otherwise, to see how you were doing. Of course, to others it may have seemed like I had no authority. But in practice my way of doing things actually increased authority and respect, both in the classroom and in the rest of the school.

I remember one parent-teacher meeting. Shortly before the parents in question arrived I was roughhousing with a student in the cafeteria. They walked in right as we hit the floor. They walked around us and the mother announced to Frits, "We have an appointment with Mr. Van Maaren."

I whispered to the student that he should probably release me. That way I could use the arm that had been pinned underneath me to prop myself up and draw their attention.

"Sorry, folks, that's me," I said. The student helped me to my feet, and I shook their hands while busily dusting off my clothes. They regarded me with somewhat surprised looks, but said nothing. I gave them coffee and we went to a classroom to conduct our meeting. Nothing was said about the wrestling match. After our conversation I reported to Frits for a cup of coffee.

"That's completely out of line," he said. "What will they think of the school now?"

"They'll think that the students here have young and quick-witted teachers," I said.

"Huh, you aren't exactly young or quick-witted," he said with a smile. "Just watch it the next time you have an appointment with some parents or anyone else."

Incognito

Not standing out from the students as far as your clothing is concerned can have certain advantages for a teacher. Especially when you want to play a joke on a group of new arrivals. Of course, certain jokes could only be played on the business students attending night school. Our school offered classes during the day as well as the evening. Night school attracted adult students ages 18 to 65. These were individuals pursuing the necessary certificates to start their own business, for example.

Obviously I could drink coffee in the teacher's lounge before class, but there were so few teachers around in the evening that hanging around all by myself in the big empty room was not appealing. Instead, I joined the new students in the cafeteria line. I got my coffee, some sugar and a spoon and made a beeline for what I was sure was my new class.

The group of aspiring hair stylists from the cosmetology department had already exited in a loud chatty swarm and these students were the only ones left. A couple of them glanced at me, but most simply carried on their conversations. I sat down in their midst and started asking questions about vacations and other subjects to prompt conversations. Meanwhile, I looked around to take stock of the group in terms of age and gender. The men outnumbered the women, and most were older than 25.

Presently I looked at my watch and noticed that it was already seven o'clock. Time for class. I stood up and announced, "Ladies and gentlemen, welcome to school. Business class is about to start. Would you kindly report to room number 14?"

Everyone sat there, staring at me and exchanging surprised looks with their neighbors. Some of them scrutinized me from head to toe and I could see them thinking, *Who are you to tell us what to do?*

"Oh, excuse me," I said. "May I introduce myself? I'm Peter van Maaren, your teacher for Business Law." Their eyes widened further in surprise.

"May I now kindly ask you to head to class?" I asked, seeing that most of them were making no move to leave. Clearly they were not sure that I was really the teacher; maybe I was just some crazy guy who wandered in off the streets. Eventually they went to class. Not necessarily at my request, of course, but because some of the other students had already gotten up and left.

I took a head count and noticed that we were missing four students. I went outside and found a group of guys who were about 18 years old. One of them was standing in the doorway smoking.

"Are you enrolled in the business program?" I asked.

He gave me a look that said, *What's it to you?*

The scornful and arrogant look prompted me to introduce myself.

"I'm your business teacher, and we're about to start the business law class."

He looked at me with surprise, and headed off to the classroom.

"Are you guys coming to class, too?" I called to the other three.

Hesitantly they entered the school. I walked with the first boy and asked, "Didn't you think I was a teacher?"

"To be honest, no," he said. "I expected someone older. And your clothes are in style. You don't see that much with teachers."

"Thanks for the compliment," I said.

Together we entered the classroom, followed by the other three. Everyone sat down and I took my place in front of the class, leaning against my desk. I was their teacher. This was where they normally expected to see a teacher. Class could begin. From now on we would spend our breaks together. The distance between us had diminished.

The Creation Story

Many students are inclined to believe practically everything that a teacher says. As if teachers have the knowledge market cornered. But what I wanted to do was to teach the students to question as much as they could. This included regularly sharing a totally made-up story in order to see if they were really listening critically.

"Kids, today I am going to clear up some misunderstandings surrounding the Creation story. After extensively studying the Bible, researchers have arrived at the conclusion that the story is in fact very different. It actually goes like this: in the beginning, God created the earth, the sky and the animals on the land, in the air and in the water. When he was finished he saw that it was good. Now it was time to create a divine man in his image from the mud. Using his creative skill he created Adam. But this striking young man, made as if he had just walked out of a gym, was very unhappy in paradise. 'What am I supposed to do with all of these animals? They are so boring. They can't even play basketball. And shooting hoops into a homemade net all by yourself? That's no fun.'

'What's wrong?' God asked. 'You look so sad.'

'I always have to play basketball by myself,' Adam replied. 'Even the monkeys are bad at it. I want a real sports buddy who is a lot like me.'

'Go to sleep,' God said. 'Everything will be fine when you wake up.'

So God created Adamo. Because Adam was the first, Adamo could not be more handsome. After all, that would make Adam jealous; it would only lead to fights. Maybe they would even beat each other up during a game.

But God did make sure that Adamo had an impressive physique. After all, he had to be in good shape in order to play sports, right? And appearances are important, too. Together they played basketball, one game after another. They never stopped. One ball after the next swooshed into the homemade net in the apple tree. Then one day after a match they were tired and hungry. What now? They did not know how to cook. They did not feel like eating apples. Besides, they were not allowed to touch the fruit on the apple tree. Otherwise they would be in for a spanking. It was time to appeal to God again.

'Hey, God, we sure would like to eat something, but we can't cook.'

'Go to sleep,' He replied.

While they were sleeping, God plucked a rib from Adam to create Eve. She was a beautiful woman, of course; after all, Adam was a good looking guy. Now Adam and Adamo could play basketball for hours on end. They were not concerned with Eve. She simply took care of the food every day.

They would have lived long and happily had Eve not decided it was time for some variety in their diet. She thought applesauce sounded good. Adam was so focused on his game that he completely forgot about telling Eve not to touch the apples. The mistake put an end to the fun. They were kicked out of paradise. From now on they would know that they were naked, that they did not have any clothes on. Ashamed, they used fig leaves as makeshift underwear."

The story was over. Maybe it was the tone I used to tell the story. In any case, they had listened closely and when I stopped speaking there was a momentary silence.

"No way," a girl spoke up. "That's not true, is it?" she asked.

"Why not?" I asked.

"I don't know," she said. "I'm not religious, so I don't know the Bible. But I don't think that's true."

Other students nodded in agreement.

"So you guys think I'm making this up?" I asked.

"Yes," was the skeptical reply.

"Well, you're right, the story isn't entirely true," I said. Then I switched to discussing the actual Creation story, and the ensuing relationship between man and woman. The man as the boss and the woman as the subordinate. The role of Satan. That sort of thing. I do not know for sure whether the story took on a life of its own like so many of the other stories I told. My students always loved listening to my stories, but there were so many that sometimes they were unable to relay them accurately. In many cases they combined two or three anecdotes into a single story and it would eventually get back to me in a completely unrecognizable version. The real problem, though, was when one of these distorted tales ended up making the rounds in their places of work. According to one manager, "If these are the kinds of stories that our employees have to listen to, then they might as well skip school altogether!"

Test Stress

After every semester I felt obliged to meet with all of the students who had failed their preliminary exams and offer them the opportunity to take them again. Incidentally, this was met by loud protests from the students in question, since they were invited for a do-over on what was supposed to be a day off from school. My fellow faculty members handed in the grades for all of the classes, and I would go through the lists looking for retake candidates. It was a long process of weeding through stacks of paperwork for each student.

On the re-take day I would sit down with the student and grade their efforts. Another failing grade meant another do-over. It drove the students crazy, but it drove me crazy, too. There was so much to check and the students had to sit around waiting for ages. And of course there was lots of cussing and frustration if they had not managed to pass.

My coworkers thought it was ridiculous; a huge waste of time and clearly a type of masochism, but the deal was that everything had to be up to scratch before the students could take their finals. At the end of the day I decided whether a student was qualified. In almost every case they had the necessary passing grades.

If I denied a student permission to take an exam in a given class, I knew I was in for a barrage of verbal abuse, first from the student as well as from the parents either later that evening or the next day. But no matter how much abuse my ears had to take, I stood by my decision. No finals. Otherwise we might as well get rid of our rules. They would pass next semester, I was sure of it.

Ultimately, our team was in charge of maintaining the quality and level of the program. As a teacher you automatically developed a thicker skin to deal with all of the verbal abuse.

Of course I was a nervous wreck whenever the students had to take a final. On those days I would report to school early with another teacher to set up the classrooms. After that, it was important to just be there for the students, and drink coffee with them.

"Chill out, Mr. Van Maaren," they would tell me. "We're the ones who should be nervous, not you. We'll pass, for real."

Still, I was a mess. Especially when a fun but rowdy and unmotivated group emerged from taking their Product Range exam just 10 minutes after entering the room.

This was the class in which I had to work with 10 different product ranges in a single semester. It was a virtually impossible job. Preparing for class took hours. Every Sunday I had to struggle through ten books to create multiple choice tests. With all the different product ranges the class itself was often chaos. In many cases I used stories and conversations based on the students' own work experience to get them back on track again.

Still, sometimes a student would announce, "Mr. Van Maaren, it's always fun in your class, but we aren't learning jack."

"We'll see whether you have learned anything when you take the exam," I would tell them, not quite believing what I just said.

"Peter, they really were done in just 10 minutes," Iris told me, who had overseen the test.

"It went fast, for everyone. There's no way they're going to pass. You can be sure that this group is going to bring down the pass rate."

"It was a breeze, seriously, teach," one student said. "I know I'm going to pass."

We received the results two weeks later. Gnawing on my nails I checked the scores for the Product Range exam. All but one student had passed! Amazing news, not only to me but especially to my coworkers.

Auditing Duty

Jan Pieter, the vice-principal, along with a couple of my coworkers, would sit in on my classes from time to time. Jan Pieter's visits were always unannounced. The other faculty members came to listen and watch to see how their students were doing.

What they did not expect was that I would actively involve them in the lesson.

"Just go ahead and teach your class like you would normally do, Peter," Jan Pieter said, walking into the room. "Don't pay any attention to me."

Of course I felt like he was checking up on me, but I pretended to ignore it.

"Good morning, ladies and gentlemen," I said to the class. "Today our vice-principal is in class to follow one of my lessons. Maybe he would like to learn something about social studies."

Everyone turned around to see just what exactly this man looked like. When they turned back to meet my gaze I could tell by the looks on their faces that they understood that something was expected from them. Like always I covered the lesson material with a pause every 10 minutes or so to discuss what we were learning. However, Jan Pieter did not like how I kept asking him to share his opinion on a certain topic. He played along like a good sport, but you could tell by the look on his face that he did not appreciate the attention from me and the students. He did not mention it after class and I never asked his reasons for auditing my class. Apparently he was satisfied. He had not caught me discussing homosexuality with the students. I did not receive any further complaints.

A couple years later a fellow teacher, Ella, had a daughter. Soon after she returned to school she stopped me in the hall and said, "Peter, I finally understand you. Now that I have a child I talk about it a lot to others and with the students. In class, if my answers to questions are not always exactly relevant or I never stop talking about my daughter it certainly doesn't mean I'm propagating motherhood. I'm presenting myself as a mother without doing so on purpose. It's my life, and I want to share it with others. It's not like I'm fighting on the barricades for something. I'm doing the same thing that you do in class when you talk about your life."

It had taken six years for one of my coworkers to "get" me. And this was only one. But that is what it is all about, right?

Sexual Assault Awareness

During my years at the remedial and learning disabled group I often asked Boukje if perhaps there was something we could do for young people who had been in trouble with the law. It took a while but eventually she managed to assign a group of three Surinamese boys to my drop-out project group. In addition to lagging behind in language and math, all three likewise did not have much in the way of social skills.

Given their lack of prior education and arrested level of intelligence they were initially placed with us. The assumption was that after completing some remedial education they would be able to enter a vocational program.

Two of them lived in the Bijlmer part of Amsterdam, which also happened to be my home at the time. One of them, Clifton, had dealt drugs, threatened someone with a gun, and committed robbery, which had led to him being placed under supervision in a home. The other one, Tommy, had participated in a gang rape in a community center. His punishment was only a few weeks' community service as a garbage collector.

The third boy had been caught dealing drugs in Amsterdam on numerous occasions. I could tell right away that he was not the sharpest crayon in the box the first time I saw him: he was over six and a half feet tall. Every police officer in the city knew him, and you could pick him out of a crowd in a heartbeat. But as clueless as he was, he would simply stand around, blatantly dealing, and immediately get picked up. Plus, he always had plenty of dope on him.

The court had ordered all three to attend school. Avoiding school meant facing tougher penalties. For the first two it was also important that they enrolled in a school somewhere outside of their normal surroundings.

The halfway house where Clifton was living was run by two "parents." The male and female counselors were there to help the residents lead more structured lives. I was drawn to the idea of being able to play a part in this process and with that in mind I arrived at school feeling optimistic and excited.

No sooner had I arrived when Jeanette ran up to me. "Peter, Barend called to say that there were problems yesterday in the lab. It seems your new student may have done something terrible over there. Cora says that Clifton tried to rape her in the bathroom at the lab. You need to talk to him. This kid is simply too dangerous to be at this school."

I had not even met Clifton yet and already we had such a huge problem!

"I'll go talk to him now, before classes start," I said. "I want to talk to both of them. Can you first show me which one is Clifton?"

Jeanette pointed to the boy seated quietly at a table across from the coffee bar. He was a black, athletic, almost six feet tall guy and looked very tough and manly. Clifton had everything working against him, considering his criminal record and of course the stereotypes about sexually insatiable Creoles. Cora, the victim, was a short, stout, flirty girl, and not exactly the brightest of the bunch. I struggled with the image of Clifton trying to rape Cora and thought, unwillingly, that he could get anyone he wanted. Then again, Clifton was likely suffering from a lack of sexual gratification afforded by living in a halfway house, which may have prompted him to assault the first girl that passed in front of his *tollie* [Suriname slang for dick].

"I'm going to talk to Clifton first and then Cora," I told Jeanette.

I walked up to Clifton, introduced myself and asked him to come with me. Obediently he followed without saying anything. We went into the classroom, I offered him a chair and I also took a seat.

"Not such a good first day, hey fella?" I said calmly.

Clifton sat there with his head hanging down.

"Give me your account of what happened," I said.

"I didn't even know the girl," he said, raising his head. "She was getting all grabby in the cafeteria, all hangin' on me. I pushed her away a couple of times. I couldn't even talk to the others in a normal way. Then Leroy came in with the fries he'd got for everybody.

That girl, Cora, she sits down next to me to eat her fries. We just started eating right when she gives her fries to the girl next to her and asks, 'You want to do it with me?'

Look, teacher, I'm a red blooded guy, see. I'm not gonna say no to that. So I put my fries down and I walk all nonchalant with her to the bathroom. We only just got started when she's all grabbing my crotch. She takes her pants off and I take my *tollie* out. Right as I'm about to nail her we see Leroy all looking in the window. Freak's trying to enjoy himself by getting a look at the action, or maybe he wants to join in. When Cora sees Leroy the girl starts screaming. I was shocked, man. She wouldn't shut up. I can see there won't be any more action happening now, so I put my *tollie* back in my pants, I open the bathroom door and I get back outside. I gotta make my way through this big group of students who all come running cuz of the screaming.

Then this morning I hear I raped this girl. Teacher, I would never do that. I don't want any trouble, or else I gotta go to prison. That girl wanted it herself, and now I'm getting the blame."

Clifton looked me in the eye the entire time and never turned away once while relating his side of the story. It seemed very plausible what he was saying. Not only because of his body language but also because I knew Cora. Or could it be that I was overly taken by his looks and his presence? After all, I am just a red blooded guy, too.

"Go back to the cafeteria," I said. "I want to talk to Cora before I decide what we are going to do with you."

"Teacher, I don't want to go to jail because of that girl!" he protested.

"I'm going to talk to Cora first. You've done some stuff, so it's not like you are totally innocent. But hopefully I'll know more once I hear Cora's story," I said.

I walked with Clifton to the cafeteria and summoned Cora.

I let her go into the classroom first. She made a beeline to the windowsill, which was not quite wide enough to accommodate her behind. However, the weather was nice and the window was open, so she managed to worm her way onto the sill after all.

"Okay, Cora, tell me exactly what happened," I said.

She turned her head slightly to cast a look outside, and then returned her gaze to me.

Calmly and with a smile she began. "All of us were sitting in the cafeteria in the lab when Leroy comes in with the fries. Everyone who ordered something started eating. Clifton came over and sat down next to me. I was still eating my fries when suddenly he's all taking them and giving them to Lucy. Then he grabbed my arm and pulled me out of my chair. The chair tipped over on the floor. Then he pushed me over to the bathroom. I suddenly realized what he was up to and I tried to get away. I got away for a second but he grabbed me again. He was way too strong for me, teacher! When we got to the bathrooms he pulled the door open and tried to get me inside. But I held onto the door, trying to shut it again. It took him three tries but he managed to get it to stay open and push me inside. He locked the door and pulled down my underpants right away. He took his cock out of his pants to screw me, and when I saw it I started screaming. I backed up behind the toilet so Clifton couldn't get me. He was trying to get me when Leroy looked through the window. Leroy asked what we were doing and I yelled for help. I was hoping Leroy would go get Barend to help me get away from this guy. That's when Clifton got scared, cuz he opened the door and ran away fast. Barend came and got me out from behind the toilet. Teacher, it was horrible."

As she spoke I tried to pay close attention to her body language and her eyes.

Surely the impact of this awful event would be plain to see. She would be sweating, her eyes would be huge, and she would be clenched up tightly. I had also imagined that she could very well start crying while recounting this attempted rape. But there was nothing. It was like she was telling me about a scene from a soap opera. There was no real emotion, no anger, no tears, nothing but her usual monotone, whiny and somewhat husky voice.

I was confused. I had never dealt with an attempted rape involving any of the students. And yet my gut said that Clifton's story was more credible than Cora's. Was I subconsciously choosing sides with him because I was a man? Was it because I found him more attractive than Cora?

"I don't know what to make of this," I said to my coworkers later. "Clifton's story seems more plausible to me. But I don't know how a woman who has been assaulted reacts. Let's see how they act towards each other today. If she fearfully avoids Clifton then I'd say Cora's story is credible. And if that's the case, then we'll have to contact the home where he's staying. It's too bad, but he'll have to be sent to prison."

Everyone agreed.

I went to the smoking lounge for a break. Presently Jeanette came in. "Peter, come and look at this," she said. "You aren't going to believe what's going on in the non-smoking lounge right now."

She had such a huge grin on her face that I immediately sensed that it was nothing serious.

Walking into the non-smoking lounge I could hardly believe my eyes. There were Cora and Clifton, sitting next to each other, drinking coffee and chatting away. The victim of a vicious assault in a friendly and flirty conversation with the perpetrator, the criminal.

"I don't think anything happened," I said to Jeanette. "Shall we give Clifton the benefit of the doubt?"

Peace had been restored, and the coffee suddenly tasted a lot better.

That day I decided to sit down with the class and talk about sexual harassment and assault. I was astonished that the boy who had been assigned community service for his part in a gang rape admitted to it during class without batting an eyelash--and without any visible sign of remorse. After all, he had not done anything wrong, had he? He was not the one who raped the girl? All he did was hold her down so his friend could have his way with her. I certainly had my work cut out for me. I had a lot to say to this group--and especially this kid.

It suddenly became clear that this school year would not be like any other I had experienced so far. But then again, I was the one who had asked Boukje to get me a couple of juvenile delinquents…

Because You Are Black

Just when you think you are on the right track with re-socializing "innocent" juvenile delinquents, it all falls apart. During one cooking class Clifton and the other Surinamese boys were allowed to make *roti*. They had been nagging about it for weeks. Two of the three had done all the shopping for the meal and did their very best to achieve results worthy of their mom or grandmother.

The flatbreads back at home were probably not as burned, but judging from the enthusiastic reception this was not a problem. Clifton did not help; however, he certainly ate the most. The other two did not make a fuss about it. Obviously Clifton was higher on the totem pole and the other two looked up to him.

The other students had made a different dish. They were finished with their meal and had already cleaned up and done the dishes. The boys' table and countertop was still a mess and they were getting ready to leave. I let the two cooks go, but I held Clifton back.

"You aren't going anywhere, son," I said. "You didn't lift a finger except to eat everything. Look at this mess. Clean it up."

"Oh, sure, I have to clean it up because I'm black, right?" he asked. "I'm not gonna do it. You're a racist!"

"That's right, I'm a racist," I said. "Now get cleaning!"

He looked at me and walked back to the kitchen, where he made motions to start cleaning. I was momentarily distracted by a student who wanted to ask me something when my intern suddenly screamed, "Peter, look out! Clifton is going to jump out the window!"

Without thinking, I ran over in front of the window to block him.

It wasn't that I was afraid he would injure himself in some kind of suicide jump - the kitchen was on the ground floor--but I sure as heck didn't want to be stuck cleaning up the mess.

He saw that he was trapped. The intern was standing in front of the kitchen door and I was in front of the window. He looked me right in the eye, grabbed a large knife from the counter and brandished it in my face.

"If you don't move it I'm gonna stab you to death!" he shouted.

"Okay," I said, raising my arms. "Go on, stab me to death. The school doesn't care and tomorrow there will be someone to take my place. Put the knife down and clean up that mess."

He shook the knife at me again. "Don't even think I'm scared of you. I could kill you."

"Stab away," I said, "but you are still going to have to clean up."

We stood there a few seconds longer staring at each other. "Put the knife down and get to work," I instructed him.

Without losing eye contact for a second I was hoping to determine whether he was really planning on stabbing me to death. So far I had seen nothing to indicate an affirmative answer. He was not threatening out of anger, but to get power. To get his way. Apparently this was the only way he was used to doing things.

It might work with others, but his approach did not cut it with me. Consider it one of the advantages of growing up in a violent neighborhood. When he realized that I was not impressed by his threat he put the knife back down on the counter.

"And now get cleaning," I hissed between my teeth.

He picked up a rag from the sink and walked towards the garbage can.

The whole episode lasted about 30 seconds but it certainly felt a lot longer. My intern had been there the entire time, too, watching in stunned horror. I went over to try to calm her down a little. I was completely confident that Clifton would do as he had been told. And he did. Well, Creole style, at least. Still, he was allowed to leave, and we could finally have a coffee break.

In order to prevent Clifton from being sent to jail I waited a couple of years before telling the other faculty members about his stunt. I never contacted the police. Our job was to re-socialize these juvenile delinquents. I did not want to immediately give up on him on account of this incident. After all, I won the first round, right?

The position of power had been clearly established. He had lost to a gay. I suspect that this changed his outlook on homosexuals, because now he treated me with respect. He did not morph into a well-behaved, mild-mannered student, but he did make an effort.

Human Pincushions

My drop-out project group included a white kid with learning and social disabilities. Harry really was not that different from the rest. There were calm, quiet kids and hyper kids, but everyone had some kind of dysfunction. One day a student came up to me and said, "Mr. Van Maaren, Harry sometimes pokes us really hard in the arm or leg or butt with a knife or a pair of scissors. We don't like it."

"Why didn't anyone tell me about this earlier?" I asked.

"We're afraid of him," she said. "We don't want him to go after us when he finds out that we told you."

"I'll talk to him," I said.

Of course Harry denied everything when I confronted him. Teachers were not allowed to search the students, so I had to take his word for it that he was not carrying a knife. There was little else I could do aside from wait for him to strike again. The class was aware that I would intervene.

Shortly after our conversation I heard someone call out during cooking class, "Mr. Van Maaren, he's poking me with a knife in my arm again."

I marched over to Harry, grabbed him and pulled him off to the side. Then I noticed the paring knife in his hand.

"Put that knife down," I said.

No sooner had I said it he pressed the knife to my chest. I felt the point against my sternum.

"Go on, you bastard!" I yelled in anger. "Stab me! If you've got the guts then just stab me!"

Suddenly his eyes started rolling around in his head and I saw the whites. Whoa, I thought to myself, this is not good. I immediately pulled away and let him go. Obviously this was the right thing to do to bring him back to earth. His eyes returned to normal.

"Put that knife down," I called. "You are suspended for a week. Don't ever let me catch you cutting a student or even having a weapon on you."

Harry left with his head hung down. I would have to talk to him when he returned to school but right now I did not have the energy. During the confrontation I did not feel any fear. It was like I knew instinctively not to take it any further. The consequences would have been disastrous.

A week later he returned to school. We sat him down and spelled out the rules regarding his stabbing problem. I was naive enough to believe that that was all it would take. I was wrong. One day the poker picked the wrong pincushion.

Class had already started when Tommy, the boy who had been given community service on account of his role in a gang rape, arrived late. He was about to sit down when Harry called out, "Hey negro, sit here." He grabbed a chair and shoved it into the wall as hard as he could. "There's your seat, nigger."

"Knock it off," I yelled, but Tommy was already in front of him. He stood there calmly and asked, "What did you just say?"

The poker leaned back and said, with a little less bravado than before, "That's your seat. You don't belong here."

I sensed that things were about to get out of hand and was about to come out from behind my desk when Harry reached out and grazed Tommy's stomach. In one swift move the much smaller Surinamese student smashed Harry's nose into a pulp. It happened so fast that there was no way for me to intervene. The sound of bone breaking was so loud that it sent shivers down my spine. I ran over to Tommy and hollered, "Dammit, get out of here! You are expelled!"

Tommy went pale and left. Now I turned my attention to the victim and looked right into his bloody face. Reeling in shock Harry pressed his hand to his nose to try to stop the bleeding. I quickly took his arm and led him to the bathroom to wash his face. Tommy was standing in the hallway, still pale as a ghost. I didn't know that someone from Suriname could turn so white. Stuttering he asked, "How come you're expelling me? He tried to stab me in the pool when I was leaning on his changing room door. I had to hit him, sir."

I was not listening. The most pressing job at hand was to help this kid. Cleaning his face I noticed a bone sticking out of his nose. I ran to Boukje and said, "Come quick. Someone has a broken nose and needs to be taken to the hospital."

"How do you know that?" she asked, as if she were the lone expert on serious injuries.

"Because a bone is sticking out!" I said, a little louder than intended. "And check him for a knife. I think he grazed Tommy with a switchblade."

On the way to the hospital she managed to get him to spill the entire story and voluntarily surrender his knife.

You should have heard the parents of the "victim." Their little darling had been beaten up by a Surinamese! Oh no, their precious son would never stab anyone. He did not even have a knife. They were shocked when we showed them the switchblade. Suddenly they saw their child in a completely new light. Without any protest they agreed that we would allow Tommy to return to school as soon as their son's nose was healed. Within a week both boys were back in school.

A Sense of Safety, Bijlmer Style

There are times when teaching juvenile delinquents comes in handy. One night I was walking through the Ganzenhoef shopping mall in Amsterdam-Zuidoost. In those days it was the kind of place you avoided like the plague. The kind of place to get away from as quickly as possible. This is why most of the people you saw there were rushing to get home from the subway. I was walking through the parking garage towards the mall when all of a sudden I saw I loud group of Surinamese boys headed my way. I am not prone to fear by nature, but for the first time in all of the years I had lived in the Bijlmer housing projects I sensed that this could turn out badly.

They approached quickly and menacingly. I looked around and saw no one else in the vicinity. They drew closer. I remember hearing in the blue collar neighborhood where I grew up never to run away in this type of situation. To do so would basically mean signing your own death warrant. Simply face the confrontation. So I continued walking calmly as if I had not noticed them, and waited for the inevitable.

I noticed a short little guy leading the group. The leader of the pack. They walked directly towards me. Suddenly the little guy piped up cheerfully, "Hey teach, is that you?" It was Tommy.

"Hey guys, this is my teacher! He's a *buller* [faggot]. Come on, let's go. See ya on Wednesday, Mr. Van M."

The group headed towards the subway station. With a sigh of relief I walked on.

Later, anytime I walked through the mall some Surinamese kid would call out, "Hey, it's Tommy's teacher!" Their friendly waves told me that Tommy had nothing but good things to say about me.

Thank goodness.

Act Normal

Even though somehow Tommy was proud of me I managed to gravely embarrass him once. The school was organizing a camping trip and his grandmother could not afford it. She was raising him and could not afford such a luxury on her meager social security check. I tried to get his father to contribute. He also lived in the Bijlmer housing projects, so it was not out of my way. But it was futile. He considered Tommy a delinquent and wanted nothing to do with him.

"He is your son, you know," I said.

"I know," he said. "But he always gets himself into trouble. He has to deal with it now. I am done with him."

That kind of attitude could really make me angry: bringing a child into the world and then refusing to take responsibility for it. And do nothing but bitch when things went wrong. The kind of father who believed that his child should be the one to take responsibility, without ever once feeling personally responsible.

Eventually I made an appointment with the social services office in Reigersbos. Of course Tommy showed up late and I lit into him before we entered the building. Inside I took a number and gave it to him. He took a seat across from me, headphones clamped to his ears. Clearly he was not interested in the sign announcing the numbers. When it was our turn I tore the headphones off his ears and said, "Hey, dickhead, can't you even pay attention to see when it's your turn? Do I have to do everything for you?"

He silently followed me to the little room where a social services employee was waiting to help us. She listened to a brief explanation of the situation, accepted the paperwork and disappeared for a moment.

"You sit like a gay," Tommy spat. "Put your legs the way they're supposed to go. A real man doesn't cross his legs. Act normal."

"But I am gay, aren't I?" I asked. "You're fine with asking me to help you go on welfare, but you can't deal with the fact that I sit like a gay?"

I was not doing what he wanted me to do, which prompted him to sit and glare into the distance.

The lady came back to tell us that his welfare application would be processed, and we left.

"Sorry, teach," Tommy said before we parted ways. "But I really can't stand it when men sit that way."

"Why do I embarrass you so much?" I asked.

"I feel like people are looking at us," he said. "Maybe I'm just worried that they're gonna think I'm gay, too."

"That's your problem," I said. "If you aren't, then it shouldn't bother you. In any case I hope you get on welfare so you can join us at camp. Bye, Tommy."

"See ya, teach," he said, and walked back into the projects.

He received the money and right before camp he dropped out. He had fulfilled his community service obligation and apparently no longer saw the need to go to school. Try as I might, I could not get him to change his mind.

Six years later I met him on the train. He was very excited to see me. No sign of embarrassment now. He was doing well. He had a job working as a sorter for a transport agency. He was carrying a bouquet of flowers for his girlfriend.

He said he hoped to get married soon.

The Love Letter

One day I arrived at the school, got my coffee and peeked in my mailbox to see whether I had any important papers from the central building. Instead I found a letter personally addressed to me. This was unusual; we hardly ever received any personal mail at school. If anything like that arrived at the central building it was always opened. This letter had been sent directly to this address, and was waiting in my mailbox, unopened.

I turned the envelope over to see if there was any return address. Nothing. Could this be an anonymous fan letter?

The handwriting was on the large side, like a child had written it. I figured it must be from a student. I opened the envelope and was shocked to see it was a threatening letter. It said something like, "I know who you are, you filthy faggot. You raped me in Groningen and I'm going to get you. I'm going to kill you, you disgusting queer. That's right, I know you from Groningen. You probably don't remember who I am. But I'm going to kill you. If you want to save your life you have to pay 5,000 guilders. Or else I'll kill you, nasty faggot."

There was Turkish writing on the back of the paper. I gave it to a Turkish coworker, who indicated that it was a Turkish translation of what was written on the other side In Dutch. I showed the letter to Boukje and she was horrified.

"We have to contact the police," she said.

"No," I said. "We don't know who wrote it. It's pretty weird that he knows I'm from Groningen. The only people who know that are the teachers and the students. So it could very well be from a student. The handwriting, too, seems to point to that."

We compared the handwriting in the letter with lots of students' work but could not find any matches. We decided to forget about the situation for the time being. I did not want to make any fuss about it. But it was not long until a second letter arrived. I was disturbed to find it. I opened the letter. The handwriting and the message were the same as the first, except that now the author was demanding more money. Once again there was Turkish writing on the back of the paper. Still, I did not think it was necessary to get the police Involved over such a ridiculous threat. Clearly this person was unbalanced. Not someone to take seriously, right?

A third letter arrived, ordering me to wait by the bridge near the school with the money on a certain day, otherwise I would be killed.

What an idiot, I thought, and ignored the instructions. But the threats seeped into my subconscious. A few days later I was walking through the shopping center near the school when all of a sudden I heard the chainsaw-like roar of a moped engine. I looked behind me and watched the moped roar up over the curb and onto the sidewalk, heading right towards me.

I felt like I was having a heart attack. The driver aimed right at me, and just before plowing into me swerved to the side and roared off, towards the bridge.

Good grief, I thought, it cannot be true that someone is trying to kill me? I did not recognize the moped driver. I only saw that it was a Turkish guy. Despite getting the fright of my life I still did not think it was necessary to take action. This could have been a mere coincidence.

I did not receive any more threatening letters.

About six months later Boukje approached me and said, "Peter, I'm not sure how to say this, but I did something foolish. This is a letter to you and I opened it. I apologize."

"What's going on?" I asked. "Why did you open my mail?"

"After the third letter there were others," she explained. "Because you didn't want to do anything about it I forwarded them to management. They sent them to the police.

We were terribly concerned about your welfare and safety. But when I read this letter it turned out to be something completely different."

She giggled a little and added, "It's a love letter from a student. I'm so embarrassed to have opened it and read it. I'm sorry. I didn't know."

Actually I really couldn't care less. I had nothing to hide from my fellow faculty members. Besides, they opened all of our mail.

Curious, I pulled out the letter. It was a long missive from a 17-year-old Surinamese student who had been in the program briefly, in the Salesclerk group. I had not even noticed that he was gay. But generally speaking I tend to pick up on that more accurately among whites than blacks.

Reading the young man's professions of love gave me a warm feeling. Clearly he now felt secure enough to be able to express his feelings for me. That takes quite a bit of courage. I immediately wrote him back that I thought he was very brave and hoped he would find a nice guy. I made it clear that I was his teacher and that he was much too young for me.

He must have been so infatuated that he misunderstood my letter. His reply was even more impassioned. I decided it would be wise to meet with him in person to make it clear that we had no future as a couple.

Even though I was no longer his teacher, I still felt like he was my student, and you do not have intimate relations with a student. Plus, I personally am not attracted to younger men. We had a long talk in a bar in Amsterdam. He was not very familiar with the gay scene, so I helped show him the way a little. Perhaps it could help make it more accessible to him so that he could start exploring on his own and find a boyfriend. That would help get his mind off of me. We went to the IT club and a few other cafés. We had a great time.

Of course he tried to persuade me to change my mind. To no avail. At the end of the night I took him to the station and never heard from him again. I hope he found a nice guy.

After the love letter a few more threatening letters arrived, but soon stopped. We assumed that we would never find out who the author was. Years later, however, we were in for a huge surprise. A coworker received a Christmas card from one of her students. He was a silent kid who displayed extreme behavioral disorders and sexual frustration, too. At first she wanted to throw the card away because he gave her the creeps.

Luckily she had opened it, though - looking at the handwriting she could not help but think it looked familiar somehow. She brought the card to school and showed it to Boukje. They compared the handwriting with copies of the threatening letters. Sure enough, it matched.

We finally figured out who the perpetrator was.

We agreed that although it was an unfortunate situation the best thing to do would be to put it behind us. There were no more threatening letters. What kind of punishment can you give a severely mentally retarded, socially handicapped boy? It was probably impossible for him to grasp the effect of his letters.

The Evidence

A new school year had started. The students from the previous year made a beeline to me, excitedly sharing their stories about their summer romances. At the same time other students tried to show me their vacation pictures.

"We'll look at those later," I said. "Let's get to class. We'll see if we have time for show and tell."

One of my groups was a class of 16-year-old boys and girls in the Salesclerk program. You could tell by their attitude that they had little faith in education. It was no coincidence that they had been placed at level 1. They had either failed to complete or had insufficient prior schooling.

Some had already attended numerous schools, only to drop out each time. Voluntarily or otherwise. It was as if the educational system had failed them. We had to prove to them that we could be the exception. That we could offer them something: a job and a diploma.

I was their teacher for Social Studies and Theory & Practice. As usual on the first day of school I had the sense that they already knew who I was based on the other students' stories. Just like with all of my other classes I introduced myself and went over school rules.

After fielding a round of comments including "Jesus, this school is like a prison" or "So you aren't allowed to skip class at all?" I was able to begin.

The students needed a few moments to recover from hearing everything that was expected of them, though. Nobody dared to ask me any personal questions. They never did at first. But they would. Sure enough, a couple of weeks later the students had sufficiently gotten acquainted with one another to feel at home in the group.

Class had just started when one of the less timid girls raised her hand. Here we go, I thought. So far none of the students had raised their hand to ask anything about the material we were covering. You simply did not do that if you were a student. After all, it might actually look like you were trying to learn something.

"Yes?" I asked.

"Mr. Van Maaren, I heard that there are gays at this school."

"What?!" I asked, pretending to be horrified. "Who?! Gays aren't allowed at this school! It is explicitly against the rules to be gay here!"

Clearly this young lady was not expecting such a sermon. Nobody said anything, and I resumed the lesson. A couple of weeks later she raised her hand again.

"Mr. Van Maaren, when did you know?"

I acted surprised. "Know what?"

"Well, when did you know that you were gay?" she asked.

"Now where did you get that?" I asked.

"My sister said you were gay."

"Which sister?" I asked, with the same mystified look on my face.

"My sister is in one of the Salesclerk Groups and she had you last year."

"Oh, so you guys want to hear a story," I said. "Okay, if you really want to hear a story, about how it all started, then I will tell you."

I spent 20 minutes telling them the whole story, just like I often did during one of my gay awareness presentations.

You could hear a pin drop. But the silence was quickly shattered by a Surinamese kid, Armand.

"Come on, I don't believe a damn word of that, it's not true what you said."

"What isn't true?" I asked.

"Well, everything! If you were really gay you wouldn't be all talking about it," he called out. A ripple of déjà vu came over me. I had heard this before. It would appear that people only accept a confession about your homosexuality when delivered with your head held down and a remorseful tone. The students had already learned from their parents and society that being gay was the worst thing that could happen to you. Calling someone gay as an insult could serve as sufficient provocation for receiving a punch in the face. And there you were as a teacher presiding over a group of students who not only thought that this was acceptable but funny as well. Obviously this caused quite a culture shock.

After Armand's remark I asked, "You guys wanted to hear a story, right? I don't care whether you believe it or not. A story is a story."

He called out, "You gotta prove to me that you are a gay for real!"

"Kid," I said. "I'll get fired if I have to prove that to you!"

The whole class burst into laughter. Armand looked around, surprised; he did not get the joke.

The girl sitting next to him felt obliged to explain exactly what I had meant by what I said. Finally, the light went on.

Good heavens! There he sat, staring at me fearfully with wide eyes. Just to mess with him a little more I said, "Armand, after class I would like to speak to you in private."

This unsettled him even more. He scanned the room for help, but the rest of the class made it clear that he was on his own. Finally the bell rang. Armand could not wait to get out of there. He practically knocked the table over as he sprinted to the door with Olympic-worthy speed. Everyone roared with laughter. Once he quickly realized that I was in no way a threat he was able to peacefully finish the school year.

Hunting Season

August 1993. Back to school. This year I was going to have Turkish students who had been in trouble with the law. While it was Boukje, our beloved department head at our building, who had done all of the networking to secure a place for this new group at the school, it was Floris and me who had to actually recruit the kids.

It was the first time we had to earn our keep by visiting the local hangouts. Obviously we couldn't do it during the day. These were the kind of kids who, by virtue of unemployment and lack of enrollment, slept all day and spent their nights in hash bars and pool halls.

This was no job for us to take on alone. We would look like two Dutch dog catchers trying to nab a pack of young and unruly hounds. When in fact we were just two smart-alecky white Dutch teachers determined to motivate these Turkish kids to trade their precious time for a year of voluntary incarceration in an educational institution.

Consequently we made an appointment with a man named Tuncay, a Turkish self-appointed social worker of sorts who had already established contact with the Turkish kids. He was also the one who knew which kids were not enrolled in any school.

He had dedicated years towards earning their trust. He did so by frequently visiting the gangs where they spent most of their time. This made it easier for them to approach him with their problems. They would never take the initiative to go to any of the various social services offices in the city. This was partly due to a lack of trust in the Dutch system and partly due to sheer ignorance. Of course their lack of Dutch skills, too, played a major role.

Tuncay could act as an interpreter as well as an expert when it came to dealing with the various agencies. If he trusted our school then it would be easier to persuade the kids to enroll.

If we could give them sufficient tools for finding work they would most likely be well equipped to resist choosing or falling back into a life of crime.

It was nighttime when we met Tuncay and Esat, his assistant, for the first time. Both men exuded utter calm and authority. We were immediately hugely confident in them and could see why the Turkish kids felt the same way. The four of us walked along the deserted streets of the city.

Around here you never saw ordinary citizens out and about after the stores closed. The side streets and alleyways were populated mostly by young people out partying. The scene was a veritable melting pot: Dutch, Surinamese, Antillean, Moroccan and Turkish. It was like we were on safari in the Dutch savannah of juvenile delinquents.

Our first stop was a combination hash bar and pool hall tucked away in a dark alley. The only clue was a neon sign over a door that gave off just enough light to see the kids hanging around the entrance.

We walked into the smoky room. It was a regular beehive of activity inside, mostly from the pool players and not so much the barflies with their joints. They sat quietly enjoying the effects of what was smoldering between their lips and whatever was going through their mind (or not).

Suddenly I saw movement at the other end of the bar. Someone ducked down at the kind a speed you do not normally see among the stoned. Out of curiosity I went to see who was still able to move.

It was Marvin, one of my Retail students. He regarded me with shock and asked, "What are you doing in a hash bar, teach?"

"I didn't see a sign that says 'no teachers allowed' did I?" I asked. "And teachers smoke a joint now and then, right?"

He rose up tentatively, followed by Jan, who had ducked down with him. I hadn't seen him. They looked at each other and then back at me.

"Listen, the other teachers can't know about this," Marvin said.

"It's not the business of other teachers what you and I do in our free time," I said, "so this will remain between us."

Jan offered me his joint but I politely turned it down and said, "Sorry, Jan, I'm here on business tonight. We are looking for new Turkish kids to put together a group. Apparently these guys hang out here sometimes. Carry on with what you were doing."

Tuncay had returned to my side and informed me that the boys we were looking for were not around, so we went back outside. We walked towards the market, behind the Hema and Vroom & Dreesmann department stores, where supposedly there was another hash bar that they frequented. We went up the stairs and entered a neon-lit room. There was a pool table surrounded by four Turkish guys.

"Tuncay! Esat!" they called enthusiastically. Vigorous handshakes were exchanged and a string of friendly Turkish greetings and salutations. They use more words and phrases to communicate how happy they are to see someone than we Dutch.

To me it felt like this exchange took five minutes. Then we were introduced to the group. Floris and I elicited no more than a quick uninterested glance. In the meantime a couple of other Turkish boys arrived who likewise went through the endless greeting ritual with Tuncay and Esat. Both were led away for a moment to discuss a number of problems, leaving me and Floris alone with the four pool players. I was impressed by the toughness and masculinity that they already exuded at such a young age. Despite my years of teaching experience and working with young people from so many different nationalities and walks of life suddenly I felt uncomfortable and even insecure. What did we look like to them? What did they think of us? How would they react to us? The initial moment of contact was crucially important: if they could not trust us then we could forget it. So there we stood, alone and unprotected in the lair of the Turkish juvenile delinquents. We were the strangers here.

The boys were the ones to break the ice. Soon we were involved in a friendly conversation. At a certain point we were obliged to tell them why we had come with Tuncay and Esat. When we explained that we were teachers and would love to have them at our school the room went silent. But it was quickly over. Basically they were interested. Only they wanted to discuss it in detail with Tuncay first. They were such friendly and polite boys that I was immediately excited about teaching them.

After the initial meeting we spent another evening visiting some hash bars and a youth center in their neighborhood, which the locals referred to as "Turkenburg," as it was populated almost entirely by Turks.

Everywhere we went we met friendly and enthusiastic people. Of course it was not unusual to be regarded initially with suspicion; after all, we were Dutch people who normally never ventured into these types of places. More specifically, we were Dutch people between the ages of 35 and 40. We were on their turf, which was away from the scrutiny of parents.

But thanks to the trust that they had in Tuncay and Esat everything went smoothly, and slowly but surely we started getting used to these kids. Kids who basically were no different from Dutch kids. In fact, they came across as friendlier and more polite. They would form the ALOP group, the at-risk ethnic minority students.

The Pink Problem

"Peter, I need to talk to you for a minute," Boukje said right as I was about to lock my classroom.

"In two weeks you're going to start working with the Turkish kids and we have a problem. The kids are Muslim. It could be difficult for them to accept the fact that you are gay. So I would think it was best if you kept quiet about it. If you tell them, it could keep the entire group away. We can't afford to take that risk. So zip your lip!"

"Come on, Boukje," I said. "The whole school knows I'm gay. They'll talk to each other and it won't be long before they find out."

"They'll be in a different building, so that's not going to be a problem," she said.

"Boukje, the students aren't idiots. They'll find out soon enough. Anyway, the couple of Turkish kids we already have here at school know that I'm gay. If they find out that we're going to be teaching the new group, they'll just tell them. They live in the same neighborhood, and go to the same community center. You can never keep this under wraps."

"If you just keep quiet everything will be fine," she said, and walked off.

Dammit, I thought, here we go again with the same crap as six years ago. We're taking on Turkish delinquents, and suddenly I'm the big pink menace.

The poor dears with their records could end up the victims of my sexual inclination. And the school, too. It could cost them students. It could earn them a bad reputation. Oh how blind I was! Here I thought that I had made inroads into gay liberation, or at least achieved a degree of tolerance towards gays. There were no more discussions on the subject, which led me to believe that all was well. The emphatic orders from Boukje cut so deep that I had to talk to Tuncay. I arranged to meet him that very same day.

The plan was to look at the room where the new group would be having class. I was uncharacteristically quiet, which prompted him to ask: "What's going on with you? You're so quiet. Did something happen?"

"Tuncay, I have to tell you something. I'm gay. Boukje feels that this could have a negative impact on the group." I told him the whole story and to my surprise he was shocked. Not that I was gay, he could not care less, but because of the way Boukje was acting.

"That's ridiculous," he said. "I mean, it's not like I can pretend I'm not Turkish. You don't have to tell the boys on the very first day. But if they ask, you should just tell them. If they have a problem with it, they can leave. They have to learn that they are in the Netherlands and not in Turkey. Don't listen to Boukje and do what you feel is most important. You will be able to tell for yourself whether it is safe enough to talk about it or not."

"I am relieved," I said. "I am so glad that you are so positive about this. Based on everything I've read about Muslims I thought you would object, too,"

"Peter," he said, "believe me; lots of Turks in the Netherlands accept more of the Dutch culture than the Dutch think!"

I never dreamed that a Muslim would be so understanding. Silly me, I had expected more support from Boukje than him. She wanted to shove me back into the closet, all in the name of being friendly and protective, when in fact she had no knowledge of - let alone experience with - Islam. I was going to be working closest with Tuncay and therefore his opinion meant the most to me.

Communication problems

Loaded down with books I boarded the bus headed to the Turkish quarter. It was still early. I wanted to have everything ready before my "motivated" group of at-risk ethnic minority students showed up. The bus stop was across from a low makeshift building surrounded by tall trees and low shrubs. The air was filled with Turkish music coming from balconies adorned with satellite dishes. The street was lined with all kinds of Turkish markets and shops. It was like Little Istanbul!

It was also the perfect place to make our kids feel as comfortable as possible. After all, it was their turf. So we hoped that the psychological barrier they faced would prove surmountable, even though it was downright early for them.

I had a key to the building and let myself in. There were a few advertising brochures scattered on the floor of the foyer. I picked them up and turned right. Here was the room that I had to transform into a classroom. I did not have much time. There were tables everywhere littered with empty cups, playing cards and checkerboards from the night before. A slot machine stood to the left. Before rearranging everything I decided to make some tea. I would have to make do without Frits' nectar of the gods for the time being. It did not take long before I had tidied everything and lined up the tables. I set up a portable blackboard at the front of the class. There were two pool cues leaning against the wall. These would come in handy later. I sat down to enjoy my fresh cup of tea. The students should be arriving any minute now. In fact, they were already 15 minutes late.

It was good that we had chosen a site away from the school to get started. They could come here for regular lessons and we could evaluate their behavior and decide whether they were suitable candidates for joining our school later. The disabled kids would be in for a huge shock if they were suddenly confronted with this rowdy bunch, even though they had more or less become accustomed to the Retail students. However, the Retail students had been removed from the building in the meantime. Despite the considerable investment in the building and the classrooms they only spent two years in our building. Order had been restored, and we wanted to hold onto it as long as we could until the time was right to unleash the Turkish kids on the building.

It was not the first time I was teaching a class made up entirely of ethnic minority students. In addition to my regular job I gave free Dutch lessons to African and Pakistani illegal aliens in the Bijlmer housing projects twice a week. But you could not compare my language students with this bunch. The Bijlmer group comprised adults who were eager to learn Dutch. They felt it would help them find employment faster, albeit illegally. The Turkish kids, though; they represented an entirely different culture and religious background and motivation.

Still, it was interesting for me to teach a class made up entirely of individuals who were not from the Netherlands. One by one the drowsy students drifted in. I stood up to greet them. I had seen a couple of them in the hash bars, but most of the faces were new to me.

It was obvious that they knew each other well, however, and a lot of time was lost to what I assumed was the need to discuss the previous day's events. Their conversations were in Turkish, which made me feel excluded. "Okay guys," I called. "We're going to start class now," and I handed out the teaching materials. Silence descended on the room.

We started out with a lesson in grammar and vocabulary. I gave them lots of examples on the blackboard and then had them do various exercises. This would help me determine their fluency in Dutch. I quickly saw that there was a huge range of levels. Some could not speak or write a single word in Dutch while others had already taken Dutch classes. Consequently, a number of students felt obliged to act as impromptu interpreters, explaining everything in Turkish to those students who could not follow what I was saying.

"Come on, in Dutch," I would call out. "We only speak Dutch during class."

"But teacher, Youssuf doesn't understand it. I have to quickly explain, otherwise he can't do his work," one of the students said.

I tried to read the innocent look on his face to see whether he was pulling my leg. See, I suspected that the students were discussing topics not even remotely related to the lesson. But there was no way for me to prove it, so I had to take his word for it.

Sometimes I walked around the room during class and would tap a student on the head to get their attention again. This would get them back on track at once. The tapping usually elicited a round of laughs, but according to some of the students it was not hard enough. Someone called out, "Teacher, you have to use that stick. That's what teachers in Turkey do."

"Sorry, kids," I informed the class. "We aren't allowed to do that in the Netherlands. That's why I don't use a stick."

Sometimes, if two kids started gabbing again, I would slowly walk over to the wall where the pool cues were. I would pick one up and turn around. The potential targets were oblivious to my actions, but the rest of the class could see what was going on. I would casually stroll up behind them. Then, standing at cue's length, I would administer a light tap on their heads. They would drop forward, holding their heads. The looks of surprise on the faces would cause the entire class to erupt in laughter.

"Mr. Van Maaren," someone called. "You need to hit harder. In Turkey you get hit really hard. In wintertime, after you just spent a long time walking in the cold, you get smacked on your cold fingers with a stick. Now that really hurts. And just for showing up late. Sometimes," the boy continued, "there isn't even a bus to take to school. When you have to walk you always arrive late, and you always get hit. You even get spanked."

He stood up, turned around and threw himself across the table and made spanking gestures. Once again, the entire class erupted in a fit of laughter. This time it was more a collective sign of recognition. Apparently everyone had endured this type of corporal punishment at some point. Perhaps this explained their reluctance to go to school.

Whereas I was learning plenty during these classes, the same could not be said for the students. In fact, they were getting nowhere. Because the location was really more of a recreation room it felt more like a course arranged by a community center instead of a serious educational program. One day, a new student named Nesdet arrived late for class. He reported to me directly and said, in broken Dutch, "Mr. Van Maaren, I want to leave early this afternoon."

"I don't think so," I told him. "This isn't a clubhouse. Take your seat."

"But teacher," he said, "I have to go with my mother to the hospital."

"Sure, sure," I said. "I saw you from the bus with your girlfriend. You were walking through the shopping center. You want to hang out with her in the city this afternoon. Sit down. You're going to participate in class, just like everyone else."

He fell silent and stared at me, almost viciously. If looks could kill. Despite his poor Dutch he understood that I had his number. After I told him where he could sit I turned around to take out some books from my bag. I heard a click and felt someone grab my forehead from behind. Nesdet was clutching me to his chest, and the tip of his switchblade was poking my Adam's apple.

"Okay, teacher," he said. "Do I get to leave early today or not?"

With my eyes trained on the blade I said, "That's a nice switchblade. Put it back in your pocket and take your seat. You are going to be here all afternoon."

I heard another click; he released my head, put the knife back in his pocket and took his seat as if nothing had happened. Aghast, the class first looked at me and then at the new student. He remained in class without any further ado.

By continuing class I made it clear that this incident had made no impression on me whatsoever. I was not even shaking. I was not scared. It seemed and felt like it had not even happened. And I think that was what impressed the other kids. It had never been so quiet in the classroom. The fact that he would not be allowed to leave early was sufficient punishment for him, I decided. If I were to report the assault to Tuncay or the police he would most certainly be sent back to jail. And I was not ready to offer him a school career behind bars. I wanted to see whether his behavior could be changed. He needed to learn that there were other ways to express your displeasure. Using words, not weapons.

Anyway, I had not sustained any emotional damage, right? I did not lose any sleep over it. Our job was to do more than just teach these kids Dutch. This special group needed to be socialized. They needed to learn how to act differently. Ultimately, this was not a normal group of students. If an average student behaved this way around a teacher, there would be severe consequences. Expulsion at the very least. Why bother thinking about their future? But I felt that these kids required a different approach. I got the impression that Boukje and the other faculty members disagreed, so I kept this switchblade incident under my hat. Besides, the school administrators had already made it clear that I was supposed to return any confiscated weapons to the owner at the end of the day. Without anyone to watch your back it seemed that it was up to you to decide how to deal with such situations, so I did what I thought was best.

Nothing I had learned at teachers college had prepared for me this. Intuition, resilience, flexibility and creativity got you farther than any program out there. The classroom was your personal training academy. Except that the students were unaware that in some way they were my teachers, too.

The Door and the Window

We did not teach in the community center for long; it was soon decided that these kids should be taking regular classes in a regular school during regular school hours. This was good, because carting all the books and materials back and forth was really a pain. Sometimes I would accidentally forget to bring something and would have no choice but to improvise. That of course did not exactly encourage the students to learn.

The group was like this high strung pack of dogs. You often had to raise your voice to keep them under control. But the little masochists were not always content to leave it at that. According to them, we should have beaten the tar out of them, just like in Turkey. Our words had little effect. They did not understand us. Evidently they wanted to *feel* like we were the boss, not just hear it. I am guessing that there were certain teachers who would have accommodated their disciplinary wishes. All too gladly, in fact. Especially when they got on your last nerve. But we happen to have laws here, and our own cultural values. I am happy to report that sadistic physical forms of punishments are no longer allowed, although some teachers simply turned to mentally abusing their students. Whether that is less traumatic I have no idea.

Although the move was a blessing, there was one problem. Namely, how was I going to be able to keep my homosexuality a secret from the new group, considering that the rest of the school was in the know? Luckily, the Turkish kids did not speak or understand much Dutch yet. However, it would not be long until they did. Or at least that was our goal.

As I had already told Boukje, the Turkish kids who had been in school for years would not be able to keep quiet. They spoke both Dutch and Turkish. And I had really good contact with these students. I regularly walked around school arm in arm with male Turkish students. They would say, "Dutch people might think I'm gay, too, but we know it isn't true. We walk around like this in our culture, so it's fine."

You could be pretty sure that what Boukje insisted had to be kept a secret would be public knowledge within a matter of hours. I did not understand in the first place the need to cut off Turkish kids from the rest of the student body.

The moment of truth came a few weeks later. My classes proceeded as usual. But when I visited the group during their other lessons, for example in Home Ec class, I heard hostile whispers of *ibne* [faggot]. I could feel the tension that the word spread throughout the group.

"Anything wrong?" I asked, doing my best Alice in Wonderland impression. "What does that word mean?"

"Nothing," they hissed.

Everyone turned around and resumed what they had been doing. They did not know that I had already learned the Turkish words for "queer" and "faggot" from my Turkish students in the Retail class.

While I am sure that Boukje's intentions were good concerning her orders to keep my sexual preference quiet, the situation was reaching the boiling point. Every time I felt the tension created by the word *ibne* I suffered a humiliation within myself. Anyone who says that you should just ignore it, rise above it, or otherwise turn a blind eye to it either does not understand or has never experienced this type of feeling. The way the word was uttered made me feel like a piece of garbage.

The same situation kept repeating. Despite the hateful comments I resolutely persisted in visiting my class during their other lessons. I went looking for it. I wanted them to accept me. So I had to rise to the confrontation. But at a given moment the anger rose from the tips of my toes, flooding my entire body. I walked out of the Home Ec room, slammed the door behind me and went to the teacher's lounge.

Boukje and Frits were sitting there having coffee.

"Goddammit, enough is enough!" I shouted furiously. "I'm going to talk to my class about homosexuality this afternoon. I'm sick of being called *ibne*!"

Two other faculty members walked into the room.

"I don't think that's a good idea," Boukje said. "That could only create more problems for yourself. They're difficult kids. You really need to think twice about what you are doing."

"I'm going to give a general talk about homosexuality. I want to hear what they have to say about the topic. I'm not going to start off with making it all about me. I'll see what happens. But I'm really sick of this. In this way, I can't teach this group anymore. I have to do something. I don't know what else to do. Anything is better than this."

Apparently, the determination I felt could be heard in my voice. Nobody tried to stop me. The break was over and my students were already standing outside the classroom waiting for me. I did not want to look at them or greet them cheerfully in the normal way. Everyone filed in and immediately took their seat. It was silent. They seemed to sense that something was bothering me. They really should have known exactly why I was seething with pent-up anger.

"Kids, today we're going to talk about homosexuality," I said, arguably a little too forcefully.

One of the tough guys slouched back in his chair raised his arm and announced, "We don't want to talk about that. Gays are disgusting. They use the window to go inside, and the others, um, how do you call them?"

"Heterosexuals," I said.

"Yeah, they use the door to go inside."

"Right," I said. I did not need any clarification of the chosen sexual imagery. It did not take too much creative thinking to understand he was talking about vaginal and anal contact.

"But you know," I continued, "I've heard that in many Islamic countries the men use the window before they get married, and the door after they get married."

Silence. The class sat intently thinking over the scenario.

"Yeah, that's true!" someone called out. "So actually there's nothing weird about gays. We all use the window to get inside sometimes. The girls have to stay virgins, obviously." Knowing smirks were exchanged. Everyone seemed to grasp the theory. Until a boy posed a question that had been on his mind for weeks.

"Mr. Van Maaren, are you an *ibne*?"

"Yes," I said. I looked at each boy expectantly.

I could tell by their faces that some were not bothered by this fact, whereas others clearly had a problem with it. The floodgates were open and they bombarded me with questions. The same questions that Dutch students would ask.

These were simply young men who, although they knew gay people, had never been given any information or explanation about homosexuality. They asked how and when I knew I was gay. When did I do it for the first time. If I had ever slept with a girl. And many more of the usual "superficial" questions, which I answered with as few personal details as possible. See, the idea was not to talk about me; the goal was to discuss homosexuality in general. The tension had dissipated, the truth had been told.

Cultural Confusion

Now that we had addressed my homosexuality freely, openly and honestly, we could talk about other things, such as the way they viewed Dutch culture. Compared to Turkish and Islamic culture, they thought ours was much too liberal. Girls walked around here free as they pleased without the protection of a father, uncles or brothers. They explained that letting our women walk around like that indicated a complete lack of respect. They also said that it was terrible how Dutch girls were allowed to have sex, while adding that they were quite pleased about it, too. But they announced that it did make the girls whores. Consequently they agreed that there was nothing wrong with harassing a Dutch woman or girl. "The Dutch women like it," they said. "And their boyfriends are afraid to do anything about it." Laughter.

"Right," I said. "That's because you guys are cowards. The only time you dare to do it is when there's a whole bunch of you. And you know, we know that if we get into a fight with a Turk then other Turks will immediately jump in. Without asking who did what."

"Well, we have to help each other out!" someone called.

"Yeah, but not when it's ten against one," I said.

We continued our discussion about the difference between the Netherlands and Turkey. They said that boys and girls in an Islamic society simply do not interact. Everyone makes sure that the girls are protected. They must retain their virginity at any cost. This was why the guys only associated with guys. In Turkey, men and boys are true friends. They have no problem with all of the kissing that goes on as part of the greeting ritual. Not on the mouth, of course; on the cheek. It was what you did with your father, uncles and brothers. Walking around arm in arm or with you're arm draped around the other's shoulder was perfectly normal. You did not do that with girls or women. If you did, you would be in huge trouble with her family.

"But Mr. Van Maaren," someone called out, "in the Netherlands they say you're a queer if a guy kisses another guy or holds hands with him. But we aren't queers! We also do that in Turkey. Nobody calls us *ibne* if we do that. Our fathers, uncles, cousins and friends think it's normal, too."

"Of course you aren't *ibne* if you do that in Turkey," I said. "However, in our culture you only kiss a woman or a girl, not a man or a boy. Plus, we hardly ever touch each other. Guys don't do that at all. You only kiss your dad or your uncle when you're a little kid. Here, we think it's very normal for girls to physically display affection. They can kiss without us assuming they are lesbians."

During the discussion one of the wanna-be tough guys felt obliged to announce, "Gays must die by the sword. I should kill you. That's what it says in the Koran."

"Well," I said, "I don't think that's a very good idea. First of all, because I'm such a cool teacher with nice green eyes. Second, because it would be very messy. Who would clean it up? Frits?"

This was the only mention of the Koran. They were likely as unfamiliar with the Koran as many Christian and Catholic kids were with the Bible.

After class I joined the group for coffee and a smoke in the lounge. Liberated and relieved I was able to sit down with them without having to hide anything. The atmosphere was friendly now. They were back to being fun, wild and uninhibited boys. They would grab my shoulder or walked through the hall with me, arm in arm. Having opened up to them I was no longer a threat. Nevertheless, I would soon be confronted with an unexpected threat from their side. Just when I thought things were going so well.

Russian Roulette

One day I was sitting in the smoking lounge having coffee with the Turkish students. One of the students said, "Hey, Mr. Van Maaren, Nesdet has a gun."

I turned to look at Nesdet, staring him down. He gazed back disinterestedly. I resumed my conversation and calmly finished my coffee. But out of the corner of my eye I watched as Nesdet stood up and headed towards me. I kept talking until suddenly I felt something cold against my temple.

"Okay, teach," Nesdet said. "Do I get to leave early today? I could shoot you dead this instant, it's loaded."

Ignoring Nesdet and his gun I tried to carry on my conversation with the other boys. Only there was one slight problem. Everyone was staring at me and Nesdet in terror, and nobody was saying a word.

"It's a real gun, I swear. I could shoot you dead just like that," Nesdet said, surprised by the lack of serious response.

"Oh, get out of here," I said, holding my head perfectly still. "It's not real."

"It is too. I could shoot you dead this instant," Nesdet repeated with a little more force and astonishment. I said something to the other students, who were still staring at us in silent horror.

"Mr. Van Maaren, I want to leave early, or else I will shoot you dead. I'm going to play Russian Roulette with you. For real. I swear. I am going to shoot you," Nesdet repeated.

"Take that phony thing out of here. It's not real, so sit back down. You aren't leaving early," I said.

Suddenly he took the gun away from my temple to show me. It was my lucky day; the gun was resting in the palm of his hand. In one swift move I grabbed it away from him.

"What are you doing?" Nesdet shouted. "That's my gun, give it back!"

"Nope, it's mine now," I said. "Thanks."

Grumbling he sat down and did not say another word. He did not try to take it back from me. I stood up and walked over to our office to call the main building. Regrettably, there was nobody from the board available at the moment to deal with the problem, and I was instructed to wait until the next break. When I finally managed to reach the administrator I simply said that I had confiscated a gun. I brought up the first incident several years ago. He told me to return the gun to the student. He did not even ask how I was. Obviously my mental state was of no concern. As if disarming someone was no more than taking away a Walkman or an apple. At the end of the day I grudgingly returned the gun.

Strangely enough, the entire incident made a huge impression on the boys. More so than the confrontation with the switchblade.

"Hey, Mr. Van Maaren, you weren't scared at all, were you?" They asked.

It seemed like this had all been some kind of test. A test to see whether I would be scared off by the boys. Apparently I had passed the test. They would never forget it. Neither would I for that matter.

The Alarm Gun

I seldom encountered the use of weapons at the other schools that were part of this regional system. Enrollment among ethnic minority students was increasing, but mostly in full-time programs. You did not see very many in the combination work/study programs. Apparently the idea of spending four days at work and one day at school did not appeal to them. Of course, there was also the fact that only full-time students were eligible for student aid. There were very few Turkish or Moroccan students in the part-time groups, which meant that there was not much of a language problem. Their Dutch was good and they did not have others to converse with in their native language during class. Slowly, however, that started to change. The school was becoming more ethnically diverse. But that only made things more fun. At least in the beginning.

The entire process was so gradual that at first we did not notice the shift in mentality. We simply taught our classes. In the beginning, none of the higher ups instructed us to take the Islamic faith into account. These were simply youngsters who were here to take classes.

The only violent episode that occurred at school in the early Nineties involved a Turkish student in the Mechanics program. The kid had been acting out and the teacher warned him several times during class, threatening to send him out of the room. After yet another warning, he completely lost it. He pulled an alarm gun out of his bag and aimed it at the teacher. The student was as high as a kite. His utter mental confusion and temporary insanity made his behavior all the more terrifying and imposing. The teacher had never been confronted with this type of situation and instinctively grabbed the nearest student to use as a human shield.

"I'll shoot you dead!" the young man shouted.

Nobody dared to make a move. Eventually, the boy fled the classroom and ran towards the train station. One of the students phoned the police, who managed to pick up the assailant at the station. But this call also put the school in an incredibly embarrassing situation.

The problem had been made public. This time, the school would not be able to take care of it behind closed doors like it had always done before. The media descended upon the school. The news stories and the cafeteria rumor mill revealed that the boy had used an alarm gun. He never would have brought it to school if his mother had not been planning to clean his room. He was afraid that she would find it, which was why he hid it in his bag. If he had not been so high and the teacher had not given him such a hard time, nothing would have happened. We were instructed over the intercom not to talk to the press. The board would take care of it.

That night we saw two of our board members on the evening news. The look on their faces made it clear that they were uncomfortable with everything that had happened and all of the publicity. But I was appalled at how they completely ignored the trauma suffered by the teacher. They earnestly explained that every effort would be made to avoid ruining the student's future. All of their attention was on the perpetrator. He, not the teacher, was portrayed as the victim. The teacher was out on disability for months. The student was eventually transferred to another school.

Turkish Shooting Gallery

I arrived at the station unsuspectingly. I descended the stairs to the buses and saw Ibrahim standing in the distance. He saw me, too, and dashed towards me.

"Mr. Van Maaren," he said with a big grin, "no students today." He held his hand up in front of his eyes, fingers spread.

"What are you talking about?" I asked.

"Don't you get it?" he asked, gesturing more adamantly with his hand in front of his face.

"No, I have no idea," I said. "Explain it to me on the bus. Hurry up, it's going to leave without us."

We found seats in the back of the bus and he excitedly began telling his story.

"All of the students are at the police station! Everyone got locked up." He gestured with his fingers in front of his eyes again. I finally understood his little pantomime, but I could hardly believe that everyone was in jail.

"Last night," he continued, "everyone went to the fair downtown. I wasn't there, but I heard the whole story. Nobody had any money to do anything, so they were bored. Then they started talking about weapons and somebody said he had a gun at home. Nobody believed him, of course. He kept going on and on about that gun and the rest of the guys started laughing at him. He got so mad that he went home to prove it. He came back about a half an hour later with the gun. Everyone was really excited about it, you know, a real gun and all. Everyone got a chance to hold it but then the youngest kid started playing with it. He aimed the gun at each of the guys and said, 'Bang, bang, bang!"

According to Ibrahim's account, everything was okay until he put the gun in one guy's face and suddenly there was a shot. Bang! The victim dropped to the ground and lay there, bleeding. The kid who had shot him stood there, shocked--and still holding the gun out. The owner of the gun did not hesitate a moment, lunging forward and grabbing the weapon and making a run for the river. He threw the gun in the water and went back to the group. The kid who had been shot was still on the ground, surrounded by the others. The bullet had entered his jaw through the side of his nose.

The police quickly arrived on the scene, along with an ambulance. The situation further escalated into a fight between the police and the group. As the victim was being loaded into the ambulance, the rest of them were trying to take on the police. In all of the commotion it was impossible for the police to figure out who had actually fired the shot, so everyone was arrested and thrown in jail. The questioning went on all night. The police were also interested in finding out the owner of the gun. Nobody was talking, of course. They knew they would all be released.

"The kid who got shot," Ibrahim concluded, "He isn't going to turn anybody in, teach. He's a Turk, too. A Turk isn't going to rat out another Turk, is he?"

I listened to his story incredulously. Of course I knew that these kids were hardly Boy Scouts, but seriously I could not believe that they could go this far.

We got off the bus and the topic of conversation changed. However, when we arrived at school it was obvious that word had spread fast. Sure enough, everyone was in jail. The entire group would be back in class within a couple of days. Nobody was about to give up the assailant, and the police could not hold them any longer.

Their intense solidarity, the whole code of honor, as well as their proclivity to play dangerously with human lives -- it was all clear to me now. It would be very difficult to socialize these boys. At school they did not usually make any serious threats. Yes, they were rowdy and at times out of control. But at least there were no more incidents involving guns. They had gotten the message that I was not going to let them intimidate me that way. Apparently the fun was over.

Raging Hormones

When you have spent years teaching mostly Dutch students it is hard to imagine that you must suddenly abandon your whole way of dealing with a class. To me, adolescents were adolescents, period. It did not matter where they were from. If you knew how to capture their interest then you could get them to learn. Or at least that was how it had worked for years before the arrival of this Turkish group.

We taught Dutch, math and social studies, to the extent that it was possible. The language problem remained a stubborn barrier for really being able to get through to them about the intricacies of Dutch society.

In order to provide them more insight we organized a field trip one day. No big deal, right? We went on plenty of field trips with our classes. An easy train ride, nothing more. Gert, one of the 16+ group teachers, volunteered at a local radio station in his free time. He thought it might be fun to show them. Maybe they could talk about their experiences in the Netherlands on air. Fun idea.

We gathered at the station early one morning. As usual, most of the students were late and some of them did not bother showing up at all. We finally boarded the train an hour behind schedule. Of course a school field trip is a noisy affair. Regardless of their biological age they all morph into a bunch of children during an outing. Plus, this was our first trip with these students and likely their first school trip ever.

No sooner had we boarded the train the students had disappeared. Dutch students usually took their seats immediately. Of course, these were not Dutch students. These walking overdoses of hormones promptly set out to find the Dutch women on board and see if they could quickly make a multicultural score. Using their newly acquired Dutch skills they started hitting on young and older women alike. They were so obnoxious that no woman would have taken the bait. We had to practically drag the boys away.

Obviously we had forgotten to check their hormone levels prior to departure. Perhaps we could have done so by putting a pressure gauge next to their crotch. It would have made more sense to pack cold washcloths and ice cubes for lunch instead of *börek* and *baklava*. We had never witnessed this type of behavior taken to such extremes. They were like wild animals in mating season. As soon as we managed to get them into their seats in our car, off they went the moment we turned away. It was enough to drive you insane.

There were only four stations left to go before we finally reached our destination, but at every single stop a group of boys would block the exit. As soon as a woman or girl tried to pass, they would press forward, desperate for even a fleeting moment of exciting physical contact. The women could not get off the train quickly enough. Our warnings had lost all effect by now. They listened only to their hormones, which were as palpable inside the train as the ozone smell after a summertime squall. Far less refreshing, though. Finally it was time for us to leave the train. Along with quite a few women.

Five boys ran ahead of us. They proceeded to molest every woman on the stairs in front of them, grabbing them between their legs or their breasts. The women tried to swat them away like flies. I quickly ascended the stairs and smacked them on the head to push them back down the stairs. Really all I wanted to do was go home, but Gert was waiting for us in his car outside the station. The idea was to take them to the radio station, one carload at a time. Of course, that meant that a group would have to stay behind at the station. We had not foreseen any problem with that.

"How was the trip?" Gert asked, beaming.

"I'd rather not talk about it," I snapped.

Confused, he started the car. We left five boys at the station. Gert figured they would wait. I hoped they wouldn't.

The radio station was actually too small even for the first group, but we tried to squeeze everybody in.

"Peter, there's fresh tea and coffee," Gert said. "I'll go pick up the rest of the group. Help yourselves to chocolate cookies, too. I'll be back in 10 minutes."

He left and I poured the tea and coffee. I told the group that they could take a cookie. Despite the language barrier, the instructions could not have been any clearer. I held up one finger and pointed to the open package. Four of them obediently followed the instructions. Then there was Osman, a student who just could not get the hang of Dutch. He took a cookie, shoved it in his mouth, and quickly grabbed another. Bad move. With my free hand I smacked him right in the face.

"I said ONE cookie," I hissed angrily.

He looked at me with surprise. Shocked, he rubbed the spot on his cheek where my hand had struck him. He quickly put the cookie back. Suddenly all was very quiet and hostile inside the radio station.

Gert finally returned after an hour. Of course the boys had not waited at the station. He had felt obliged to drive around town looking for them. In the end, he found only three.

"At least the other two will learn how to get back on their own," I said.

The broadcast was very brief, mostly because the students had very little to say. I guessed that their reticence had something to do with the cookie incident. Basically, it was not worth the huge waste of energy.

What I could see, however, was that we would have to start taking a different approach to field trips by train. And it was high time for teaching these kids sex education and Dutch values and standards. This was completely unacceptable. Their behavior was utterly disrespectful towards women. Well, except Turkish women, of course. They had respect for them. Or more accurately, they were scared silly of the fathers and husbands of these Turkish women.

They were not afraid of Dutch men. Their behavior was unheard of in Turkey, so the logical conclusion was that they must have picked it up here. And now it was up to us to cure them of it.

The two missing boys eventually made it back on their own. Their time spent in the Netherlands so far had shown them that it was pretty easy to travel without a ticket. If you ended up getting caught, all you had to do was make a huge scene.

Exhausted, I returned to our building. Luckily there were a few teachers still in the lounge. I told them what had happened, gesturing wildly and not leaving out any detail. Including the part about slapping Osman. I thought my colleagues would understand, but my honesty had the exact opposite effect.

"Peter, are you okay?" Ingrid asked. She taught sewing class.

"Never been better," I said. "I needed to get tough with this group. It was quite a relief."

"You can't hit a student!" Frits exclaimed. "I'm pretty sure it's against the law to hit a student."

"Well, they don't know that," I said. "And I'm not going to tell them, either. It was necessary to take action. And clearly the wimpy Dutch way of talking everything out is not always effective. Not with this group, at least. They went totally quiet after the slap. Thank god we weren't live on the air. The entire region could have heard how we teach our Turkish students."

"This has to be reported," one of the newer teachers announced.

"Don't even think about it," I said. "It's not in my nature to go around beating on problem students. It was necessary this time. Let's just leave it at that."

I was disappointed by their reactions. And I also understood why some teachers did not talk about what went on in class. You could give others the impression that you did not have any control over yourself or your students. Showing weakness was punished immediately. I had to explain to Boukje what had happened, but that was all. It was also a lot easier to handle the group in the wake of the incident. Clearly these kids were more prone to testing the boundaries than their Dutch peers.

Prayer Break

The school paid very little attention to the students' religious background. They were supposed to take Dutch as well as social studies, P.E., Home Ec and swimming. The initial problems with putting Islamic girls in with the boys already clued us into the fact that these students were not exactly the same as the Dutch kids. Now I had another problem to deal with.

During one of my classes, suddenly and without any explanation all of the girls stood up. It was a simple grammar lesson, without any offensive verbs. Surprised, I asked: "Ladies, what are we up to?"

"It's 2 o'clock, Mr. Van Maaren. We have to pray. We have to pray to Allah five times a day and now it's time again."

That was the first I had heard of it, but I let them go. Who was I to deny them their mandatory moment with Allah?

"They're crazy, teacher," the boys informed me. "They never pray. So why now?"

I began to wonder what exactly the praying was all about, as well as other aspects of the Islamic faith. What was allowed, and what was forbidden? What was required, and what were the followers allowed to decide for themselves? Boukje had no advice to offer, so I had to go looking on my own.

I bought a Dutch-Arabic version of the Koran on the following Saturday. I was interested in finally seeing what kind of rules it prescribed, particularly with respect to prayer rituals. I began reading. God is great, He is all-knowing, and He is all-seeing. Having been raised Roman Catholic, none of this was new to me. That saved a lot of time; I breezed through it.

I tucked a piece of paper between the pages to mark the various passages that I thought might come in handy during class. I began to wonder whether any of the students had ever actually read the Koran. For example, the head scarf. According to the scriptures, a woman is obliged to cover all of the desirable parts of her body. But what qualifies as desirable? I did not find anything about the female body desirable. But then again, I cannot speak for every man.

I thought it would be fun to talk about these things in class. After all, a lot has changed in the Netherlands over the centuries. More and more of the body was revealed; in some periods there was practically nothing covered. I had also noticed on television that the situation varied tremendously among the different Islamic countries, ranging from everything covered to very little covered: each individual country clearly had a great deal of influence on the matter. The topic of head scarves was intriguing, just like many other things I read in the Koran. But I could not find anything about prayer breaks.

Eventually I called Tuncay about the need to pray during class. "They're messing with you," he said as soon as I asked.

"How?" I asked.

"While it is true that every Muslim is supposed to pray five times a day, not everyone has to strictly follow those guidelines. If a Muslim lives or works in a non-Islamic country, Allah will take it in stride. It is understood that you cannot always follow the five times a day schedule. If a believer cannot pray during the day for whatever reason, he or she can make up for it in the evening. You have special prayers for that. The third prayer can be said between two and three, it does not have to be exactly at two o'clock. If you can't pray because you're on your way somewhere, that's fine, you will be forgiven. The Islamic faith takes many exceptions into account, as well as difficulties that believers may encounter. So what those girls told you is nonsense. They don't *have* to do anything."

Armed with this knowledge I was looking forward to the upcoming confrontation with plenty of confidence. It was Wednesday again, and the girls immediately rose for their prayer break, fully expecting to receive my permission. You could tell by the pious looks on their faces that they had already been preparing themselves mentally for intensive religious contact.

"Wait just a minute there, ladies!" I called. "What are we doing?"

Surprised, they looked at me and said, "But Mr. Van Maaren, you know what we're going to do! We have to pray now."

"You're going to stay in your seats," I ordered. "You can pray at 2:30."

"No, we have to do it at TWO o'clock," they protested.

"Ladies, I spent some time reading the Koran," I informed them, using my best poker face. "You have until three o'clock to pray. This gives you plenty of time if you do it at 2:30." Of course that was not completely true, but I was hoping to sound authoritative. And to be honest I was guessing that none of them had ever read the Koran.

"But that's during our break!" they said.

"Watch out," I said, as I raised my finger. "Allah can hear you. He hears you and sees that you are not willing to give up your break for him. Is tea more important than Allah?"

"How do you know that, Mr. Van Maaren?" asked one of the girls. "The Koran is in Arabic. Can you read Arabic?"

"It's in Dutch and Arabic, so it's not a problem," I said. "But you can read and understand Arabic?"

"Well, I can kind of read it, but I don't understand it," she answered. "We read it in Turkish."

"Have you read the entire Koran and understand it?" I asked.

"No, Mr. Van Maaren," she said. "It's really hard. None of us have really read the whole thing."

And so it was clear that the girls had indeed been messing with me. They were no different from the Dutch students after all. They, too, had to obey what they had been taught in school or at home. They had been hoping that as an ignorant Dutchman I would agree to anything that had to do with their religion. This knowledge would play a significant role in how I would go about dealing with them. And vice-versa, too. We were becoming increasingly candid with one another. Far more candid than I had ever imagined could be possible. Incidentally, the girls never prayed at school again. The tea break took priority over Allah after all.

Veiled craftiness

Unexpectedly, and for an unknown reason, our At-Risk Ethnic Students group was doing pretty well. Most of the credit goes to Turkish social worker Tuncay and his coworker Esat. Thanks to them we managed to gain more recognition and trust from the city's Turkish community. The girls were starting to feel more comfortable at school, in spite of the boys behaving like an uncontrollable pack of dogs. They managed to stake a claim for themselves, mainly by making a habit of verbally putting the boys in their place. However, their boldness experienced a momentary lapse. A refined, self-confident young woman was introduced to the group. Dilara wore a traditional Islamic gown with a veil that hung over her shoulders. She had a somewhat stuck-up appearance yet at the same time there was a kind of sweetness and serenity to her. Clearly, she was not to be messed with. She was the paragon of a devout, self-assured and ambitious Muslim woman. From day one she had the annoying habit of arriving two minutes late, every single time. She refused to join the other Turkish girls in their social tea breaks. Every time this queen of little Istanbul finally entered the classroom, she would hiss something in Turkish through her teeth and glare disdainfully at the other girls, who were already seated. One by one they bowed their heads in shame. "What did she say?" I asked. "Nothing, teacher. Never mind. It was nothing," they replied. Then everyone would resume what they had been doing. Miss Islam would scrutinize each assignment for any *haram* or sinful words before deigning to put a pen to paper. If the assignment failed to meet her approval, she would refuse to fill in anything. To my extreme irritation she was completely consistent about this.

Gradually, my patience ran out. It was pretty much inevitable that I would reach the limits of my Dutch tolerance at some point. On the day in question I handed out reading material to the students that I had carefully checked the night before for any potentially disputable words or sentences. I had not been able to find any. The students were instructed to read the passage and pick out any unfamiliar words. Their next task was to find and underline all of the verbs. Everyone immediately set to work. Then Dilara arrived. Late, as usual. And, once again, hissing something through her teeth. The reaction from the other girls was the same as always. I handed the lesson material to Dilara. Without even looking at it she set her paper aside and announced, "I do not want to read this; it is *haram*."

"That is impossible," I said. "I checked everything."

"I am still not going to read it." She immediately began rolling up her paper.

Infuriated, I told her, "I go out of my way for you all the time and now I've had it with your refusals based on religious reasons."

"I am still not going to read it," she said, dramatically tearing up the paper.

More than anything it was that arrogant look of hers that made my blood boil. I felt like I was about to explode. I gave her a new sheet and she tore that up, too.

"I have completely had it with you!" I shouted.

She took the corner of her veil and covered her face. I could see in her eyes that she was mocking me. Her eyes smiled triumphantly. Apparently she had been trying to drive me crazy and she had finally succeeded. "Take that veil off!" I shouted angrily. "I want to see your face!"

She kept the veil over her face. I was this close to smacking her. I ordered: "If you have even the slightest inkling of respect left you will take that veil away from your face. Otherwise get the hell out of my classroom!"

I had totally lost control of myself. I felt so incredibly humiliated by that veil. Her stare became even more defiant, more piercing, and I could no longer keep it together. I completely exploded. Enraged and powerless I stormed out of the classroom and slammed the door with a thunderous *bang!*

I needed good old Frits and his coffee to help me settle down. Out of the corner of my eye I saw Dilara rush out of the classroom, her veil and gown flapping. I was shaking so badly that the coffee spilled over the edge of the cup. I could not even get my lips to work properly to take a sip. "I am never teaching those Turks again," I raged to Frits. "I have had it. My tolerance has reached the limit. Who do they think they are?!"

After a few minutes two of the girls from my class showed up and said, "Teacher, don't be mad anymore. We just want to continue the lesson. Come back to class, okay?"

"Ladies," I said. "Where were you when I was in trouble? You did not help me. I was up there alone. You did not say anything, which means that you agree with her. Go back to class. I feel abandoned. I am not ready to do any teaching just yet."

They silently returned to class. A little while later a couple of boys arrived. "Teacher, come on. We want to have class."

"Not yet," I said. "I am still shaking like the string of a bow after the arrow has been shot," I said, pantomiming an archer's moves. "Wow, cool way of putting it," they told me. "Please come back to class. Please?"

After I finished my coffee I returned to the classroom. Everyone was silent. "Now I want to know what Dilara said every time she came in late," I announced.

"She called us whores, teacher, because we do not wear a headscarf," they answered.

My blood began to boil all over again. Suddenly I was so utterly sick of that girl. What on earth was she thinking? It was like she was some kind of Turkish-Islamic secret police in charge of deciding whether everything at this school was being done in accordance with Muslim law. But apparently my meltdown made a big impression on Dilara. She never came back to our school. And in spite of my professionalism I could not make the effort to bring her back.

The Hymen

Who would have dreamed that my orientation would have a positive effect on Muslims? After all, the Islamic faith is very clear about the perversion and sin of homosexuality! But judging by the students' attitudes Boukje's fears were unfounded. Enrollment was on the rise and not a single Muslim left the school on account of having the likes of me for a teacher.

I think their aggression at the outset had more to do with my forced silence. These kids simply wanted to be treated honestly. They figure out quickly enough whether they can trust you. If they feel like you are putting them on, they will give it right back to you and then some. And feel no whatsoever compassion. By being open about who and what I was, I took them into my confidence with respect to a personally sensitive matter. I made them equal to the other students who already knew about my orientation. And I loved them, despite their criminal backgrounds in some cases.

Clowning around and incorporating plenty of theatrics in class helped everyone let go and relax. This was necessary in order to help them momentarily forget about their situation, which was pretty dire for some. Perhaps it was because I had managed to establish this trust with the students that I was allowed to teach sex ed to the Islamic girls. Of course I discussed it with Tuncay first on account of the potential problems. His only condition was that I would have to separate the boys from the girls. Scheduling-wise this was no trouble. I thought it would be best not to let the groups know about the lesson plan in advance. First of all because it would make it more difficult to get the boys to go along with dividing the class for a day, and secondly because they might say that Islamic girls were not allowed to learn about sex. It would take just one of them to object and spread the news around. Not that I was anticipating too many problems, but still, an ounce of prevention beats a pound of cure.

Break was over. Or at least it was according to the schedule. The boys did not agree. Again with the same old whining! By the time you managed to herd all of them into the room a good 10 minutes of teaching time had passed.

"Guys, today we are going to have class separately. It's really important!" I called.

"What are you going to talk about?" one kid asked.

"You don't need to be concerned about that," I said. "It's women's business. You won't be of any help to me."

"I wanna be a girl today!" someone else called out.

"Okay, just follow me to the kitchen then," I said. "First we'll chop off your *jarak* [dick]. Then I'll make a girl out of you. Otherwise you can't participate."

"No way," he said, grabbing his crotch. "I'll go sit with the others."

I waited outside my classroom, trying to get the girls in my class into the room and keep the boys out and into the room next door. Finally I had achieved the impossible and could shut the door.

"Why do we have to be separated today, Mr. Van Maaren?" one of the girls asked.

"I want to talk to you about sex today," I told them. "You already told me that you wanted to discuss it, except not around the boys. Now you can decide whether you want to or not. If it's a problem and you don't, we'll just carry on with our usual Dutch lessons."

They looked at each other. For a few minutes it seemed like it was too scary after all and they were not ready. But Ayca quickly piped up: "It's fine, teacher. Just don't let our parents find out about it. Otherwise we'll be in big trouble. We won't say anything, but you have to promise not to tell them, too."

"We are more concerned with you than we are about your parents," I said. "Tuncay is aware of my plans to teach this class. I'm sure that he's not going to say anything. Actually, he told me it was okay to do this. But are you okay with it, having a man lead the discussion?"

They started laughing. Then someone explained, "Oh Mr. Van Maaren, you're *ibne*.

You're not a man the same way as other men are. You can talk about things the way women do."

"Uh, thanks," I said, although I could not decide whether their take on my manliness was meant as a compliment or an insult. At any rate, I could start the class. Without any formal teaching materials, I should add; we could not risk having any evidence that we had ever talked about this subject. It might end up in the wrong hands. My drawing teacher experience came in handy, though. I could draw the necessary illustrations and quickly erase them in one fell swoop.

I started out by talking to them about the way in which contact between Turkish boys/men and girls/women normally occurred in their community. As expected, it was very difficult if not downright impossible for them to have any such contact on account of the immense social control exerted by neighbors and family. The girls were supposed to go home immediately after school. They obeyed. Nobody liked following this strict rule, but it was better than getting into trouble for breaking it. All but one of the girls expected to have an arranged marriage. Whether they wanted to or not. The exception was a young woman whose parents had always been very progressive, even before they moved to the Netherlands. Actually, she was already married to a man from Turkey, whom she had met when she was still living there. They fell in love and she knew she wanted to spend the rest of her life with him. Their biggest problem had been that it took a long time for him to be allowed into the Netherlands. However, she was working as a hairdresser, with her own income, and eventually he was granted entry.

A major difference between the Turkish and the Dutch girls was that these young women were not allowed to experiment with love, dating, affection and sexuality with boys. Their first sexual contact took place on their wedding night.

"But the boys told me that some couples experiment before marriage by having sex the rear entry way," I said.

They exchanged surprised looks.

"How do you know that?" one of the girls asked.

"The boys told me they sometimes go through the window before marriage, and use the door afterwards."

"Well, some girls want to do that, but you have to be really careful," another girl said. "I mean, you could end up not being a virgin anymore."

"Is that still so important?" I asked naively.

"Are you kidding? If you don't bleed on your wedding night, your husband is allowed to leave you! That's not only bad news for you, but for the entire family, too."

"Do you have to hang the bloody sheets out the window?"

"No, thank goodness. Well, in some rural villages they still do that sometimes. An aunt or the mother-in-law visits the next day to inspect the sheets. But if you're not a virgin sometimes your husband knows about it, too. You know, if you've already had sex with him. Then you put a little blood on the sheets and everybody's happy."

"Okay, so what do you think a hymen looks like?" I asked.

Everyone gave the exact same answer that I had already heard from Dutch students so many times: a membrane that covered the entire vaginal opening. I drew a hymen on the chalkboard. Now they could see that it was no more than a thick edge or fold that would be damaged by penetration and subsequently start bleeding.

"Look, everyone's hymen is different. Sometimes it's very thin and a man can go right past it without causing any damage. And then he accuses you of not being a virgin anymore, even though you have never had sex with anyone before. Plus, if the man has a small or thin *jarak*, chances are he's not going to damage that membrane, either. And who gets the blame? Right: you do."

"Well, that's not fair," they agreed. "Is there anything you can do about it?" they asked.

"No," I said. "Which is why it is wrong that you get in trouble when it's not your fault to begin with. But what if you have already had sex?"

"We know someone who can help us out," they said. "With the right tools and stuff."

"Sometimes it hurts but at least it makes you bleed. That way everyone is happy. And you can get your hymen reconstructed, too. A lot of families are willing to pay big money for that. It's a much bigger outrage if you don't bleed on your wedding night."

"What I think is really unfortunate for you, though," I said, "is that Muslim men ejaculate so quickly. There's no enjoyment in it for you."

"How do you know about that?" someone asked.

"I've had Muslim boyfriends," I said. "They told me that it's like when you're really hungry. So when you get something to eat, you wolf it down as fast as you can. If you want to have sex, then you want to have fun as fast as you can. The quicker you come, the more of a man you are."

"Well, that's not a problem for me," volunteered the married student. Everyone laughed.

"But it's hard work for men," I said. "They have to really sweat over it. All you have to do is walk around with a baby in your belly for nine months. No big deal. And then when the baby arrives, why, it's like you ate something that disagreed with you. That's it. You get the stomach cramps, the diarrhea. There's something in your body that wants to get out of there by any means necessary."

I lay down on the table, legs bent and spread wide, and started huffing and puffing.

"See," I called out, "no big deal. Even I can do it!"

Everyone was laughing so hard that a boy walking past our classroom was prompted to stop and open the door to see what was going on. He quickly shut it again as soon as he caught a glimpse of me on the table.

"Don't you want kids?" one of the girls asked.

"I would love to have kids and I keep trying and trying but I still can't get pregnant," I answered.

"Oh come on, you can't have a baby!" they exclaimed. "You're *ibne*, right?"

Now was a good time to talk about my homosexuality. The nice thing was that they did not start preaching at me with Islamic quotes and denunciations. In fact, sharing my own personal stories made the discussion even more enjoyable and open.

"Do you know who is Turkish and also *ibne*?" I asked.

They named a female singer who had undergone a sex change.

"No," I said. "Tarkan, the singer."

I used him as an example after seeing a Turkish pop magazine on one girl's desk. Tarkan was on the cover. I had never heard of him, but I could tell instantly that he was "on the team."

"No way!" they shouted.

"Why not?" I asked.

"Because he's really cute and he has lots of girlfriends. Everyone loves him!"

"Oh, so only ugly guys can be gay?"

"NO, Mr. Van Maaren, but Tarkan is not gay."

End of discussion.

They were no different from the Dutch girls who refused to believe that a pop star like George Michael could be gay.

Deadly Candy

In our multicultural society, the month of December is a time when certain people get on their high horse--and I am not referring to "Sinterklaas" astride his dapple gray steed. They feel the need to blow off more steam than the boat that ferries Sinterklaas and his horse around the country. As soon as the friendly old bearded man and his cheerful black-faced helpers set foot on land to treat our kids to presents and sweets, the whole discussion about the discriminatory nature of the holiday shifts into overdrive.

But a veritable rainbow nation of kids gathers on the shores to eagerly vie for candy. Muslim, Christian, Hindu, you name it. Of course, the detractors keep their children at home to protect them from this pagan, oppressive festival. I celebrated Sinterklaas with the adult students in my Bijlmer Dutch class, too. There were Christians and Muslims in the group, including Ghanaians, Pakistanis and Moroccans. In keeping with the Sinterklaas holiday tradition I had them draw lots just like we did at school in order to introduce them to Dutch culture. I hid poems with their names in balloons and decorated the room accordingly. I brought lots of sweet treats, too.

Once everyone had arrived, I explained the rules. I popped a balloon and unrolled the poem. The person in question was obliged to read the poem out loud and then choose a gift. Then it was his turn to pop a balloon. To be on the safe side I brought a few extra presents in case anyone conveniently "forgot" to buy something. As it turned out, we had a new Moroccan student in the class, so it was a good thing that there were enough gifts. He did not speak any Dutch, but I could make myself reasonably understood in French. The other Moroccan students helped me out, too.

After all of the balloons had been popped and everyone had opened their present, I took the bag of candy and enthusiastically started flinging the traditional miniature gingerbread cookies, marshmallows, chocolate and other sugary treats around the room. That was a mistake. The new student turned a ghastly shade of pale and flew across the table right towards me. Suddenly the 5 foot 7 inch solidly built 25-year old was in my face, staring me down with a menacing glare.

Clearly I had done something so wrong that the only appropriate punishment was death. But why? Luckily, before he could get to me he first had to make his way through the piles of wrapping paper, punctured balloons and cups. This gave four fellow Moroccans a chance to grab hold of him. They dragged him away from the table, but he kept me locked in his sights the entire time, not about to give up any opportunity to crush me.

I stayed calm, refusing to avert my gaze. I stood my ground. By now I was used to dealing with these kinds of situations in the classroom. The others spoke to him in Moroccan. Luckily it did not take long to calm him down. His eyes started to go back into their sockets. The threat was over.

"What the heck was that all about?" I asked.

"Mr. Van Maaren, according to our religion it is forbidden to throw food on the ground. It is considered a mortal sin. He hasn't been in the Netherlands that long and he didn't understand what you were doing."

"So I have to die for a couple of gingerbread cookies?" I asked. "Isn't that a complete overreaction?"

"He got so mad that he couldn't control himself, sir," one of the students offered. "He's sorry."

"It's okay," I said. "Let's get back to the party."

Everyone had brought music and there was lots of dancing. Luckily, the lack of women was not a problem given their cultural background. All of the men happily danced with each other, waving their handkerchiefs in the air. I refrained from playing traditional Dutch Sinterklaas songs. It's fun music to get into the holiday mood, but you cannot really dance to it.

Even the self-appointed defender of Islam grabbed me by the arm and danced with me as if nothing had happened. He likely did not understand our cultural heritage, but at least he was okay with that. Personally, the whole episode taught me that while it is fine to throw Sinterklaas treats in the air, it is a good idea to explain the custom to the Muslims ahead of time.

Incidentally, the Turks love the fact that the bearded Saint hails from the Turkish island of Mira. There are years when Sinterklaas (December 5) coincides with the end of the Islamic Ramadan month, when Aïd el Fitr ("Festival of the Breaking of the Fast) is celebrated. I always liked to celebrate both holidays together. I also loved to see Moroccan kids celebrating St. Martin's Day (November 11), going from door to door singing and receiving candy. They could not care less if it was a Catholic holiday; after all, as long as there was lots of fun and treats in store, why not?

Haram rolls

Cooking class was one of the most fun *and* labor-intensive classes at our school. First you had to find out the students' religion, then figure out who would be in charge of getting the necessary ingredients and finally who would do what in the kitchen. This would not have been such a challenge were it not for the attitude of the Turkish boys, who insisted that the division of tasks between the boys and the girls was clear. Namely, that the girls were supposed to cook and clean up, and the boys were just there to eat. However, in Dutch society we have been trying to move away from those traditional roles since the Sixties, and therefore the boys were expected to help cook, clean up and do the dishes. Before we could do any cooking it took 10 minutes to deal with the brainwashed views and stubborn culturally-based indoctrination.

One day I decided that we would prepare crepes. In addition to the Muslims there were a couple of Christian and non-religious students in class, too, so we agreed to make separate batches of crepes with ham and cheese filling and with cheese only and put them on separate serving dishes.

Everyone started cooking. In the midst of the activity the Turkish girls spoke in their native language to let their male peers know what they thought of their behavior. It did not take much imagination or even fluency to understand that they were not mincing words.

As soon as the crepes were ready they were topped with the various fillings, rolled up and arranged on trays. Gradually, the kitchen filled with the smell of hot cooking oil and the trays with crepes. Two boys set the table and two girls brought the trays in.

"Which tray is *haram*?" a student asked.

I did not know. Each tray contained the same number of crepes, and you could not tell the filling from the outside. See, I had chosen the burrito folding method as opposed to the enchilada.

"Um, this tray is *halal*," I said, hoping my guess was right.

Everyone started eating, and the boys in particular were enjoying the crepes. They descended on the tray as if they had not eaten in days. Several of them had already wolfed down two crepes by the time Murat asked: "Mr. Van Maaren, what are the chunks in the sauce?"

A piece of crepe stuck in my throat. It was like my entire body froze.

I cannot lie, I thought. I just could not do that to them. I picked up the half-full tray and said solemnly, "I'm sorry, you guys; you have been eating the ham and cheese crepes."

The room echoed with gagging noises as the boys pretended like they were spitting out or even throwing up what they had just eaten.

"That's *haram*," Mustafa said.

"No, you guys," I said, "it's not. You didn't know that there was pork in it, so Allah is cool with it. You don't have to go to the bathroom and force yourselves to throw up. Here, just take the crepes from the other tray."

Crisis averted, the kids continued eating. Of course, after the meal the boys proclaimed that eating pork had made them so weak that they were unable to do the dishes. It was their lucky day; the girls had already started cleaning up.

Murat came up to me and whispered in my ear: "You did it on purpose, didn't you, Mr. Van Maaren?"

"Of course not," I said. "I want all of you to go to *Jehennem*."

"You mean *Jennet*, sir," Murat said.

"Oh, sorry, my mistake. I always get the two mixed up."

"Aw, come on," he said. "*Jehennem* is with an 'h', and Hell starts with an 'h.' That will help you remember."

Of course, the word 'heaven' starts with an 'h', too. Still, I managed to stop confusing the terms thanks to Murat's earnest speech. From that day forward the class always asked me whether the food was truly safe. They did not want to make the same mistake again. They also made sure to carefully inspect the food before shoving it into their mouths.

Racist?

"Mr. Van Maaren, you failed me because I'm Turkish, huh?" One of the students from the retail group was clearly unhappy with his grade.

"That's right," I nodded. "Because you're Turkish."

He cocked his head and smiled wryly.

The ethnic minority students were prone to making these kinds of comments, even though both of us knew that racism had nothing to do with a failing grade or being sent out of the classroom. However, addressing an entire group could quickly be seen as discriminatory. We had a huge problem with a dozen or so Turkish kids in our building. To get to Frits' coffee bar, you had to walk down a long hallway. The restrooms were located there. The Turkish boys insisted on loitering by the girls' bathroom. And my colleagues and I kept shooing them away. One day, I had had enough. No matter how many times you sent them away, they kept coming back.

"Listen, dammit, enough is enough!" I shouted. "It's always the same routine with you guys. Leave the girls alone! None of the girls dares to use the bathroom during the break because all of you are always hanging around in front of the door. Beat it. If I catch even one of you trying to pull a girl into one of the stalls, then you are out of here, finished."

"But sir, why are you singling us out?" implored the smallest and most devout of the boys.

"You're a racist! You only pick on the Turks, and you leave the other students alone."

"Well, that's because the Turks are the only ones hanging around the girls' bathroom! Look around, do you see any other students? I don't see any of the boys from Iraq, Morocco, Somalia or Iran!" My voice continued to rise. "I'm not going to single out students who aren't doing anything, am I? Am I?"

"You're still a racist," he insisted.

"Of course I'm a racist." I said. "And the Turks aren't doing anything wrong and still you get picked on." I stormed off to the smoking lounge, eager to get away from their indignant protests.

They honestly did not understand what they were doing that was so wrong. And that was the worst part of all. No matter how many times you tried to teach them about how they were supposed to act around women and girls in the Netherlands, it simply did not get through to them. To them, any female without a head scarf was a whore. And calling them on their behavior made you a racist.

Fine, then I was a racist, but their behavior was completely inappropriate – even though I could understand where this delusion that Dutch girls were whores came from. But I cannot tolerate certain behavior. Yes, this behavior may be intrinsic to a certain segment of the population. And yes, I walk around with certain stereotypes in my head, but I always try to see everyone as human beings first. When I meet with someone who confirms those stereotypes, I tend not to watch what I say and not to stop to think that it might come across as discriminatory.

One of the kids in my retail group was a Creole boy named Harold. The only reason he came to school was because Dutch law required him to. He had never managed to graduate, and he was unemployed. The students who did not have a job had 10 weeks to find one. If they failed to find work, they were no longer allowed to stay in our program. Or they had to switch to the full-time program. They had job search training every Wednesday. The idea was for them to learn how to write a letter of application and acquire interview skills. My coworker had spent 10 weeks trying to help, and a number of students were still unemployed.

Against every rule and agreement I welcomed the problem cases in my class on Wednesday. I was willing to hold their hand while they looked for work. They were not even supposed to be in school anymore, so they were allowed to attend my class "voluntarily." This greatly upset my fellow faculty members, who felt that these kids had no reason to stay in school any longer. Despite my help Harold continued to be a problem. He did not make any effort whatsoever. Instead, he harassed the girls in class, calling out: "Hey baby, you want to see my big *tollie*? I'll make you scream!"

During the break I went out for a smoke with five Creole boys. A former student from Suriname joined the fun. He had dropped by the school to see how I was doing. We were gathered near the exit and Harold catcalled to every girl who walked through the door. Once again, he started up with the macho nonsense: "Hey baby, I'll show you my *tollie*. I swear, I'll make you scream!"

I stood there listening to his tireless harassment until finally enough was enough. "You know, that is exactly what white people expect from blacks: not doing a damn thing except going on and on about your *tollie*. What do you actually think you have to offer them? Just your *tollie*? Well, guess what? That's not what they're in the market for. No education, no work, and no money. You know what you are? A lazy negro. And if you want a girlfriend you are going to have to start doing something about that!"

My former student burst out laughing and said: "See? I told you my teacher talked like that!"

A week later Harold had gotten a job in a supermarket and went on to graduate, too. And no one in that class accused me of racism or discrimination at the time.

Angels and Devils

Despite the huge increase in ethnic minority students in our building, we continued to uphold the annual Christmas party tradition at the end of December. Like always, I was given carte blanche to decorate the room. I was under no restrictions; the only condition was that it could not be too expensive. No problem; we got the cardboard for the giant decorations for free from a cardboard factory in the city. A can factory provided shiny scrap tin. The only thing we had to spend money on were transportation and big bottles of Ecoline paint.

This year I had decided to use a plaster cast to make a life-sized angel and devil.

Had I known what I was getting into I never would have started the project. Not because of cultural problems, but because of the tremendous amount of labor involved. The idea was to suspend both figures from the ceiling so it would look like they were floating in the air. They had to be in a certain position to make it work.

I started out using a student as a model. I figured strips of gauze and plaster would do the trick. We packed him in and covered him in plaster. I had help from a big group of students. Of course, I had to make sure they did not get carried away and end up covering his face. I really should have done a trial run first. It was one huge mess and the plaster would not dry. The poor kid really suffered. He could not move and the heat was too much. Boukje observed the entire process and finally said: "Peter, we better put him out of his misery. Just look at how uncomfortable he is."

I was forced to agree. The results were a relieved student and a mess of gloopy plaster all over the room. On the ground lay the broken carcass of what was supposed to be an angel. Eventually, I still ended up using plaster. To prevent another student from becoming the victim of my creativity, I decided to sacrifice myself. The students helped wrap my arms. I attached the plaster arms to the torso of a female mannequin. For the legs I put on shorts and took a seat in the smoking lounge, where a fellow teacher wrapped my entire lower body. Even the Turkish girls did not avert their eyes to the spectacle of me sitting half-naked on a stool in the lounge.

For the devil, we plastered my torso. Abdulah from Zaire had a suitably devilish face and he agreed to be the model.

"You know it's for the devil, right?" Harmen asked me. "Don't forget, he's a Muslim."

"I didn't tell him; he'll see the result afterwards."

"No, Peter, you can't do this," Harmen said, the panic rising in his voice.

"Oh, relax, Harmen, it will be fine," I assured him. "He had fun doing it. Let's just leave it at that."

A coworker came up with the idea to put two red bulbs in the eyes. We rigged it with a few wires and a couple of batteries: the effect was perfect. Once the figures were finished I could start painting. After two weeks of hard work everything was ready for the big Christmas party. Then, to my extreme dismay, I discovered that the angel had been badly damaged. A couple of the Turkish boys had been messing around with it, mauling the breasts and crotch. The plaster was not harassment-proof.

I got the idea that they would literally grab anything they could. Their sexual frustration was off the charts! To prevent further molestation I went ahead and hung the figures from the ceiling. It was quite a breathtaking sight, the floating angel with wings, halo and draped in white and the devil with red eyes, red horns and a red cloak over his chest. One of the arms jutted outward, pointing dramatically.

Abdulah was proud that he looked so imposing. He did not see any conflict between the figure and his faith. Harmen had gotten all bent out of shape for nothing.

On the day of the Christmas party the food was arranged buffet-style on rectangular tables. Everyone helped with the cooking. The background music included English Christmas carols, Turkish and Arab music. The buzzing of the students chatting and eating added to the good spirits. Our Christmas was a festival celebrating all cultures.

In the following year I had a lot less work to do. I was able to re-use many of the decorations, even though the angel had clearly been subjected to additional pawing.

This time, I came up with the idea to make a huge angel using chicken wire and papier-mâché. I wanted the ethnic minority students to help. First I used the chicken wire to make the frame in the basement of our building. The Muslim kids helped cover it with strips of newspaper dripping with slimy wallpaper paste.

Of course this caused plenty of hilarity and messing around. They constantly played around with the paste, pointing out its similarity to snot and other substances, dipping their hands into the bucket and letting it drip from their fingers. As a result of all the clowning around we only managed to cover the frame with one layer of paper by the end of the day. I also had to spend a while patching up the parts that needed help. Harmen showed up unexpectedly. Now that Boukje had launched a political career he had taken over as our department head.

"Peter," he said, sounding tired, "last year I already spoke to you about the devil. Do you find it necessary to taunt the Muslims by making an angel?"

"What are you talking about?" I asked. "The Muslims weren't bothered at all by the devil and the angel last year. Why would they have a problem with it now?"

"Peter," he said. "I would just rather have you make a snowman."

"Harmen," I said, "I think an angel is prettier and more appropriate for this party."

"Listen to me, Peter! An angel is something Christian, and a lot of Muslim kids will be at the party. It is inappropriate."

"Harmen, please. If you read the Koran you would know that Allah had messengers in the form of angels, too. The two religions have more similarities than differences!"

Harmen turned and left.

The next day I told the Muslim students about our conversation. They were mystified.

"But sir, we have angels, too. We just call them something different. In our language an angel is called *mellek*. Are we not allowed to work on it anymore?"

"Of course you are," I assured them. "We are going to carry on putting together the slimy mess."

The new angel, a woman with flowing blonde hair and rosy cheeks, wearing a light blue gown, looked down from the ceiling during the Christmas party. Hundreds of Christmas lights surrounded her and the other two figures. Abdulah pointed to the devil and shouted to the others, "Look, that's me!" Doing his best devil imitation he tackled a couple of the other students. Once again, it was one big multicultural celebration.

Stifled

One of the highlights of my job was meeting with parents, whether it was us who asked to see them or it was the parents who requested a talk. The Dutch parents usually agreed to come in. In talking with them it was always clear that our students shared a lot of what went on at school with them. In most cases they were very positive.

I remember meeting with one mom and her daughter. As often was the case the discussion concerned grades and behavior. When the girl excused herself to go to the bathroom, her mother confided: "My daughter talks about you a lot. She told me that you are very fond of black guys. So am I!"

Clearly, my orientation was not a problem for her, and we chatted about good-looking men like we were old friends.

Other parent-teacher meetings were equally surprising. One father turned out to be a transvestite. He arrived for the meeting, daughter in tow, wearing a synthetic wig, a cheap dress and a five o'clock shadow. He was a big man, too, with broad shoulders, thick wrists and arms like ham hocks. His thick hairy legs looked rather charming in a pair of pumps. His daughter sat there, visibly embarrassed and uncomfortable, but the ice was quickly broken. After all, I had pretty much seen it all in the gay scene.

With the Islamic students, simply having the parents show up was a major victory. And when they did show up, language often proved to be a barrier. Using the kids as interpreters seldom helped.

For example, I told one couple: "Mohammed has screwed up again. He is disruptive in class and doesn't do his homework. Mohammed, can you translate that for your parents?"

Expectantly, the parents sat there blinking at Mohammed.

As soon as he finished it was plain to see that his version painted a very different picture. But you could not always find a reliable interpreter.

I would regularly drop by to visit parents in the evening. Each time I was given a warm welcome, surrounded by friendly and kind people who generously brought me one cup of tea and slice of baklava after the other. The advantage of these house calls was that there were more people around, and therefore the odds were good that somebody in the group spoke Dutch. The student in question was not always happy about that, but it worked for me. And the parents were always pleased to have these informal chats.

I always tried to be as prepared as possible for the meetings at school. Am I going to share good news, or bad news? Does the conversation involve a student prone to violence? In that case I would always seat the student and the parents by the window, on the other side of the table. I would sit as close to the door as possible. That way, if things got out of hand I would hopefully be able to make a run for it and call Frits or another teacher for back up. I let them know in advance whenever I was going into a potentially risky situation.

I was not the only teacher who had to worry about violence. Tessa taught a group of students aged 16 and up. One time she met with the parents of a difficult student. They were unhappy with the way their "darling" daughter had been kicked out of class. Tessa had failed to correctly size up the situation. She took a seat by the window and the parents sat by the door. It did not take long before the mother became enraged and lunged for her. She grabbed Tessa by the throat and pressed down on her windpipe, choking Tess almost to death. After a violent struggle Tessa managed to break free and escape. Frits and another teacher rushed to help calm the parents down while others tended to Tessa.

The daughter was allowed to return to school after this incident, the reasoning being that it was the mother who attacked Tessa, not the student. Tessa was completely traumatized. She was out on disability for six months. Once again, the police were not notified.

Harmen had something similar happen to him, except it was a student who went after him, not a parent. The boy was big, strong and mentally disabled. He was chronically late for school. One day when he showed up late again the teacher decided that enough was enough and ordered him to report to Harmen. He obliged. Harmen was in his office with a faculty member. The boy walked in and explained the situation.

"Okay, son," Harmen told him. "Go back to class. But from now on you need to make sure you get here on time."

The boy left the office. Seconds later he threw open the door and stormed over to Harmen, grabbing him by the throat and slamming him to the ground. There was no way Harmen could free himself from the boy's vise-like grip, even with the help of the other teacher. Two additional teachers arrived on the scene. They tried everything they could to get the boy off of him, but to no avail. The female coworker gripped the student where it counts so forcefully that all of the blood drained from her hand. He did not even wince. Finally, he let go. Apparently he had had enough. Harmen gasped for air, fighting for his life.

The boy was suspended for a period of time. We agreed that he was mentally disturbed, but obviously he was lucid enough to understand who to go after. He would never hurt me, the wimpy gay guy, or Frits, the friendly janitor. He know exactly who he liked and who he did not. If he did not like you, then you were at risk of being attacked. To what degree is it possible to say when someone like that has gone completely crazy? This kid was disturbed, but not completely crazy. What is the point of slapping on a suspension?

At some point I had a big, burly Italian guy in my group. He, too, was not entirely all right mentally. He was a terrible disruption during class.

"Okay, and now you are going to be quiet for a while," I told him one day. "I can't even hear myself talk, let alone anyone else in the class."

"Yeah, well the hell with you," he spat in a mixture of Dutch and Italian.

He knocked over his desk, kicked the chair over and charged me. I refused to budge an inch. Suddenly, he stopped. He was a mere two inches or so away from my face. He was taller and I had to look up to see his eyes. Rolling up the sleeve of my t-shirt, I said calmly, "Look at this. You have a lot of nerve. I have no muscles in my arm at all. You have more than enough for both of us. Would you please pick on someone your own size--and strength? Go back and pick up your desk and your chair and sit down. And I do not want to hear another peep out of you."

He stood there, looking down at me for a few seconds. Then he turned and went back to his seat and did as he was told.

They do not teach you how to deal with these kinds of situations. You have to fully trust your intuition. After all, it would be pretty horrible to have to take a self defense class just to be able to teach your class, right?

Do Not Touch

It was 8:30 when I arrived at our building one morning. A tall Somali kid came over. "Good morning, Mr. Van Maaren," he said, hugging me before continuing on his way. He wasn't even one of my students. I had grown accustomed to this greeting from the ethnic minority students. For them, especially the Muslim boys, this was an everyday way of saying hello to someone.

"We do that in our country when we like our teacher," I had been told.

However, everyone noticed that I was the only faculty member that was given this friendly greeting. They never hugged any of the other teachers. Sometimes I was a little embarrassed when students would call out "Bye Peter, see you tomorrow!" while I sat drinking coffee with their teachers. Of course, I took it as a sign of appreciation, even more so because they knew I was gay. Maybe it meant a lot to them that I always spent the breaks with them and we could use the time to casually discuss the various things going on in their lives.

Someone was always hugging me, or throwing his arm around me. Walking hand in hand was no big deal to them. Generally speaking, the ethnic minority students were far more physically demonstrative than the Dutch kids.

Of course, the Dutch girls loved to hug me, too. I was not a threat to them, either. And of course this did not escape the attention of the other staff members in our building. Now that Boukje was gone and Harmen was in charge of the department I was subjected to the old criticisms and comments.

"Peter," Harmen said one morning, "could you come to my office during the break?"

"Sure," I said. "What's up?"

"You'll find out when I see you later."

No sooner had I walked into his office or he dove right in.

"Peter, I can't help but notice that you are constantly touching the students. I cannot tolerate that kind of behavior."

I was utterly perplexed.

"Oh come on, open your eyes. The students greet me in the morning with a hug and then they let go. What am I supposed to do, stand there like a statue? I hug them back quickly, and then they take their seat. I'm not making the first move here."

"Just stop touching them," he ordered. "I don't want to see this kind of thing at school. It just leads to gossip. We can't afford that here."

"I'll talk to the students about it," I said, and left.

But how was I supposed to explain this to the students? They simply acted out of enthusiasm.

"Boys and girls," I announced. "We have to agree that you will no longer touch me. The 'principal' would prefer to have no touching."

"But we like you. There's more to it than that, right?"

"Well, in the Netherlands we shake hands; we don't throw our arm around someone. A man sometimes does that with a woman, but men do not do it with other men. It's just a different culture. We also have different ways to shake hands.

"If it's your boss, or somebody important, you extend your arm all the way forward. This indicates that you wish to maintain a respectful distance. Sometimes you can extend your arm all the way out to let someone know that you don't really like them that much. Kind of like, 'stay away from me' but then in a polite way. If you are better acquainted with someone, like a coworker or a neighbor, you can bend your arm a little. That allows them to get closer.

"If you really like someone, say a girlfriend, you keep your hand practically next to your body and while you shake her hand you place your free arm around her shoulder, and you can kiss her three times on the cheek, alternating sides. But a man does not do this with other men. Okay, I do it with my friends, but they don't mind. I'm gay, they don't think it's strange. My friends greet each other this way, too. But it's not 'normal' in the Netherlands."

"So we can only shake hands with each other from now on?" they asked.

"Yes," I nodded. "I think it's better that way."

They did not understand it at all, but were game to try to uphold the agreement. They lasted about, oh, a day.

The next morning I was walking down the hall near the teacher's lounge. Harmen happened to walk past right as a Turkish boy approached me. It was like he had been waiting for this moment. He made a big show of kneeling and extending his arm dramatically to offer me his hand.

"Good morning, Mr. Van Maaren," he announced, looking at Harmen.

Harmen did not get the joke. Before he could reach his office I had been approached by another three boys, and each demonstrated the same exaggerated interpretation of the new rule.

"Was that better?" the first kid asked.

"Mmm, it was a little over the top, but that's how the Dutch like it. Except you should skip the kneeling part. That might give people the wrong impression."

After that day they simply resumed their affectionate behavior, unless Harmen was around. Then they would make a big deal out of shaking my hand.

During class, Farzad, a student from Iraq, showed me another way of greeting teenagers. He walked up and stuck out his hand. We shook, locking hands using our thumbs and index fingers, pulled our hands back so our interlaced fingers stayed locked, then we let go, clenching our hands into a fist, and knocking our fists together before pounding our fists on our chest, on top of our hearts. It took a little practice, but I learned the special handshake. The whole ritual struck me as very cool. I had seen lots of young men greet each other this way.

A few days later I ran into a Moroccan student at the train station. I immediately greeted him using the cool, streetwise handshake. He automatically went through the motions. Suddenly it hit him that I knew about the special greeting and he exclaimed, "Huh?!"

We stood there talking a few minutes until my train arrived. I glanced over my shoulder as I dashed to catch it. He was standing there, clearly puzzling over what had just happened. A teacher who was in on their brotherly greeting code. That was impossible…or was it?

Am I An Ibne?

Of course, different cultures have different views when it comes to public displays of affection or greeting. Perhaps I am incredibly naive, but I thought it was important for the students, not me, to take the initiative. The exception to this rule was if I happened to see a student in the hall who appeared to be visibly upset about something. In that case, I would escort them into an empty classroom and offer a sympathetic ear and if necessary a shoulder to cry on. Hugs and sobs were a part of the exchange.

After Harmen's lecture about no touching, I found myself feeling kind of paranoid. I wondered what would happen if someone were to walk in on us. I always kept the door closed; after all, the personal problems or sorrows of one classmate were not the rest of the student body's business. This paranoia was exactly what I had experienced back in 1987 when I hugged one of the kids with Down syndrome in hopes of offering some comfort. My reaction came straight from the heart, and yet I still had the nagging feeling I was doing something wrong. Luckily, a student in tears was not likely to pick up on this.

I remember one time when Youssuf, a Turkish boy, came up to me. It was so touching. He was a short and slight kid, and he stood very closely next to me, looked up at me and announced, "Mr. Van Maaren, I think you are really nice. Does that make me an *ibne* now?"

"No, Youssuf," I assured him. "You are an ibne if you only love men. You can still think I'm a nice person."

He wrapped his arms around my waist and rested his head against my stomach. "Thank you, sir." And off he went. I was so choked up. They certainly never addressed these types of situations in teacher's college.

Then again, maybe it had something to do with the times. The Eighties were not the same as the Nineties. There were not that many cultural differences at the time; it would be stretching it to say that we lived in an ethnically diverse society back then. I mean, the first time I saw a Turkish or Moroccan person was after I moved to Amsterdam.

When I was going to school, there were no discussions about whether it was appropriate to touch a student, or to comfort them. To me, sometimes it seemed like the rule against students making physical contact with teachers and vice-versa was largely a personal choice. We never received any memo about it at school.

Locker Room Antics

In addition to learning Dutch, we felt it was essential for the ethnic minority students to learn how to swim. During one of my first years as a teacher, the only Turkish boy in my class nearly drowned in a swimming pool. He had simply followed the other students' example and jumped into the pool, and we were not aware that he did not know how to swim. Thankfully, a lifeguard managed to rescue him in time.

Of course, the Islamic backgrounds of the students posed certain issues when it came to organizing swimming lessons. The boys were not the problem; we had to figure out how to convince the girls to partake.

Olga, our short, perky and self-assured Dutch teacher, approached the girls about taking swimming lessons. The results were surprising. They actually really wanted to learn how to swim, but they had made a collective decision not to tell their parents. They decided that this was a school matter, and therefore none of their parents' business. Incidentally, the Turkish girls were far less concerned about swimming class than the Afghan and Moroccan girls. All but one of the Ethiopian and Somali girls had already distanced themselves from the group, but we did not want to force anyone.

We met at the pool on a Friday morning. As a team we had agreed in advance that Alex and Ester, two PE teachers, and I would supervise the group. The manager of the pool had approved our use of the facilities on the condition that they would provide a certified swimming instructor. Alex would be in charge of the best students and the swimming instructor would coach the kids eligible for their beginner's swimming diploma. Ester would teach the girls who could not swim, and I would be in charge of the boys who could not swim.

The girls went to the girl's changing area. Alex and Ester used a separate changing area. I joined the boys in the boy's changing room. We did not think anything of it. After everyone had changed, I collected all of the watches, jewelry and other valuables to prevent theft. There was enough theft at school. I collected all of the girls' things, too.

Poolside, we saw for the first time what the rules for going in the water according to Islam were for girls: they were fully dressed! The boys were in swimming trunks or boxers. That was modern, and had nothing to do with religion.

I jumped in first, only to have all of the boys follow, trying to jump on top of me. They felt the need to prove that they were stronger and could easily dunk me. Despite all the horsing around they stopped as soon as I sputtered that enough was enough.

Before we could start the lessons we had to determine whether the kids could swim. Of course the boys protested loudly, claiming they could swim. But I was not about to relive the experience of watching a student sink to the bottom of the pool like a stone.

The wild splashing did not show much in the way of swimming prowess. The African boys in particular could do no more than doggy paddle, thrashing their arms and legs but basically staying in one place. They were exhausted within a minute. And of course their masculine pride had been wounded. They were assigned to the beginner's group, with me.

Fifteen boys were immediately allowed to report to the deep end to start preparing for their beginner's swimming diploma. The lifeguard, Ester and Alex instructed their groups from the side of the pool. I was the only instructor who got in the water with my group.

Their first task was to learn how to swim breast stroke. Some of them picked it up quickly. Maybe it was my teaching method: I would hold them by their mid-sections, pushing them upwards, allowing them to release their feet from the bottom of the pool and practice the right leg motion.

The first day at the pool was promising. Except of course that the girls spent more time gabbing than swimming, much to Ester's irritation.

I entered the changing room, where I observed each and every one of the boys wrestling with his towel. It was absolutely essential to keep their buttocks and genitals hidden from the rest of the group, hence their Houdini-like contortions in an attempt to stay completely covered during the transition from swimming trunks to underwear.

Both the Bible and the Koran state that you are not allowed to show your "shame," in other words your private parts, to anyone else.

Of course, we Dutch used to go through this same complicated towel dance decades ago, but In the meantime most of us do not have a problem with changing in front of other people. My clothes were hanging at the other end of the changing room and I walked past the students without saying anything. Instead, I simply turned my back to the students, removed my trunks, grabbed a towel, and started drying off. When I glanced over my shoulder at the boys, I was surprised to see that everyone had untied their towel from their waist. Naked, facing away from each other, they went about drying themselves off like it was no big deal.

I imagined that they were even relieved about not having to make such a fuss about it. I was really proud of them. These were Islamic boys who, according to some people, had a huge problem with gays. There were no further complicated clothing rituals in the changing room after that. Well, as long as I was there. Whenever another teacher came in, for example to talk to me, they were quick to put their towels back on.

At a certain point, they were so comfortable with the situation that we would horse around the changing room, chasing each other and snapping towels at each other's butts with as much force as possible. We were wearing underwear, I should hasten to mention.

Sometimes we had so much fun that we ended up making too much noise and a fellow teacher would have to come in and tell us to settle down. Those were moments when I truly was just one of the gang.

After swimming class, Alex and Ester returned to school by car and I rode the bus with the students. We always stopped by the local supermarket first, though, and loaded up on candy and sugar wafers. Despite my less than mature conduct, I still always remained the teacher to them. In class, in the hall and in the pool.

Afghan Nymph

While I tried to expand my personal boundaries and accept what other cultures and religions had to say, there were times when it all fell apart. It had to do with irritation and a lack of patience, while patience is supposed to be a trait for which we teachers are so admired. But hey, teachers are people too.

Some of the girls in Ester's swimming lesson group were not doing so well. This had nothing to do with Ester's merits as a teacher, however; it was mainly due to the endless chattering of the girls. Being around them was like being stuck in a henhouse. They never stopped yet Ester's patience was boundless.

Eventually I was left with only two kids in my beginner's group. I left them in the shallow end to try to improve their technique, and turned my attention to an Afghan girl. After months of lessons she was still unwilling to stop touching the bottom of the pool with her feet and float. I tried to encourage her, but she refused to listen. At a certain point my patience ran out and I extended some unsolicited assistance.

I never asked the boys ahead of time whether it was okay for me to touch them. Any time they started to sink towards the bottom I simply grabbed them around their midsection to keep them afloat. Perhaps I should have remembered that this was an Islamic girl I was dealing with, and asked her in advance. Instead, I placed my hand on her abdomen and pushed her upwards, just like I did with the boys. Her legs automatically went up and finally, after months of trying, her feet left the bottom of the pool.

"Arms, legs, arms, legs!" I yelled.

At first, she did not seem to have a problem with the hands-on instruction, and when she asked me to stop, I stopped. After several weeks she was still not making any progress. It was really bothering me. We did not have much time left. Camp was about to start and everyone was expected to be able to swim with at least some basic competency. So I put my hand on her stomach again.

One day, Alex, the PE teacher, came up to me and said: "Peter, Hannah does not like having you hold onto her while she is swimming. She's a Muslim, and men are not allowed to touch her. Would you stop doing that?"

"While she is *swimming*?" I asked, unable to mask my annoyance. "She hasn't made any progress the entire time we've been having these lessons! And what's this about 'men aren't allowed to touch her'? I'm not a man. I'm her instructor. I want to teach her something. This is why there may be times when I need to touch her stomach. If she wants to go to camp, she has to be able to swim. This is the Netherlands, not Afghanistan."

Alex wisely kept quiet. Clearly I had gone too far. I left Hannah alone. After all, whether she learned how to swim was her responsibility, and Ester's, too. I went back to my two struggling boys.

That was the end of that, or so I thought. Back at school, Harmen summoned me to his office again. At the rate things were going we would be living together any day now.

"Peter, Alex told me that you touched an Islamic girl against her wishes. If she doesn't want you to touch her, then you need to respect her wishes. It's against her religion."

"Well, I think she needs to learn that I am not touching her as a man," I said. "I don't want to have sex with her; I want her to learn how to swim. I'm her teacher. And I think she's using her religion as an excuse to avoid making any real effort to learn how to swim."

"If she doesn't want to then you need to back off," Harmen said.

"I'm not touching her anymore anyway," I said, and left.

I ran into Alex out in the hall. "Why did you go to Harmen instead of talking to me about this first?" I asked.

"You seemed to be pretty bent out of shape. I thought it would be best to let Harmen know what was going on," he answered.

"Next time, let's try to solve things together," I said. "Next time, if you come to me with sound arguments, I'm sure I will listen to you."

The Magic Finger

In the old days, when the principal of the school walked into the cafeteria, you could hear a pin drop. The king of the school jungle. You had respect for him. And for all of his royal subjects, the teachers. You did not mess with them. Those were the days!

I had to firmly slap myself upside the head to bring me back to reality: those days are over. Not only are Dutch kids considerably more outspoken nowadays, the advent of ethnic minority students really opened the floodgates.

The administrators and faculty in our school responded by adapting. They were clearly intimidated by the students' aggressive behavior. They seldom dared to open their mouth, especially if the kid in question was not one of their students.

I continued to subscribe to the belief that young people needed to be taught certain standards and values, and that teachers could help instill these. The help could come from an index finger: Merlin's finger. Abracadabra and suddenly the world looks a lot different.

The buildings and lunchrooms had become bigger and more impersonal. I hardly knew most of the students. The school was like the arrival hall of an airport, with people from all different cultures crossing paths.

One day I was walking down the hall behind a burly coworker. We were both headed towards the cafeteria. First we had to walk through the students' part of the cafeteria to reach the swing door to the teacher's area. I saw a group of four Surinamese boys with their feet up on the table. And the table was positioned right across from the entrance to the teacher's dining area. My coworker glanced at the group and quickly walked past.

What the hell? I thought. He must have seen them. Why didn't he say anything? I approached the group and said: "Listen, gentlemen, on behalf of this regional educational institution would you be so kind as to remove your feet from the table? It looks more appetizing."

They stared at me in surprise, but removed their feet from the table. I went to get my coffee--minus any knife in the back.

It was perhaps two months later that I encountered another group in the cafeteria with their feet on the table. I went over to them, stuck my left hand under my right arm, and started rotating my right arm. I began telling them why it is unhygienic to put your feet on the table, and informing them about basic table manners. Less than 30 seconds later one of them interrupted me.

"Yeah, yeah, enough already. We get it. We'll move our feet off the table."

Sitting there in the middle of the cafeteria, they probably did not like being made the center of attention. And obviously they knew that they were not supposed to sit with their feet on the table.

These were not my students, incidentally. I had no idea who these kids were. But I believed that you should be able to address someone about their behavior, whether it was positive or negative.

Not too long afterwards, I spied from across the student's cafeteria a huge kid sitting on top of a table with his feet on a chair. He was flanked by a number of students. They were listening to him attentively. I stood there with my arms folded across my chest, observing the scene for a good minute.

He did not see me, but the kids at the table in front of me did. Curious, they followed my gaze. The next table did the same, and the next. Eventually, the group I was watching caught on. One of them tapped the kid on the knee, gesturing that I was staring at him. I stood about 50 feet away fro him. Once again, I stuck my left hand under my right arm, extended my right arm, and used my finger to gesture for him to take a seat in the chair. I alternately moved my finger and flashed my open palm, and gave him a look that said, "Come on, kid, you know the rules."

He took his seat, without looking at me. I went to get my coffee.

That just went to show that you can get a lot done without even saying anything or by asking nicely. In any case I did not have to raise my voice.

Of course things at school changed with the arrival of the first Muslim students. In many cases they demonstrated an utter lack of respect for women in general and Dutch women in particular.

One day, Anna, who was the head of our complex, watched Husamettin, a Turkish student with aggression issues, throw a piece of paper on the floor in the hallway. She called him on it. Several coworkers and I observed the scene, starting with Anna talking to the kid, gesturing wildly. She looked really upset by something he had said to her. Husamettin stared at the floor, as if she was invisible.

"And now you are going to throw that paper in the trash can!" she yelled.

"You can't tell me anything," the boy called, gesturing with his arm and sneering at her.

"What do you want, who are you?"

Anna was so angry she turned beet red.

I got up and went over to the pair, instructing Husamettin: "Pick up that paper <u>now</u>, and throw it in the trash."

He bent down, picked up the paper and threw it in the trash can next to him.

"And now get out of here," I spat. "I don't want to see you around here anymore today."

He left without another word.

Anna was happy that I had managed to overcome the deadlock, but she was also furious that he had refused to listen to her solely on account of her gender.

Later, I went to have a cup of coffee in the smoking lounge in our building. A couple of my fellow faculty members were sitting around. There were two boys seated at the next table. One was a skinhead, listening to music on his walkman. He was leaning back in his chair, but what really bothered me was the fact that he had his feet propped up on the table.

I set my coffee down in front of the other teachers and went over to him. I pointed to my ears, gesturing for him to remove the headphones. He did not see or hear me. The kid across from him gestured that I was trying to get his attention.

He looked up and again I pointed to my ears. Finally, he removed the headphones.

"Would you be so kind as to remove your feet from the table?" I asked calmly.

"Sure," he said, and took his feet down.

"And would you also perhaps like to scoot your chair in a little closer to the table and sit up straight? It looks better that way."

Again he obliged, and then went back to listening to his music.

I turned around to grab my mug and found my coworkers staring at me in amazement.

"Peter, how do you do that?" Olga asked. "He is the most aggressive student that we have in the entire school!"

"He's an adult, right?" I asked. "Which means you can address him calmly in an adult manner, right?"

I thought it was too bad that my fellow teachers let him get away with whatever he wanted simply because they were afraid that he might become aggressive. Three or so years later we were sent to a class to learn how to deal with these kinds of situations. We were told that kids actually want to be talked to about their behavior, but it is good to know what to do in case a disciplinary remark is taken badly.

Sewn Up

In 1995 I started teaching a group from the Fashion Merchandising class, which was a new addition to the Fashion department. It did not surprise me that there were more girls than boys in the group. In addition to a dozen or so Dutch students there was a Surinamese boy, a Turkish boy, two Turkish and two Moroccan girls in the class. Everyone had been born in the Netherlands and spoke perfect Dutch. The boys were somewhat shy, but that was compensated by the girls' confidence. These students were never in the main building, where rumors about my sexual orientation continued to circulate. Still, they were students, which meant they were curious about their teacher's domestic situation and within two weeks of starting class they asked whether I was married.

"No, I'm not married," I said. "But I do have a boyfriend."

Confusion clouded their faces. Did they hear that right?

"What, so you're gay?" The most confident girl spoke on behalf of the class.

"Yes."

They exchanged wide-eyed stares. A couple started to giggle. A couple of the boys squirmed in their seats. The Turkish boy simply stared out the window. I wondered whether I had embarrassed him. I had a feeling he might be gay. It had nothing to do with the fact that he was a Turkish male and taking Fashion Merchandising; there were other male students in the class and I did not assume or think that they were gay.

"Wow, you really have the guts to come out and say that?" someone asked.

"Aren't you afraid it might get you in trouble?"

"No," I answered. "I mean, everyone already knows, and I never had any problems with any students."

Once again, it was time for some education. Nothing had changed in all the years I had been teaching. It would always be a shock to some people. I am often the first "real" gay person they have ever met. Like every other group before them, these students were fine with it. I did not pose any threat, although it did take a while for them to recover from the shock.

Something else I noticed was how quick the girls were to get physical with me, grabbing me, hanging on me. Just like ET, I went from being an alien to a big teddy bear.

Now that the news was out, I could carry on with the regularly scheduled social studies curriculum. Of course I taught from the book, but sometimes I also brought up things I had seen on TV.

One day I brought up a documentary that I had just watched about female circumcision in Eritrea. The mother interviewed said she considered the tradition cruel and inhumane. She did not want her daughter to be subjected to the same suffering as she had at a young age. She was a Muslim, but felt that the practice had nothing to do with Islam. Her sisters disagreed.

The following scenes were grisly. A seven year-old girl, playing in a courtyard. The sun is shining, she seems carefree. She waves to her mom, who is on her way to the market. Suddenly her aunt appears.

"Come with me," the aunt says. "Today is an important day for you. Today you will become a beautiful woman in the eyes of Allah."

The girl trusts her. She reaches for the woman's extended hand and walks beside her.

They arrive in a dimly-lit bedroom. There are several women waiting in the room. The girl knows them. The aunt picks her up and lays her down on the bed. The girl has no idea what is about to happen to her.

The women bend over her, gripping her arms and legs in order to hold her still. Her legs are spread. The aunt lifts up the girl's thin dress, folding it back. The girl is still smiling but she seems surprised. Her underwear is carefully removed. The aunt in front of her picks up the lid from a tin can and brings it down in the direction of the girl's genitals. Her smile disappears. The woman quickly cuts away the outer labia and clitoris. The girl screams in agony. It is a piercing scream that bores deep into the brain. The images and sounds are unbelievable. I have never heard a human being scream like that. Even as I write this I can still hear her cries. She keeps screaming.

After the aunt has finished the butchering, the girl is sewn up with long needles from some kind of shrub. No more than a small opening is left. The sound and images fade from the screen, but I cannot get them out of my mind.

The narrator explains that the girl's husband will have to cut her open again on their wedding night if his organ is too large for the hole, which is hardly enough to accommodate a finger. If he cannot manage, then he will leave the room and an aunt or her mother will take over. There is no anesthesia involved; none of the instruments or materials are sterilized.

It is a well-known fact that both Jewish and Muslim men undergo circumcision. The procedure is done mainly for hygiene reasons. It is also far less intrusive for men.

Male circumcision is also practiced in many African tribes. For women, it is presumably commonplace only among certain Islamic tribes, and the only reason is to eliminate sexual urges. The prevailing system of beliefs indicate that women are not supposed to have a sexual appetite. Sometimes the clitoris is cut off with scissors; in other cases it is perforated. This practice continues in Egypt. In other tribes, the outer labia are also sliced off. The practice of sewing up the genitalia primarily occurs in Eritrea.

After I finished relating this gruesome story to the class, there was a long silence. It was a lot to digest, and it took a while before we could discuss the topic of circumcision.

Even the Islamic boys were open about it. They also made it clear that they objected to the practices in question. This led to a discussion about sexuality for men and women, and the functions of the sex organs. Of course, the various cultural differences with respect to the roles assigned to men and women were mentioned, too. They also talked about what were considered religious laws, and the role that culture plays in various rites and customs. Time flies during this type of class discussion, and before you know it the bell was ringing. Everyone left the room calmly, and the topic was never raised in class again during the rest of the year.

I had completely forgotten about it until one day Halima, a Turkish woman who taught sewing, came up to me and said: "You teach social studies to the fashion merchandising students, right?"

"Yes, is there anything wrong?"

"No, not at all. But do you know who Frieda is?"

"The sweet, chubby girl, kind of slow, doesn't really belong in that group?"

"Yes, that's her. She came up to me the other day and said, 'I feel sorry for you.' So I asked, 'Why do you feel sorry for me?' and do you know what she told me?"

I shook my head.

"She said, 'because you are all sewn up.' I couldn't believe my ears! I asked her where she got that, and informed her no, I was not 'all sewn up,' and she said that the teacher had discussed the matter during social studies class! I asked her, 'Did that teacher happen to be Mr. Van Maaren?' and she said, 'Yes, how did you know that?' So I said to her, 'Frieda, I am not sewn shut. That only happens in a very few cultures. Most Muslim women are not sewn up.' She left, but she certainly looked doubtful."

Halima paused, and smiled.

"You know, Peter, you are the only person who could tell such a story. I knew right away that you were the teacher. But be careful and make sure that next time there aren't any misunderstandings."

"But I told the class that it only happens in Eritrea," I protested. "I didn't say that all Muslim women are subjected to it. The problem with sharing these kinds of stories with the students is that sometimes they get carried away--like the old game of telephone. By the time they repeat the story, it isn't at all like what I originally told them!"

Case closed. Still, it was obvious that I needed to approach sensitive subjects with extreme care in the future. Not *avoid* them of course, but I thought it would be wisest to wait and bring it up again later with the students, just to make sure everyone was on the same page.

Lactobacillus Acidophilus

So, I had decided to tackle taboo subjects with care, and then test the students to see whether they had understood everything correctly. Nevertheless, things still sometimes went off the rails.

In one of my classes I had a group of girls from the advanced fashion merchandising class. They were a great bunch from all over. Walking into the room was like walking into a henhouse. At first I really had to shout to get their attention. They had heard from other girls at school that I was gay. It was time for my informal gay awareness talk again. After that, the mood was completely relaxed. It was like sitting around chatting with friends.

Outside of class, they would come up to me and ask for my opinion on their boyfriends, especially this one bunch of Surinamese girls. One of the girls, who was a little older than the rest, would sometimes get picked up from school by this big macho guy in a fancy sports car. He looked even better than the car.

"What do you think?' she asked.

"Gorgeous," I said.

We both knew that we were not talking about the car. She was happy with the verdict.

Other girls would sometimes bring pictures of boyfriends taken during summer vacation. I was instructed to evaluate their looks, too. They also wanted to hear what I had to say about the subject's character simply by looking at his eyes. I had acquired a reputation as some kind of a psychic after I had been shown a picture of a boy in class and made an innocent remark about his character. Apparently it had been an accurate "reading," and from then on the students were forever bringing me pictures of boyfriends and girlfriends, interested in finding out whether true love was in the cards, or if the relationship was doomed. I had to be very diplomatic about it all, of course. After all, one wrong word and their tender little souls were mortally wounded.

During one social studies class I raised the subject of personal hygiene. An informal survey revealed that everyone washed at least once or twice a day with soap.

"How often do you wash with soap?" they asked me.

"Never," I said. "I use shampoo on my hair, and that's all. Soap dries your skin out, and hot water is enough. I don't stink, do I?"

They wrinkled their noses.

"Soap dries up the natural oils in your skin, and I don't want that," I explained. "And I know that women often use too much soap. Especially 'down there.' Do you know why that isn't a good idea?"

"But, wait, you have to keep 'it' clean, right? Otherwise it will start to stink."

"It's not a good idea for men or women to use too much soap between their legs," I told them.

"For women especially it can have really unpleasant consequences. It starts very innocently.

Using a little soap you want to smell nice everywhere, so you get scrubbing."

I used my hand to make a rapid scrubbing gesture in front of my crotch.

"After a few days it starts to smell a bit stronger, so you use more soap."

I repeated the scrubbing gesture.

"Then it starts to smell even more. One day, it starts reeking, a rotten fishy odor, and you notice a yellowish-white discharge. That's a symptom of a yeast infection. A woman's vagina stays healthy and yeast-free through a complex balancing act. It is important to keep the pH at the right level. Using soap disrupts the balance. The body receives a signal to up the acid production. It makes more. You use more soap. More soap, more overreaction from the body. Eventually, you start to notice a smelly discharge. It is important to see your doctor about this."

"There are different prescription remedies to restore the pH level. But I have also read that yoghurt containing L. acidophilus can work wonders, too. As long as the container says 'live cultures.' It's good for the body if you eat it normally, but you can also apply it directly to the inside of the vagina, for example using an applicator or soaking a tampon with it."

I pantomimed shooting a syringe towards my crotch.

"But seriously, avoiding soap is the best thing. If you have any discharge, burning or itching, see your doctor. Any or all of these symptoms combined could indicate some type of infection or other condition."

Of course, these were educational and appetizing anecdotes to share right before lunch. You could tell by the looks on their faces that going to lunch was the last thing they felt like doing. It was too bad that time always went by so fast in class.

A week later I had the same group again, and I had promised myself I would briefly review what we had covered in class the previous week just to make sure everyone understood.

No sooner had I walked into the room or someone called out, "Mr. Van Maaren, there is no such thing as 'acidophilus' yoghurt! We went to the grocery store after class and looked for it, but the guy stocking the shelves had no idea what we were talking about. He helped us look through the entire dairy case and there was nothing, no acido-whatever yoghurt. You lied!"

Clearly, there were a number of girls in the class who had some intimate hygiene issues.

"I wasn't lying," I said. "But I'm guessing that that kid in the store doesn't know anything about yoghurt. Go to a health food store and ask someone there. I am 100% sure that they sell the kind of yoghurt containing live cultures that I'm talking about. Or ask your doctor, see if they can help."

I was pleased that my class had proved inspiring. And obviously they felt comfortable enough around me to talk about their search with me. But maybe they did not understand that I could see what the problem was. At any rate, we did not discuss the matter again.

As it turned out, our days together were numbered. During that school year, all of the fashion merchandising students were transferred to the full-time Retail program. I didn't teach any of those groups, and in fact the entire department was moved to a different building. So I never saw the girls anymore. That is, until I was transferred to their building.

One day I was walking to the cafeteria when I was surprised to meet one of the Surinamese girls from the group. She bounded up to me, planted a kiss on my cheek and asked how I was doing. We walked together to the cafeteria, chatting away. She turned to the other girls who were with her and said, "This is Peter, he was my social studies teacher when I was in the fashion merchandising group."

"Oh, are you the acido-whatchamacallit yoghurt teacher?" one asked.

"Yes," I said, unable to conceal my surprise. "That's me!"

We chatted for a few more minutes before I excused myself. Breaks were never that long, and I wanted to get a quick smoke in while I still could. And to have a moment to smile to myself, thinking: *I'm not just the gay teacher anymore; now I'm the Lactobacillus Acidophilus yoghurt guy, too.*

The New Pink Closet

There are times in your life when you realize that you are not as tolerant as you always assumed you were. Although I demanded tolerance from others with respect to my conduct, my teaching style and the way I interacted with the students, I could be pretty intolerant with my fellow faculty members. I wanted everyone to be as closely involved with the students as I was. I felt that they needed to be involved in their lives, not just lecture them in a classroom. But that was my way of doing things. Which worked well for me, but I needed to keep in mind that others were not obliged to do the same.

I also had to acknowledge the fact that not all homosexual employees could or wanted to be as open about their sexual identity. This realization hit me like a bolt out of the blue when I strolled into the teacher's lounge one morning. I could hear my co-workers talking before I entered the room. However, one voice rose clearly above the others. I could not identify the speaker. The voice was high, and kind of feminine.

I opened the door and immediately noticed the newcomer. I was taken aback. A chunky, somewhat older man was sitting at the table, legs crossed. He was wearing a jaunty black beret. He held a cigarette between the tips of his right index and middle finger. He made a show of pursing his lips each time he took a drag, turning his face to the right as he inhaled. Now *that* is a queen, I thought to myself. No doubt about it!

I felt the fight or flight urge. I wanted to flee. His presence completely threw me off kilter. I did not know what to do, but I managed to say, "Hello, I'm Peter."

He took my extended hand limply and lisped, "I'm Rico."

"He'll be teaching Dutch to the level 2 and 3 minority groups," Olga said, brimming with enthusiasm. "He's already had lots of experience teaching Dutch as a second language."

I was not sure whether I should be happy about this. Perhaps I just needed some time to adjust to the fact that I was no longer the only queer on board. Still, I could not shake the bad feeling I had. We'll see, I thought to myself.

A month or so later we were sitting around the teacher's lounge discussing dieting and appearance.

"Peter, you seem to be very concerned about your looks," Rico said. "Why on earth do you need to go on a diet? You're already skinny enough, aren't you? You seem kind of obsessed."

"Well, Rico," I replied, "you already have a boyfriend. So you don't have to pay attention to you're appearance anymore."

I admit that maybe that was kind of a bitchy, clichéd gay thing to say. Rico shot me an angry look, pursing his lips. Immediately I decided that it would be best to cut out for the smoking lounge.

Rico followed me. He grabbed my arm and pulled me aside in the hall.

"Peter," he fumed. "That was not a very nice thing to say. The rest of the faculty doesn't need to know I'm gay. What I do in my bedroom is nobody's business."

I was dumbfounded.

"I'm sorry, Rico," I said, "but surely everyone here can see that you're gay?"

That was the wrong thing to say.

"That's beside the point," he said. "I do not wish to discuss this with the team."

I agreed and offered my apologies. He accepted. So, there was a pink closet in the building. And Rico did not want to come out of it. Of course it was his business, but given his appearance and mannerisms it was going to be difficult to conceal it from everyone else.

A week later I was on the train, reading the paper. I was on my way to work, just like all of the other morning commuters. There was a pleasant hum of voices in the car, but suddenly everyone fell silent. I looked up from my paper. Rico was walking down the aisle. He was wearing a long, wide coat and his signature beret. The remaining strands of his long hair stuck out from underneath. He strode towards me, cigarette clenched between pursed lips. He took a seat next to me.

Gradually we struck up a conversation. The sickly sweet smell of his cologne was almost unbearable at first. Clearly his entrance had made quite an impression, judging by the silence. Everywhere he went, he caused a similar reaction.

One day in class one of the Iraqi students asked: "Mr. Van Maaren, is that other teacher like you? Mr. Rico? Is he a *kunda*, too?"

"I don't know," I replied. "I haven't noticed anything. We haven't talked about it. If you really want to know, you need to ask him."

A year later it would prove even more difficult to keep his orientation a secret. We had organized a volleyball match with all of the ethnic minority students. Shortly before the game was supposed to start, the last of the students emerged from the locker room, giggling.

They hunched over secretively, leaning into each other and whispering. Then Rico walked out, in an oversized t-shirt and wide cotton sweatpants. He was wearing terrycloth sweatbands on both wrists and his head. The giggling grew louder. None of us had ever seen him in gym clothes.

The match started. Everyone was really fanatical, even Rico. But amidst all of the deep grunts and roars emitted with every violent smash and spike, Rico's high-pitched squeals were impossible to ignore. Every time the ball came barreling towards him he would try to dodge the projectile. Or he would turn his head, throwing his right arm up to try to stop the inevitable. Sometimes he would fall on the ground, screaming, or run into the wall.

Two Turkish boys came up to me on the sidelines.

"Are you sure that Mr. Rico is not like you?" one asked. "He looks so weird, and he keeps screeching. We're convinced that he's like you."

"Guys," I said. "I don't know if he is. A lot of men who *aren't* still act like that, too. You have to ask him yourselves."

I am pretty sure that they never asked him. Rico worked well on the team, and that was what mattered most. Still, I could not stand his swishy, effeminate ways and it also really bugged me how he tried to keep his homosexuality a big secret from everyone. But I had to learn to accept it. Not everyone benefits from coming out.

The Sexual Intimidation and Discrimination Committee

The Ministry of Education came up with a brilliant plan in 1995. The time had come to start paying more attention to safety at schools. Each school was assigned a Sexual Intimidation and Discrimination Committee. The group was tasked with handling complaints for the sake of achieving the necessary safe environment. The lavishly designed folders, complete with photos of the committee members, were presented to the faculty with a great fanfare.

We were supposed to distribute the material to all of the students. The new committee was expected to play a significant role in solving the problems that students were having at school. That was exactly what I was hoping for, too. Traditionally, we were expected to deal with bullying, attempted sexual assaults and discrimination by ourselves. We often got the impression that everyone basically muddled along. Teachers and administrators made ad hoc decisions about how to handle a problematic situation as they saw fit. Teachers and students alike had come to feel that the administration sometimes sided more with the perpetrator than the victim. This also applied to situations in which teachers found themselves at the receiving end of violence or discrimination.

The committee could help change that. Finally, we would have a safe school. We would show those troublemakers who were causing harm to others in whatever way that we were not going to take it.

In the meantime, everything was in an uproar. Our decrepit building was scheduled for demolition, so we were temporarily moved to a different location. The faculty at this building were not happy about this to say the least. To them, our students were criminals. A far cry from the adult ethnic minority students who were highly motivated.

Convinced that our students carried weapons, they wanted to install metal detectors at the entrance to the building.

The business school moved, too; they were housed in a brand new building behind the station. After all of the various mergers and changes we were now truly one big school. Everything was new and nothing was too extravagant: inviting, comfortable faculty lounges for every department; a spacious cafeteria and the intoxicating smell of new vinyl.

Everything was new, but it was not necessarily safer. That was made clear during a meeting with the faculty from the at-risk ethnic minority student program. Olga cleared her throat and said that she had an announcement to make. With a guilty look on her face, she took the floor.

"Listen, I have some very bad news that I want to share with you. I was sexually assaulted by a student."

We were stunned. All at once everyone started asking, "Who? When? Where?"

"Two weeks ago, after class had ended, I was in the room getting my things together. I had already noticed that Habib had been dawdling. At first, he stayed in the back of the classroom, loitering around, but eventually he calmly walked up to the front. I looked at him for a moment, but then went back to what I was doing. He approached me from behind, and when he got close enough he grabbed me in my crotch. From behind."

"What did you do?" Rico asked.

"I wanted to hit him, but I remembered that Peter had already done that once, and it only got him into trouble. So I simply told him to leave. I didn't even tell him he was suspended."

We conferred on what to do with him now.

"It's been two weeks," someone said. "We can't suspend him now. He won't see the connection between what he did and the punishment. You need to talk to him and make it clear that we will not accept this kind of behavior. If it happens again, he will have to be expelled."

"But wait," I said. "We have a special committee for this type of problem now, right?"

Nobody felt it was necessary to inform the committee yet.

Olga agreed to talk to the student, and Rico volunteered to sit in. The meeting adjourned.

But during the coffee break tempers were still running high. I was utterly disgusted with the final result. That little scumbag! You cannot walk up to a teacher in class and sexually assault her!

Luckily, I worked in the main building, which was also where the Sexual Intimidation and Discrimination Committee office was located. Iris, one of my former coworkers, was on the committee. I immediately went to her.

"Iris," I said. "A female faculty member was sexually assaulted by a student. Can the committee look into this? We aren't sure what to do."

"How awful," she said. "What steps have you taken? Have you reported the incident to the police?"

"No," I said. "The team feels that the student should be expelled if he does it again. But can't the committee do anything?"

"No," she said. "Our hands are tied. The government set up this committee solely to deal with situations in which a teacher does something to a student."

"What?! For god's sake, Iris! Most of the problems here involve students against students, or a student against a teacher. So basically nobody is protected, and our school remains unsafe. Have you ever stood in line in the cafeteria? The Turkish and Moroccan boys in particular like to pinch girls on the butt, or grope them in other places. They do this to all of the girls except the Islamic ones!"

"I can't help you, Peter," she said.

I could not believe what I was hearing. Just what good was this committee for, anyway?

It certainly was not helping the school!

A 'Sporting' Assault

Another case involved an even worse form of sexual assault. In reality it was more of an attempted rape. Three Turkish boys had selected an Antillean girl as their victim. She was a cheerful girl who was nice to everyone. They decided to trap her in the gym. One of the boys was in charge of standing guard outside the door. It was his job to keep a lookout for teachers. The other two were inside the gym with the girl. They pinned her down on the bleachers and one of them held her wrists while the other tried to force himself on her. They were interrupted when the kid on guard duty signaled that Ester the PE teacher was on her way. The one boy pulled up his pants and both fled, leaving the girl on the bleachers. Ester found her there, shaking and utterly distraught. So was Ester when she learned what had happened.

Luckily Ester had seen two of the three attackers. We would find out who the third one was when we captured them. But to my astonishment nobody was brought in let alone expelled.

Harmen, our department head, wanted to get a positive ID on the third participant. He refused to suspend anyone until then. These kids should have been kicked out of school immediately. The police should have been notified, too. "Are you kidding?" I asked. The two who had been identified were in my class. Was I supposed to carry on teaching, knowing that they had tried to rape a student at school? Harmen insisted that we had to find the third perpetrator.

Meanwhile the two attackers were hanging out drinking coffee in the smoking lounge as usual. I, too, wanted some coffee and a cigarette, which meant I was forced to share the same space with them. I saw them sitting there, acting like nothing had happened. I walked past them, coffee mug in hand, and said nothing. I made a show of turning away from them. I did not even want to look at them.

Someone sneered, "Oh, so we're going to be all tough?"

I declined to answer.

Nobody spoke during the break. The tension was so thick you could have cut it with a knife. And I knew full well that I was the source of the tension. Usually I am a fun, chatty and sociable guy. I could not make the effort this time. I simply felt hatred inside. Not towards everyone, but towards the perpetrators.

Right before break ended, I walked past them again. I refused to look at them. Instead, I stared straight ahead with a look of pure disgust on my face.

A boy ran after me. "Mr. Van Maaren, why are you mad at us?" he asked.

"You're sitting with the guys who attacked that girl," I said. "You know that they did it. By choosing to sit with them, you are saying that you agree with what they did. You are sitting with pigs."

"But wait," he asked. "That girl has slept with other guys, so how come not with us? That's discrimination! She won't sleep with Turks. All Dutch girls sleep with everyone, right? They're all whores, aren't they?"

My blood boiled.

"Girls and women have the right to choose who they go to bed with and when. But if they say no, then it means no. It's their personal preference and it has nothing to do with 'discrimination.' Turkish girls rarely date Dutch guys. Are you telling me that's discrimination, too?"

The kid shrugged, turned and went back to his friends.

The next day all three attackers had been identified. Their "memorable" punishment was three days' suspension. One of the days was already a school holiday, which meant that their suspension amounted to a whopping whole two days. A hair-raising and precedent-setting sentence!

I am relieved to point out that this type of physical violence was seldom; nevertheless, every form of sexual intimidation or molestation has a traumatic effect on the victim--and the climate at school.

When the boys had done their time -- all two days of it -- they were back in my class as usual. Before we started, I took a long, hard look at them.

"Listen, guys. I have to let you back in because you have supposedly been punished. I cannot excuse what happened, but I am required to continue teaching you. But do not let something like that ever happen again at this school."

All week long I just could not get in a good mood. I was totally sick of Harmen and the Turks. I had to really make an effort not to take out my frustration on all of the Turkish students. Still, it was really difficult. Especially because there was such a sense of solidarity among them, almost *pride*, about what the three boys had done.

After the swimming lesson, I joined my students on the traditional candy run to the supermarket. I saw the victim of the assault with a couple of friends. As soon as she saw me she bounded over to me.

"Mr. Van Maaren, it's no fun at school anymore. You aren't happy, you don't make jokes, you don't sing any songs. What's wrong?"

"Those boys wanted to rape you," I said. "I just can't accept this. Harmen didn't punish them severely enough. I am having a very tough time acting like nothing happened."

"But if you start being fun again, then everything will go back to normal."

It was clear that she felt that the assault should not cast a dark shadow over the school. It was more important to her that I started being the fun teacher again; that took priority over her own well being.

"Mr. Van Maaren, I can't go to the police. They can't protect me from the Turks in the city. If I do that I won't be able to go out at all anymore. So it's better if I just try to forget about it."

Still, I was not willing to simply put it in the past. I decided to pay another visit to the Sexual Intimidation and Discrimination Committee. All seven members happened to be in the office when I showed up. They were in a meeting, but I was pleased that they were willing to take a moment to hear what I had to say. My good mood quickly turned foul. After I explained what happened, they informed me that there was nothing they could do. That they did not intervene in situations like this between students. What the hell!

"You must be terribly busy," I spat, unable to conceal my sarcasm. "I mean, considering all of the abuse, rape and discrimination being committed by the *educators* in the school system."

"We're sorry, Peter, but we can't help you," I was informed. "The student needs to file a report with the police. That's the only option."

The Inappropriate Trip

March, 1996. The snow was falling on our shivering bodies. Twenty teachers, representing ten different subjects, were waiting to get our first glimpse inside a Turkish school in Istanbul. Tuncay had arranged the trip to help us get more insight into Turkey's educational climate. He had spent months preparing. I had the feeling that it was extremely important to him for Turkey and the schools to make a good impression on us.

I had actually really wanted to go because I had so many Turkish kids in my class. Unfortunately, I had lost all interest during the final week leading up to our departure. See, it had to do with the room assignments. I had already asked several male colleagues if they were interested in sharing a room. These were people I had known for years and with whom I had shared lots of laughs. People who I really respected, and assumed the feeling was mutual. However, when we gathered to discuss the sleeping arrangements and everyone indicated their choice of roommate, it turned out that nobody wanted to room with me. I was surprised and disappointed. I was left with Rico and a couple of the female faculty members. That did not appeal to me. I did not really feel it was necessary to board with women. Normally I was not adverse to such an arrangement, but this time I was against it.

I ended up being assigned to room with the other leftover coworker. I liked him okay, so it was not a big deal. Still, I could not help wonder why my casual agreement with the other teachers fell through. Standing there in the sleet and snow, it suddenly became crystal-clear: I was gay.

My roommate had just informed me that certain people had made some "cute" comments to him earlier that morning. He was asked things like, "So, did you have a good time with Peter? Were you able to sleep okay? Did you make sure you swallowed a fork?"

Oh, I had heard these kinds of comments from students. Whenever I had to take a student out of class for a private talk they were usually greeted with smart-alecky questions. "Did you put a cork in your ass? Did you make sure you swallowed a fork?" Those were the students. I did not expect this type of behavior from my coworkers.

I tried to direct all of my energy into cheering myself up and make the most of the week. I immediately perked up when I recalled how enthusiastic the Turkish students reacted when they heard that we were going to be visiting their native country. Mustafa, who had done time in prison, had a cousin who was still living in Istanbul, Muttalip.

The cousin's parents had sent him back to Turkey and confiscated his passport. They were tired of him getting in trouble with the law all the time. They thought he should leave the Netherlands and go back to Turkey. They wanted him to see just how bad it was there in hopes he would appreciate the Netherlands more. Mustafa told me he would call Muttalip and see if he wanted to go to some gay bars with me. I had Muttalip's phone number with me.

We waited obediently outside the school gates as our feet slowly froze. Finally we were given the signal to go inside where it was warm. We followed Tuncay across the schoolyard in a single file line. To the right of us was a big group of boys. I guessed they were about 14 years old. While my coworkers marched behind Tuncay to the entrance of the school, I slipped away from the group to go talk to the kids. I wanted to talk to the students before being subjected to the principal's speech.

The boys immediately surrounded me. Their English was good, so we could understand each other. They excitedly clamored for my attention, voices rising to a shout as everyone tried to ask me questions and I tried to answer. Then I realized someone else was calling my name.

"Are you coming, Peter? We're all waiting on you."

I had to go back to the group. But the students were not about to let me go. They followed, shouting in unison, "Ajax! Ajax!" Nothing like soccer to unite nations. One of the female teachers grabbed me by the arm.

"I'm so jealous of the way you do that. How do you immediately strike up a conversation with kids you don't even know?"

"Well, simply by taking an interest in them. I ask them what they think about school, and what kind of classes they take, that sort of thing," I said. "That's really all it takes."

We were ushered into a hall and once everyone was seated the principal gave us a friendly PR-speech about the school. He mentioned that the students were not subjected to corporal punishment, and that girls were not allowed to wear head scarves. The separation between church and state was clear in Turkey. The public school was secular. The boys and girls were separated, however.

Anyone who wanted a parochial education and to wear a head scarf had to go to an Islamic school. I was amazed. We have a separation of church and state, and yet there was still no end in sight to the debate about head scarves in schools.

The next stop on our Turkey trip was a vocational school. The students were busy making bronze casts of Ataturk, among other things. No sooner had we arrived I was surrounded by numerous boys. And once again, I was called to come back to the group. I cannot help it. I simply relate more to students than my adult peers. I learn a lot more from the kids than the well-rehearsed slick presentations by the principals.

After a comfort stop in an extremely filthy and smelly bathroom, I lit a cigarette to recover from the experience. A couple of students joined me. Suddenly they panicked. We had to stub out the cigarette immediately. In the distance I spied the cause for alarm. A teacher was briskly striding towards us. He angrily addressed the boys. We had done something against the rules. Smoking. They would likely get into more trouble than me. I tried to explain to the teacher that I was the only one who had been smoking, and that I was not aware it was prohibited.

I joined the rest of my group in the cafeteria. The look on Tuncay's face made it clear that I was out of line again. But I was simply doing the same things that I did at home in the Netherlands, right?

After spending three days *and* nights with my coworkers I was ready for a change. We had dined together, danced together, drank together, but now I needed some gay company. I ended up calling Mustafa's cousin, Muttalip. He was happy to hear from me, mostly because he had really wanted to talk to a Dutch person again. He and a friend were going to show me Istanbul's gay bars.

I was honestly surprised that Mustafa had arranged this, not to mention the fact that Muttalip did not seem to have any objection. He and his friend arrived at the hotel around nine that evening. I said goodbye to my coworkers and left.

I enjoyed going out with the boys, but the mood in the bars was very subdued, which did not exactly put me in a party mood. Anyway, just being around other gay men and enjoying some good conversation with the boys was enough. Muttalip's friend did not speak any English or Dutch and that complicated communication somewhat, but it was fine. I had a great time dancing with Muttalip. It was a refreshing change from having to adapt my moves on the dance floor with my female coworkers. No big deal, of course; still, it was different for me with men.

Those Kinds of People

My gay bar tour lasted well into the night and it was late by the time I returned to the hotel. I said goodbye to the boys and headed for my room. I said hello to Olga and Erwin, a Surinamese teacher, who appeared to be engaged in a rather intimate conversation.

After a good night's sleep I went down to the breakfast room and took a seat next to Erwin and one of the department heads.

"Hey, Erwin, did you sleep well?" I asked, even though he was visibly drowsy.

"Mind your own business," he snarled, looking at me like I was something stuck to the bottom of his shoe.

"Whoa, hold on there, Erwin! We can be civilized adults, can't we?" the department head asked.

"Never mind," I said, throwing up my arms. "I'm out of here!"

Shocked and intimidated, I went back to my room. I was utterly mystified by his reaction. Later I heard that Erwin had informed the department head along with a couple of others that "my culture doesn't accept those kinds of people, so I don't have to accept him."

The department head had urged him to calm down, and the others, too, tried to soothe his temper. And yet nobody bothered to mention how incredibly discriminatory his remarks were.

When I heard what had happened, I was utterly flabbergasted.

"If I had told him that my culture did not accept blacks and therefore I wasn't obliged to accept him, I would have been fired on the spot. Apparently, discrimination against gays is more acceptable than racial discrimination. I have truly had it with you all!"

All I wanted to do was go home. Not a single person in the entire group had stood up for me when Erwin broadcast his views. There was no way anyone was going to stick up for me if I confronted him about it in public.

I found out later that some of my fellow faculty members had told Erwin that I liked Surinamese men, and that perhaps he had felt threatened as a result.

Accountability

A week after the trip to Turkey I was confronted by Tuncay.

"Peter, thanks to you the school will never be allowed to go back to Turkey for another tour."

"What? Why?" I asked.

"The intelligence department was following us the entire time," he said. "You did all kinds of things that were not part of the program. They did not appreciate this. You did not follow the rules."

I was shocked. "But Tuncay, you never told us ahead of time that national security was going to be tracking us. And you never mentioned the rules that we were supposed to follow. So don't blame me for this. You were already familiar with my 'inappropriate conduct' here at school. You shouldn't have let me go in the first place."

"I should think that teachers are aware of how they should behave when they are guests somewhere. Obviously you are different," Tuncay said.

"That's right, I'm different," I said, and left without any feeling of guilt whatsoever.

To make matters worse, the video that we had secretly shot during our visit to the first school was defective. Arjan was perplexed. He had played it back in Turkey and the tape was fine. Did the Turkish secret police have something to do with it? That sounded like paranoia creeping in. After all, Turkey is a free, safe and democratic country. Mysteriously erased video tapes are the stuff of spy novels.

Yes, I could kind of see where Tuncay was coming from when he reprimanded me. I had gone overboard trying to talk to students to see whether their version of the story matched the various principals' upbeat speeches. I accepted it, and that was that. Or so I thought. However, my participation in the Turkey trip was the subject of further criticism during a meeting of the at-risk ethnic minority students' team.

"Hey, Peter," one of the faculty members said. He had not even been on the trip. "I heard from the other teachers that you didn't join in the group activities during your field trip to Turkey."

"What are you talking about?" I said, completely stunned by his allegation.

"Oh, you know, that you went to gay bars instead," he replied.

"That wasn't until the fourth day," I said, "and only at night. I happened to be very sociable with everyone and I sat with a different group at every meal. But after spending three days and three nights together I was in the mood for a change. Picture this: you go on a field trip to Mikonos with a group of 29 gay people and you are the only heterosexual. You join in all of the organized excursions and after every dinner you join your gay coworkers at the gay club--you know, to show your solidarity. Everyone is dancing, everyone is having a great time, and you even observe a couple of love connections form right before your very eyes. How would you feel after three days?"

"I would be ready to see a woman," he said.

"That's what I mean," I said. "After three days I simply wanted to hang out with gay people, and dance with men. It has nothing to do with being anti-social, or refusing to join in the group activities!"

Maybe I need to learn to quit defending myself so fiercely, or doggedly explaining to straight people why they have it all wrong. Because as soon as I reverse their comment or question, they suddenly understand. Take a simple question like: "Why do you go to gay bars?" and turn it around, responding with: "Why do *you* go to straight bars?"

Question: "Why do you say that you are gay?"
Answer: "Why do *you* say that you are married with children?"
"Why do you wear a pink triangle?"

"Why do *you* wear a wedding ring?"
"Why do you go to watch a gay pride parade?"
"Why do *you* go watch a Mardi Gras parade?"

Sometimes I get tired of explaining it, but I keep hoping that people will eventually understand.

The Mustache

During one social studies class I said to my minority students: "Ladies and gentlemen, I have to tell you something rather unpleasant. Foreigners are the butt of a lot of jokes. Especially the Turks. I think it's terrible."

"What kind of jokes?" one of the Turkish students asked.

"Oh, I'm not going to repeat them. It's racist."

There was loud protest from the class.

"Come on, Mr. Van Maaren! Tell us one of the jokes!"

"No, kids, I won't do that. They aren't meant to be funny."

"But we want to know what kinds of jokes are being told. Come on, tell us one. Just one!"

"All right," I sighed. "One. I'll tell you one. Why do all Turkish men have a mustache?"

Everyone looked at each other, seeing if anyone knew the answer.

"We don't know. Why do all Turkish men have a mustache?"

"Because they want to look like their mother," I answered. Nobody laughed, but one boy raised his hand. "My mother has a moustache, too!"

The students conferred eagerly with one another, and the consensus was that nearly everyone's mother had a mustache. Some mothers even had sideburns. The punch line was confirmed, and taken seriously. And so the lesson went from being a warning about racist jokes to a discussion about women's facial hair in different ethnic groups. The students agreed that although many Dutch women also had facial hair, it was usually blonde and downy, unlike that of their ethnic minority counterparts, which was more visible due to their darker coloring.

I Buy, You Buy, He Buys

I taught Dutch as a second language to illegal immigrants in the Bijlmer housing projects and a community center in the Pijp, a multicultural neighborhood in the heart of Amsterdam. We focused mainly on vocabulary, grammar drills and reading and listening to simple texts. The students always enjoyed the grammar drills. Some of the students in the group managed to get a pretty good grip on the fundamentals of Dutch in just two months, and others made decent progress after about six months. The classes were conducted exclusively in Dutch, while they only conversed in their native tongue at home or with their friends.

I was so impressed with the results that I decided to start using the same method at my school. Everyone enthusiastically set to work, filling in the blanks in each sentence. I had made up sheets in advance with the personal pronouns and then gave the students the verbs to use. For homework they were instructed to continue the exercise.

We quickly started doing drills to practice verb tenses: swim, swam, swum; get, got, got. Every week the students had to memorize 20 or so words and I would quiz them. We would have a competition to see who could come up with the most definitions for a word.

The best part for me was always the beginning of each quiz. First, I would hand out the papers. Everyone would wait until I gave the signal to start. "Bismillah!" I would call, holding my hands out, palms facing up, and drawing them towards my shoulder while looking up at the sky. "Bismillah," the entire class would echo in reply.

I had learned this ritual during my dinner with an Islamic family. It was kind of like their way of saying grace before a meal. Afterwards, they said "alhamdulillah," which was the equivalent of saying "Thank you Lord." When everyone was done with their quiz, I would announce "Alhamdulillah" and they would repeat after me. My blessings were meant respectfully, and clearly everyone understood my intentions. Nobody raised any objection.

During class, I liked to suddenly call on someone and ask them to recite the alphabet, for example, or conjugate a verb, or recite the present and past participle. These were my favorite lessons because the students were so incredibly enthusiastic, most likely due to the competitive edge to the drills.

Kids that were transferred to us from other schools had no grasp of grammar whatsoever, and they would sit in amazement watching the others answer my rapid-fire questions. When it was their turn and they were unable to come up with the right answer, I would reassure them.

"It's okay if you don't know the answer. They didn't either four months ago. Just try to practice a little. It might come automatically."

Not willing to be left behind, they picked up the grammar very quickly. The only time I saw them get discouraged was when we were practicing verb tenses and nouns involving spelling changes with tricky shifts from one vowel to two. *Kopen, kopte, gekopt; koppen, koopte,*

gekocht; wekken-weken; hopen-hoppen. It did not do any good to say them out loud or to use the classical approach of reeling off words with long and short vowel sounds; sometimes it was just too confusing. During class, I alternated between one hour of grammar and vocabulary with one hour of reading and listening comprehension. Every now and then we played word games on the computer, too.

Everything was fine until I was ordered during a faculty meeting to drop the grammar lessons. I was told that I should stick to the primer. The students were supposed to be learning Dutch by reading, listening and doing the exercises. I disagreed. I wanted to keep using my approach, mainly because none of us had any formal Dutch language teaching qualifications. Besides, nobody could offer any convincing arguments against my doing so. I was motivated solely by the positive responses from my students, and their progress, of course. Consequently, I carried on teaching them grammar my way.

I made the students promise not to tell anyone.

"We like you a lot more than the other teachers," they told me. "You are a way better teacher. It's a lot easier to understand you, too. The way you speak to us, and what you tell us; we can understand what you are saying; we don't get the other teachers."

To make matters worse, they let my fellow teachers know how they felt, too. Once again, I was chastised during a faculty meeting. I was supposed to have respected the "democratically" issued decision. I agreed, and simply went ahead with my grammar lessons.

Maybe I should have been more of a politician, launching a campaign to try to win their votes. But that would have taken way too much energy. Clearly, I was a born dissident; although I should hasten to point out that I was very much open to well-founded arguments. But nobody was giving me any, and I happened to be an advocate of the old-fashioned method of memorizing, drilling, taking quizzes and doing one's best. Obviously, the ethnic minority students had done so back at home, too. Being quizzed and seeing who was the best: if it works, then why not?

The Apology

Discrimination makes me really angry. I also do not like it when one of my own team mates is threatened by a class. I found out from my Surinamese coworker Melita that she was having trouble with Coby, a girl in the Salesclerk class. So far, she had been told to "Shut up and go back to Suriname" or something along those lines. Things were escalating and could potentially get out of hand.

I took the initiative to sit down and have a talk with Coby, her mother, Melita and Ines, who was the head of the Retail department. We met in the office. I shook the mother's hand and asked everyone to sit down.

"If no one minds, I would like to get right down to business," I said, looking at Melita and Ines.

"The reason why we are here is that I would like to hear Coby apologize for the discriminatory remarks she made to Melita," I said, shifting my gaze to Coby and her mother. "We cannot accept this kind of behavior. So, Coby, what do you have to say?"

She sat there silently, looking at Melita balefully.

"Look at me!" I ordered.

The hateful look on her face was what really got me mad.

"What do you have to say to Melita?"

"Sorry," she said. She turned away from us, the hateful look on her face still very much visible.

"Listen, dammit," I said, my voice rising louder. "You call that an apology? Your comments and your behavior are enough to justify expelling you from school. If you can't accept other people then you have no place here. You are obliged to treat everyone respectfully, and I want a sincere apology from you right now; otherwise you can get the hell out of here."

Coby and her mother started sobbing.

"Coby, this is your last chance to offer a sincere apology. If I don't like what I hear, you're going to get kicked out of school."

"I'm sorry," she stammered. "I'll never do it again."

"Melita, is that satisfactory?" I asked.

"Yes," she said, clearly just as shook up.

"Coby was totally out of line," I said, addressing her mother. "If this happens again then you will need to find a different school for her. This kind of behavior is totally unacceptable. I hope you understand."

She nodded, sniffling. Coby and her mother left the office.

"That was intense," Ines said. "I never dreamed that you could go off on a student like that. I always thought that you were so popular because you let the kids get away with everything."

I was dumbstruck. After all these years, she still had not caught on to how I dealt with the students?

"Ines, why do you think that all of the students show up to my classes on time? Why do you think that they don't wear their jackets in class? Why do you think that they stay in class until the bell rings?" I waited for a moment.

"Is it because the students actually want to, or because I actually have rules in my class?"

"Obviously I was wrong," she said. "I'm sorry."

Melita was likewise impressed and thanked me for arranging the meeting.

Coby wisely kept a low profile after that and did not mouth off again. She was not exactly buddy-buddy with Melita in the classroom, but at least she was no longer openly hostile.

Multicultural Survival

The annual summer camp for at-risk ethnic minority students was one of the best things about working as a teacher. There was always a body of water near the chosen camp site, which meant swimming lessons were a prerequisite. Our goal was to come home with the same number of students with which we left. Knowing how to ride a bike was likewise important. Bicycle lessons were part of PE class, and upon completion the students received a "real" cycling diploma. They were tested on their practical skills as well as theory.

At some point, the Islamic girls had finally figured out that the teacher was there to help them, not molest or otherwise offend them. Now it was okay to offer a steadying hand, or to pick them up when they fell off the bike. Still, most of the female students were not inclined to ride along because their parents insisted on them being brought home every night. That was difficult to do by bike, which meant we were expected to provide taxi service, too.

Actually that was no big deal; the most important thing was for them to join us. Finally the big day arrived. It was time to put theory into practice. The bicycles were lined up outside and the boys were inside the gym making a ruckus. As soon as they saw me, a couple of them jumped on my back, initiating an impromptu wrestling match. There was always a certain degree of nervous tension right before a field trip.

After I disentangled myself from the frisky pups, I looked for an excuse to take a coffee break as soon as possible. Some of the faculty members were already on the phone, trying to get in touch with the students who had not shown up yet. After the coffee break, we loaded the luggage into a van. The plan was for Rico to drive all of our stuff to the campsite; that would save us from carrying it on shaky bikes.

A couple of students were ready to get on their bikes and get going. We still needed to divide everyone into groups. Murat approached me, threw his arms around my waist and laid his head against my chest.

"We're going to camp, aren't we?"

Right as I put my arms around his shoulders I noticed Harmen standing at the top of the stairs. He witnessed our "intimate" conduct and moved to come downstairs and interrupt our embrace.

"Yes, Murat," I told him. "We're going to camp. Why don't you go see if your bike is ready? We'll be leaving in 10 minutes."

He let go of me and dutifully went over to his bike. Harmen looked visibly pleased that intervention had proved unnecessary.

Everyone got on their bikes and our colorful group hit the road. We had hardly made it to the end of the street before we were on the verge of cardiac arrest. Everyone had seemingly forgotten everything they had learned about bike safety, especially the boys. The only thing to do was to keep a constant watch on them and call out warnings.

Finally, two flat tires later, we reached the nature area where we would participate in a "survival" exercise.

After a short break, the students received their first assignment: they were going to be building rafts in groups of five.

Alex, the PE teacher, went from group to group, checking their lines and knots and tightening things up as necessary. When I realized how professional his efforts were, I decided I had to take action. After all, I had some sneaky plans up my sleeve for our students.

"What are you doing, Mr. Van Maaren?"

It was my turn to inspect the ropes.

"Oh, just making a few adjustments so the ropes don't come undone," I said.

Of course, I was doing exactly the opposite, loosening the ropes to guarantee some comical and unexpected situations shortly.

The groups launched their rafts. They started out rowing serenely, there was no screeching or yelling or laughing. The scene was downright romantic. Something had to be done about this, I decided. The rafts were holding together fine, and that had not been my intention.

I joined a group of Moroccan and Iraqi boys.

"OK, guys! We're going to take over that group to the right!" I called.

I did not have to say that twice.

We headed straight for the unsuspecting group. As we bore down on their raft, the group suddenly realized that something was about to happen that they were not happy about. Using their oars they started splashing wildly in our direction. This prompted us to retaliate, splashing back just as vigorously, trying to soak them. But we could do more than that, I decided.

"Board the raft!" I shouted.

Within seconds they had capsized, and everyone was bobbing alongside their raft. Luckily the water was not very deep, and everyone could swim.

We immediately set sail for a new target.

The group on another raft had quickly figured out what we were up to and they tried to flee, shrieking and shouting all the way. My fearless pirates caught up with them and they soon ended up in the water.

The third group was not as easy to conquer. In fact, they did such a noble job of defending their raft that we hit the water first. But we still managed to upset their raft.

The other teachers stood on the banks, observing the spectacle in the water. They felt it was better to stay neutral.

Everyone emerged from the water, dripping wet, victims and perpetrators alike. I decided that none of the students should still be dry, so the handful of kids who had managed to stay afloat was thrown in.

A tall student named Farzad tried to pull Zainab out of the water. He was still dry, and the skinny girl was soaked, her black hair sticking to her like seaweed. My shoes were soaked but despite the squelching sounds I managed to sneak up on Farzad from behind and push him into the water. But I was not aware that one of the boys had decided to pull the very same stunt with me. He pushed me forcefully. This set off a domino effect, with me smashing into Farzad and both of us pitching into the water, where Zainab was waiting with her arms held out, hoping to be rescued by Farzad. Instead, she plunged underwater along with us.

Farzad surfaced, brushing the water from his face. He was furious.

"Who did that?! I'll kill him!"

"That was a dirty trick, wasn't it?" I said, feigning innocence. "You try to help someone and *you* end up getting thrown into the water!"

"I'll kill the son of a bitch!" he shouted.

The water was doing nothing to cool him off, and I felt no urge whatsoever to confess. I could not admit to my childish act just yet because I did not want my week of camping to come to an abrupt end.

The other teachers tried to comfort some of the students or warm them up, briskly rubbing their arms and backs. We were not only soaking wet, we were also freezing cold. And all of our bags packed with dry clothes were already at the campsite, waiting for us.

We were resigned to spend the rest of the day in our cold, wet clothes. They suddenly weighed a ton and it felt disgusting walking around in wet clothes. The way jeans stick to your legs is especially unpleasant. The worst was riding a bike in wet clothes; the temperature felt a lot colder.

We stopped for fries along the way to try to cheer up the kids. They ate quietly, shaking and trembling from the cold. Some of them even needed help getting the fries into their mouth they were shaking so badly.

"Is this the Dutch way of having fun?" Dave asked, the English boy's teeth chattering.

The rest of the survival day, including a treasure hunt, was cancelled. Still, none of the faculty or students accused me of acting irresponsibly. I was as soaked as the students, and the high seas adventure had been awfully fun.

We pedaled our bikes as fast as we could to our campsite. As soon as we arrived we quickly changed. Dry clothes had never felt so good.

Later that night, Farzad and I were standing next to each other brushing our teeth.

"Did you find out who the son of a bitch was that pushed you into the water?" I asked.

"It was you, you arsehole," he said, turning to face me. "I knew it all along. If it had been anyone else, I would have killed you. But I forgive you."

The surprising thing about camp this year was that a couple of the Islamic girls actually stayed overnight. A few of their classmates had arranged either to be picked up every day or get a ride from us, but some of them spent the night.

We brought our week of biking, swimming and beach fun to a close with a talent show night. During camp, everyone put together a presentation about his or her native culture. The last evening was a virtual tour of the students' various countries, filled with all kinds of music, dance and fantastic costumes. The mood was wonderful; everyone was so open and sharing. These were kids to be proud of.

Family Ties

In working with the ethnic minority students in the Dutch as a Second Language program, two boys caught my attention: Samir and Sefket from Iraq. They were twins, but not identical. In fact, it was hard to tell they were related in the first place. Samir was slim, athletic and had very little body hair, whereas Sefket was this big, burly guy positively covered in hair.

But it was not their appearances that made them stand out; it was how they introduced themselves in class. The rest of the students were already seated when the pair arrived.

"Good morning, guys," I said, walking over to my desk. Suddenly I noticed the two boys were standing at attention at their table. The class burst out laughing. The brothers looked around, bewildered. They were standing to show their respect for their teacher. This was customary in Iraqi Kurdistan, and they saw no reason not to do the same here in Amsterdam. I had never seen such a thing in all my years of teaching. I liked it! Too bad that all of the other minority kids had long abandoned the tradition.

Surprised by the response from their classmates, Samir and Sefket took their seat and we started class. The boys surprised me again: they neither spoke nor understood a single word of Dutch. At home they spoke Kurdish; their parents and siblings were taking classes to learn our language, though. Despite being absolute beginners, the pair made exceptionally good progress in just three months. Samir immediately joined a Dutch soccer team. "Good for my Dutch," he explained.

Sefket was not as athletic; instead, he took on a paper route. Samir followed his example. When Samir's soccer obligations prevented him from delivering *de Telegraaf*, a younger brother would fill in for him.

They showed such initiative and energy, it must have earned them admiration from their peers. I had only seen this kind of get up and go among Pakistani students.

Several months had past and Samir came up to me in the hall one day.

"Sir, my parents are having trouble trying to fill out some paperwork. We told them about you and they want to invite you over for dinner. Then afterwards you can help them with the forms."

"Samir," I said, "don't they have a social worker to help them with that kind of stuff?"

"Oh sure, but they still can't figure it out. Would you please help?"

"Have your mom or dad call me to explain what the problem is," I said.

Their mother quickly got in touch. Her Dutch was quite impressive, too; obviously she had really applied herself. This family was one surprise after another. I wanted to help them, so we made a date for me to come over after school. The boys agreed to escort me.

We arrived at the house. I was overwhelmed by the clamor of so many children. A Dutch neighbor boy and girl were seated on the couch. A heavyset man with a large belly was seated in the chair to the right of the couch. He was the twins' father. He stood up and shook my hand.

Their mother emerged from the kitchen. She dried her hands and likewise shook my hand. Then all of the kids lined up to greet me. Samir and Sefket had eight brothers and sisters. The youngest was a handicapped girl. They had a total of two daughters and eight sons. It was simply incredible to meet such a huge family. Dad ran the show with a firm hand, while mom provided the TLC, and the oldest daughter helped with the housekeeping.

I was immediately presented with a stack of papers. The first thing was to try to put them in chronological order.

"Back in Iraq, I received a grand total of <u>one</u> form in my entire life, and within two months of living here I have gotten hundreds!" the father said, clearly defeated.

Before I could do anything else with the papers, it was time for dinner. A dizzying number of children led me over to the table. Their mother proudly stood in front of what could only be called a gigantic banquet.

"Please sit down," she said sweetly. I sat down. There was only enough room for six of us at the table. The father and the oldest sons were allowed to join me; the rest would eat later. The food was delicious. Their mother had gone all out. It looked like a special holiday feast.

After dinner I went back to the paperwork and helped them fill out the various forms. We talked a lot about the situation in Iraq and life in the Netherlands, too.

At some point I absently looked at my watch only to see that I had missed the last bus back to Amsterdam.

"I have a slight problem," I said. "I missed the last bus. What's the best way back to the city; do you know if there is still a train?"

The parents exchanged looks. "It is no problem at all. You will sleep with the boys in their room. You are family. Do not worry."

I was worried. It was not a good idea for teachers to spend the night with their students. School camp is one thing; private sleepovers are an entirely different story.

"Mr. Van Maaren, it's okay, really," Samir assured me. "We sleep upstairs; six of us share a room. And one of my uncles and a cousin, too. But we have to get up early to do our paper route. We'll be back in time to go to school."

They made up a bed for me, and I stayed over. The uncle was already asleep and snoring loudly. I had a feeling it would be a long night. Before going to sleep we talked for a long time.

At a certain point I turned to Samir and asked: "Do your parents know that I am *kunda*?"

"Yes," Sefket said. "We told them as soon as we heard about it from the other boys at school. At first we couldn't believe it, but everyone said it was true, so we figured they weren't making it up. Our parents said that everything is different in the Netherlands. So we just had to accept it, because that's how it is!"

We went to school together the next day. Of course I immediately told my coworkers what had happened. They did not think it was a wise idea, but what could you do?

There were at least three occasions when parents, including a Turkish couple, called me to ask whether I would chaperone their sons in the city. They did not like the idea of the boys roaming around Amsterdam unsupervised. I obliged, and from time to time I arranged to meet a group of students on the weekend for shopping and sightseeing. These chaperoned city trips often ended with a stop at my place for tea and cookies. Even the most aggressive student turned into the very picture of respectability and decency. And I always informed the school ahead of time to prevent gossip.

The Coming-Out Assistance Team

"Good morning, ladies," I said to the pair of girls and a boy walking towards me up the stairs. They were students of mine.

"Hello, I'm here, too!" the boy said.

"I know, that's why I said 'good morning, ladies'!"

"Get out of here," he said. Together we walked to the cafeteria.

Obviously this is not the way to help a student come out of the closet, but it worked with him. I understood that making similar remarks was like walking into a minefield, which could blow up in my face.

A week later I saw the boy in the hallway. "I was wondering if I could be excused from class 10 minutes early today. Only 10 minutes. I have an appointment for a performance, and I need some extra time to change."

"Into your drag outfit?" I asked.

He looked at me in amazement. "How did you know that?!"

"It wasn't exactly a stretch of the imagination," I said.

"Okay, but listen Mr. Van Maaren, nobody must know about this!"

"No problem," I said.

I think that by being open I gave the students, especially the gay students, the opportunity to put a face on homosexuality. Usually I could identify the gay ones, but I kept it to myself. I also avoided making any insinuations in class. It was entirely up to the student to decide whether he wanted to talk about it with me. Making sure that everyone felt safe and secure was my top priority.

In many cases gay students wanted first to see what the rest of the class thought about homosexuality. By encouraging the class to ask me personal questions and by answering them candidly, the students could see whether the atmosphere was homophobic. Sometimes all it took was one negative student to express their opinion, and the gay student would end up keeping quiet.

This is what happened in a class with Abdelmalik, a Moroccan student.

"Are you married?" a female student asked.

"No," I said. "Why do you ask?"

A couple of the students looked at each other, checking to see whether it was appropriate to continue.

"Because we think you're gay," the spokeswoman announced.

"That's right," I said. "But why did you think that?"

"Well, the way you teach, and how you interact with us," she said.

"That's enough, I don't want to hear any more about this," Abdelmalik said suddenly.

"Gays go to Morocco to sleep with young boys. They are a bunch of perverts!"

It was impossible to ignore the rage and indignation in his voice, which in turn enraged me.

"Hang on a second," I said. "Let's get something straight. You don't use the word 'homosexual' to describe men who mess around with little kids. The proper term is pedophile. And another thing: Muslims love camping it up."

No sooner had I finished my speech he was on his feet and grabbing his chair to throw at me.

I stood there and stared at him calmly.

He hesitated, but finally put the chair down with a crash and left the room.

"You shouldn't have said that!" one of the students cried. "You really insulted him! That was a really discriminatory thing to say."

"Well, I thought his remark was very insulting, discriminatory and extremely hurtful. Although I must say that it was an automatic reflex, I didn't think before I spoke." I was still shaking with anger.

"You should apologize," the students informed me. "I'll think about it."

The group returned a week later. Abdelmalik was back in class, too. He stared at me, the anger and disdain burning in his eyes. It was like he felt I did not have the right to exist.

"Abdelmalik, I wanted to apologize for what I said last week. I am sorry, I should not have said that."

He nodded and accepted my apology.

I looked at him questioningly, and gestured with my hands as if to say: don't you have something you would like to say to me?

"What do you want?" he snapped.

"Well, I would like to hear you apologize, too," I said, in a perfectly friendly tone of voice.

"I got nothing to say sorry for. What I said is true! Homos are disgusting and they go after little boys!"

Instantly I flew into a rage again. "Fine, consider my apology null and void."

Abdelmalik stood up and left the room in a huff.

The class was on my side now. His conduct was unjustifiable in their eyes, too.

I was obliged to contact Abdelmalik's temp agency to discuss the matter. They were very sympathetic. Abdelmalik had to understand that his attitude was unacceptable not only in the classroom but also in the retail sector. If he wanted to work for a clothing business he needed to understand that he might come in contact with gays, either as coworkers or customers. The temp agency also informed me that Abdelmalik was not interested in returning to school.

I did not give any additional talks on sexuality to this class. There was no need. However, the situation made an impression on one of the students.

One day Victor came up to me after class.

"Mr. Van Maaren, I don't know if you noticed, but I'm gay, too."

"Yes, I figured that," I said. "Can I help you with something?"

"I really want to tell the class that I'm gay, but first I want to make sure that nobody has anything against gays. Abdelmalik is gone now, so I guess there won't be any problem."

I wanted to help him, so I brought up the incident with Abdelmalik in class again. I asked them what they thought about homosexuality. Nobody took issue with gays, and suddenly everyone had lots of questions. I ended up giving a brief, informal lecture.

When I was done, I asked the class: "Ladies and gentlemen, what would you think if someone in the class was gay?"

"Gays are just like everyone else, except that they are attracted to people of the same sex. There's nothing wrong with that."

Everyone nodded, so I assumed that nobody had a problem. But it was still up to Victor to decide whether he felt safe enough to come out of the closet.

Suddenly he said, "I have something to tell you. I'm gay, too."

Nobody in the class looked surprised. A couple of the girls went over and hugged him. Class was officially over, so we sat on the tables and everyone had a question for Victor. The mood was great. He thanked me after class.

Later I learned that he told the people at his work, too. Once again, he did not face any problems. It was unfortunate that Abdelmalik dropped out; however, had he stuck around Victor never would have dared to come out of the closet.

Razor Sharp

Working with the at-risk ethnic minority students was usually a piece of cake. They were enthusiastic and really friendly. They were no trouble at all. Sure, they were boisterous when they arrived in class, but they quieted down as soon as the lesson started. In their eyes, you were the boss, you were their teacher. Still, every now and then there were exceptions.

It started out very innocently one day. Feisal, a young man from Saudi Arabia, entered the classroom with a cup of chocolate milk.

"Check it out, Mr. Van Maaren," he said, triumphantly holding the cup in the air. "I brought some chocolate milk with me."

"That's nice," I said. "But you know that you aren't allowed to drink it in class."

"OK, teach," he said and took his seat.

"Hey, look at that!" he said. "It's empty!"

He turned the cup upside down to make it clear: not a drop was left over.

"You can leave now," I said calmly. "You weren't allowed to drink that. This isn't a cafeteria. So off you go!"

"Huh? Since when did I do anything wrong? All I did was drink some chocolate milk."

"OUT!"

He walked up to me.

"Come on, Mr. Van Maaren. I don't know what I did wrong."

"You drank your chocolate milk after I specifically told you that you weren't allowed to. Get out. I want to talk to you after class."

Walking to the door he announced, "If I have to leave, I'll cut you open with a razor."

"Fine, no problem, but not now. I'm teaching now, so you can cut me open after class is over."

He left and then proceeded to walk past the windows of my class, pacing back and forth. After his third round, he opened the door to our room and shouted, "I'll cut you open, man! I did that before to a kid at my last school, and I'll do it again!"

He was telling the truth; he had ended up at our school after attacking a classmate in his previous school. I refused to bow to his threat.

"No problem. You go ahead and cut me open during the break. Come back after class."

"I'm going home now and I'm getting a razor!" he called.

"Okaaaay, run along then. Go home and get a razor. And then cut me open. I'll be waiting for you," I said.

You could hear a pin drop in the classroom. He slammed the door and left. I turned my attention to teaching until the bell rang. Break time.

All but two of the students had left when I saw the Saudi return. The boys asked if they should stay just to be on the safe side. I did not feel that there was any real threat, so I sent them away without a second thought. Feisal entered the room.

"Mr. Van Maaren, I don't know why I got kicked out of class," he said. He was noticeably calmer.

I explained my rules about eating and drinking in class again.

"OK, I get it now. But I could have sliced you open, you know? Whenever we go out in Saudi Arabia, we take half of a razor blade and hide it in our mouth, tucked between our top teeth and cheek." He pulled a half razor out of his cheek to demonstrate. "That way the police can't find any weapons on us, but we can still protect ourselves if anyone attacks us."

"Well, that's nice to know. But go ahead and throw that razor in the trash. You don't have to worry about being attacked here."

He threw the razor away and together we walked to the cafeteria. I never had any trouble with Feisal after that.

Thrown Out

Slowly but surely the salad days came to an end for the drop-out project and the corresponding funds that the government provided. Now we were mostly being judged by the number of participants in our department, and enrollment had taken a nosedive. The young refugees kept coming, but there was a drastic decline in the number of students with learning disabilities.

During a meeting after the summer break Harmen announced the number of students in each group. As soon as he was finished he quickly tried to move to the next item on his agenda.

"Wait a minute, Harmen," I said. "You're going a little too fast for me. Things can't go on this way. Pretty soon we're not going to exist anymore. What are your plans to attract more students?"

"I can't do anything," he said. "The funding has dried up and other schools are stealing our students."

"You should have prevented this," I said. "Boukje always managed to get new students and projects. She actively approached all of the organizations and agencies that could help us; she networked. All you do is sit around in your office. Now we hardly have any students left."

He shrugged.

None of my coworkers backed me up. Finally Rico volunteered that a brochure was being designed to help attract new students to the Dutch as a Second Language program. I kept my mouth shut during the rest of the meeting. Perhaps I was making a big deal out of nothing.

Still, the future was looking pretty dim to me. If the school continued to go the way it was going, there would be no work for a number of teachers in the near future. I was thinking about the teachers in the other groups, not the ones working with the ethnic minority students. Why weren't they sticking up for themselves? Why weren't they fighting for their jobs? Considering how long I had been teaching and all my experience, as well as my popularity among the students, I assumed my job was not in jeopardy.

But gradually the anxiety was growing among the team and at school. Storm clouds were gathering. I applied for several jobs elsewhere during this school year, but my prospects were not looking good. All I could do was have faith in the Dutch as a Second Language program and hope that I would be able to continue my work with the ethnic minority kids.

I called Harmen in April to find out how things were going and ask what kind of shape the department was in.

"I have absolutely no clue what's going to happen," Harmen said. "No decision has been made yet as to whether the department can be saved. Nothing has been said about who might get the axe or be transferred to a different department."

Basically, I had to have faith in my superiors. But no matter who I talked to, none of the department heads knew anything. I called Harmen after every single meeting of department heads. And every single time he had no news to share.

I walked into the next meeting for the remedial and learning disabled group unsuspectingly. By now it was May.

Everyone was chatting away as we walked into the meeting room. We took our seats and reviewed the agenda. I was seated next to Harmen on his right.

"Would you like a piece of cake?" he asked innocently, holding the tray in front of me.

"No, thank you," I said, likewise in a friendly manner.

The meeting adjourned. Harmen spoke directly to those seated to his left, Rico and Olga. Without bothering to look at me, he announced: "Peter is leaving us. He's going to be working in the building of the new school that recently merged with us. He'll be working in the Retail and Computer Science departments.

The impersonal delivery made it seem like the announcement was not intended for me. Harmen was quick to move on to the next item. All of the young at-risk ethnic minority students would be divided up between the adult education groups for newcomers.

"What is going to happen to the students if they get put in with the adults?" I fumed. "If our kids have to take classes with adults, the motivation to come to school is guaranteed to diminish. Kids belong together. And the adults will be thoroughly annoyed by the behavior of the younger students, and they will try to discipline them. Plus, the adults will be regarded as an Islamic surveillance group. How on earth did this decision come about?"

"The decision was handed down," Harmen said. "There is no way to change it now. Budget cuts mean it has to be done."

I was so concerned about the future of our students that I was completely oblivious to what had just happened to my job. None of my coworkers protested, despite the fact that everything that we had spent years creating had just been destroyed in one fell swoop.

After the meeting we all walked out together. I could not understand why everyone was staring at me. We were out in the hall when suddenly one of the female teachers threw her arms around me and cried, "Oh Peter! I am so sorry! This is just terrible." As I stood there hugging her back, the gravity of Harmen's announcement suddenly hit me like a ton of bricks.

I was overcome with a sense of bewilderment and astonishment that left me feeling paralyzed. I had been kicked out!

Even worse, I found out that all of my respected fellow faculty members had already known about it six weeks ago! They had not aroused my suspicion whatsoever. Nothing had changed in the way we interacted with each other. We had had plenty of fun as usual. This hurt. A lot.

I headed home alone, baffled by what had just happened. What was I supposed to do now?

The next day I reported to work as usual. Walking into the teacher's lounge, my coworkers stared at me in surprise.

"What are you doing here?" Olga asked.

"Last time I checked I was still a teacher at this school," I sneered. "The students are expecting to have class with me. Which is what I plan to do today. I am going to finish this school year."

Later I realized that none of my coworkers would have thought twice if someone in my position simply stopped coming to work out of spite. How idiotic. "The school screwed me over, so now I'm going to screw over the school"? Not my attitude!

In class I told the students that I would be teaching at a different school after the summer.

"Are you mad at us?" one of the students asked. "Don't you want to teach us anymore?"

"No, guys," I said. "I would love to keep teaching you, but it's impossible. Olga and Rico will be staying, though. You might be put in the other groups."

"But Mr. Van Maaren, we'll be in the other building in the fall, too. So we'll still see you, right? That means you'll be able to visit our department and see how we're doing."

While that was something to look forward to, I wasn't prepared to think about the future just yet. I still had a bone to pick with Harmen. I won't lie; I was still consumed with anger.

I spotted Harmen in the hall.

"Harmen, I want to talk to you. *Now*."

He offered a friendly smile and asked me to come to his office.

"Would you like to have a seat?" he asked.

"No. I think *you* should sit down," I said. My tone was smooth but at the same time deadly.

As soon as he was seated I let him have it. Launching into a venomous sermon I told him exactly what I thought about him and his performance over the years. The blood drained from his face as he sat there listening to my tirade, his eyes bugging out of his head.

After 10 minutes I walked out, slamming the door behind me.

I had just unloaded six years' worth of hatred and anger with undervaluation and homophobia in one go. Still shaking, I went to the cafeteria and informed my coworkers: "Well, I just finally got it all off my chest. I think I made myself abundantly clear. Our little meeting was more like a verbal execution."

Harmen spent the rest of the day in his office.

The Attack

The end of my tenure with the remedial and learning disabled group was near. We decided to get together one more time on the last Wednesday before the summer vacation.

Of course it was hardly a festive occasion but it was still nice to see everyone. Although nobody stood up to give a speech, several faculty members had put together a song. Everyone joined in and sang the five stanzas with gusto. There was one for each teacher who was either leaving for a different department at the school or taking a job somewhere else.

It was not how I had pictured my last day, but then again it is hard to sum up 12 years spent working as a part of this team in four pithy sentences. I was usually the one who made the speeches whenever anyone was leaving, but this time I was not in the mood for speeches.

Still, I felt optimistic thinking about the new building where I would be teaching after the summer, and the whole farewell thing was feeling less final.

Together with a coworker I organized one last field trip for the Retail department: a bicycle ride in the dunes and a guided tour of the water-collection area. The team could use a nice day of exercise and fresh air after such a relaxing school year. Most of the faculty joined in. A couple of teachers arranged to meet us afterwards at a pancake restaurant. Pancakes were part of a strenuous excursion like this. Actually, just enjoying nature was the main activity. Talk about stress relief. Standing there smoking a cigarette in the dunes I could not help but think: there is something about the invigorating sea air that simply makes all of my worries disappear.

After a fun and educational tour we brought the rental bikes back and started walking to the pancake restaurant.

Suddenly, my intestines began churning and I was stricken with crippling stomach cramps. I had to find a bathroom quick: I felt like I couldn't hold in all that digested food any longer."

As a precaution, I warned the rest of the group to keep their distance to avoid the noxious gas clouds I was producing. I ran to the most remote clump of bushes. This was a toxic spill the likes of which poor Mother Nature had seldom seen. I was pretty shocked by it myself. That's that, I thought.

But now my body started shaking, and I was sweating profusely. I had no idea what was happening. I was really worried, which only made things worse.

As soon as we got to the restaurant's patio I immediately had to run to the bathroom again. Now I was extremely panicky. I felt dizzy and I was close to fainting. Pins and needles shot through my entire body. It was like an elephant had sat on me and now every cell in my body was asleep. I could hardly breathe.

I returned to the table, pale as a ghost.

The rest of the group was concerned.

"What's wrong with you?"

"I feel like I'm having a heart attack," I gasped. "I need to get to a doctor--fast. Something is really wrong here."

They quickly loaded me into a coworker's car. My smoke break buddy, Jack, took me to his family doctor, who lived in the neighborhood. After a brief examination, the doctor informed me that I had suffered an acute anxiety attack.

"Oh, is that all?" I remember thinking.

I was dropped off at home, where I spent the rest of the day taking it easy.

The next morning I felt fine, so I showed up for our next outing. This one was for the entire staff.

"Peter!" Iris said. "We thought that you were very ill. We sent flowers to your house."

"Everything is fine," I assured her. "My neighbors will sign for the flowers. It's fine."

Like always I simply kept going. I did my best to focus my thoughts on my upcoming vacation in the south of Italy.

I should have listened to my body. The summer vacation should have been good for me, but ultimately I was still in bad shape. The new school year was just around the corner, and I told myself that I was sure to feel better once it got underway. I just needed to see my students again.

The part-time Retail team was scheduled to relocate to our new merger partner's building, too, which meant that all of my work would be concentrated at a single location. A new location, with new people and new opportunities. Finally, I would be rid of all of the homophobic hassles in the past.

Banned

The first day in a new building feels kind of strange. To get to my new workplace I had to walk by the buildings where I had spent the past two years. Now there were different people sitting in our coffee corner. I reminded myself that we would manage to carve out our own comfortable niche in this new school, too.

The entrance to the new building was wide and largely made of glass. You walked into a large space, which at one time had been a public cloakroom. Those were the days when you could still hang up your coat and leave it without a second thought. Times had changed, and chances were that any jacket innocently hung there would be stolen in a flash.

To the left was the copy room, run by my former "dance partner," Freek. We were delighted to see each other again. His decorating style had not changed a bit, I noticed. His workroom was covered with posters of attractive men. You would not want to try that in a classroom, but he was not a teacher, so it was okay.

To the right was a huge cafeteria, with orderly rows of tables and chairs.

To the left was the full-time Retail department and Esat's office. He was formerly Tuncay's assistant. He was now the ethnic minority liaison for this school. For the Turkish students, that is.

To the right was a wide flight of stairs to the other departments and the teacher's lounge. Our department was at the end of the hall. Our office was located past a row of classrooms. Starting today, this would be our new home.

After I put my things on my new desk I walked with Jack to the teacher's lounge. It was big and impersonal. The different teams had separated into their own little groups. I was not in the mood to play musical chairs and spend time at each table in hopes of getting to know the individual teachers.

I recognized at least one person. Erwin had been on the Turkey trip. I knew the people from the full-time Retail program, too. We greeted each other warmly and swapped vacation stories.

Then it was time for a group photo. Only when everyone was gathered outside in front of the school did I realize just how many people worked in such a great big building. When you look at the picture you can't even tell who is who. It was the idea that counted, of course.

The smoking area in the teacher's lounge proved to be not only the haziest but also the most fun place to hang out. It was also the only place where you had teachers from every team. It started out kind of formal, the main topics of conversation being the school and the students, but I was keen on changing that. It did not take long until we were talking extensively about personally and socially taboo subjects.

We had a week before all of the students arrived. That really brought the school to life. I was happy to see my students again. Of course, I had to bring the new kids up to speed on what I considered appropriate behavior in class and at school. The more seasoned students, too, could stand a refresher course.

Just when I was starting to feel at home at the new school I was stopped by Ines, the department head.

"Peter," she said. "I was talking to Carry and she told me that she has seen you using the student restrooms. At this school, faculty members use the restroom next to the teacher's lounge on the first floor. So I would like to ask that you do the same from now on."

"That's crazy," I said. "The student restrooms are right by our office. That's kind of silly to have to go all the way up to the first floor just to take a leak, isn't it? This wasn't a problem at the old building, was it?"

"Carry said that those restrooms are for students only, so remember that."

I thought the rule was ridiculous, and therefore saw no reason to obey it. Still, I wanted to find out whether Carry had really said this. I went to her office next to the teacher's lounge and knocked. A short, brisk, slim woman opened the door. I introduced myself and wasted no time on small talk, asking her whether what Ines had said was true. She confirmed that it was. Teachers were not allowed to use student restrooms. That was the rule.

"But there are only four bathrooms for 80 teachers!" I said. "And they reek, too."

She was unconcerned. A rule was a rule.

For some reason this was really starting to bug me, and I wanted to poll a couple of teachers to find out whether they always used the teacher restrooms. After all, they had worked here for years.

The smoking area was the ideal place for my research. "Ladies and gentlemen," I said, walking into the room. "I have a question. Where do you go to the bathroom?"

A couple of men looked at me like I had just made an indecent proposal, but they quickly saw that I was not trying to provoke anyone. I was not surprised to hear their reply.

"We always use the student restrooms. They are on our floor, and they are the cleanest."

"Carry said that the staff here only uses the faculty restrooms, and I was reprimanded for my choice of sanitary facilities."

"That's nonsense. If that's a 'rule' then everyone breaks it. You only do that if you happen to be in the vicinity of the faculty restrooms."

Apparently no one had ever been busted. In all these years was I really the first teacher who Carry had caught using a student restroom? Or when it came to bathroom visits did she perhaps think that I had to relieve myself in other ways than the rest of the faculty? Of course, there was also the possibility that the male students felt threatened by my presence.

Maybe they had complained. But I had not noticed anything amiss. Okay, the boys hanging out in the restroom talking would usually look at me, and often I would join in their conversations. They were not in my department, but I know a lot of them through my students.

Or was there a new homophobe on my case?

The Applause

Despite the whole "restroom ban" it was a nice school. I simply ignored the bogus bathroom rule. Nobody ever said anything about it again.

I loved arriving at school at eight in the morning and switching on the lights in our department. Jack often got there early, too.

I set up the classrooms for our team and cleaned up any litter left behind by the students. Some teachers, including ones who used our classrooms, sometimes had difficulties enforcing the no eating and no drinking rule in class, let alone the clean up after yourself rule. The janitorial staff cleaned the tables on one day and the floor the next, which meant that I was always finding leftover food or wrappers.

When everything was in order I would join Jack for a cup of coffee and a cigarette. The coffee here did not taste like Frits' but it was drinkable.

I was at this school to teach social studies, business organization and other subjects in the Computer Science department. Business organization was new to me, and I wanted to see the old curriculum. I met my new coworkers and asked them what they expected and which books I should use. It did not take long to get oriented. Apparently it was up to me to choose the books. That was fine with me. After all, teachers need to be flexible.

The subjects that I would be teaching were of no interest whatsoever to my coworkers. After all, the students were really only there for the computer classes.

Par for the course in an assembly line school, the class schedule was wrong. I showed up to teach my first class only to find an old English teacher sitting in my room. The class was full of Turks and Moroccans and a Dutch student who had ended up there by accident.

"This school is bullshit!"

A short Turkish student had stood up and was waving his arms. "Nothing makes sense here!"

The English teacher fled the room.

"You're right," I said loudly, likewise waving my arms. "You are entitled to well-organized education. You pay a ton of money to be here, and you are motivated to pursue a diploma. Of course you should be standing up for your rights. I say go for it. Speak up! Let your voice be heard!"

The students sat there, staring at me in disbelief.

The angry short guy, too, fell silent. He seemed to have trouble deciding whether I was being serious or making fun of him.

That was my introduction to this group.

A week later the schedule had been straightened out a bit and I was able to start teaching.

During the first week, I paid a visit to Tom, the head of the department. I deeply admired his integrity and intelligence.

"You know, Tom," I said. "There is a chance that my sexuality will come up as a topic of discussion in class. If that is the case, would you be opposed to me responding openly?"

"Yes," he said. "I would be opposed. It has nothing to do with the subject you teach. The students do not need to know about it."

I was stunned.

"Are my coworkers banned from mentioning their husband or their wife or their children in the classroom? I mean, none of that has anything to do with what they teach, right?"

"I don't want to discuss this. Homosexuality happens to be a touchy subject among ethnic minorities and you have a lot of them in your group."

I left his office, teaching material in hand and pain in my heart. After all these years nothing had changed.

I was not exactly relaxed at the start of my next class. The Muslims filed in, the aggression and rejection positively radiating from them. I scanned their faces.

"What are you looking at me for!" one of them asked.

"Because you are such a handsome young man," I said.

He shut up.

Every now and then I would hear the usual "ibne" or "zemmel" from the back of the room. I could feel the tension rising. I was not allowed to say anything, but I knew that the situation could get out of hand.

After two tense weeks I had had enough. I never wanted to have to put up with this kind of tension and aggression again.

I began our next class with an announcement. "Guys, everything you think about me is true."

"So you're gay?" one of them asked.

"Yes. I'm gay, *ibne, zemmel, buller, go mang*, you name it, that's me."

They did not register any shock. They must have already known, or at least suspected. And like so many times in the past, I proceeded to give one of my informal gay awareness talks.

The students had lots of questions and I felt that they needed to be answered. And I knew that information was crucial to clearing the air.

After class the group spontaneously broke into applause. I had never witnessed this before.

"Hey, guys, why am I being treated to applause now?"

"Because you are the first teacher to talk so openly about being gay."

From then on absences were seldom and motivation was tremendous. The students would often come to my class and ditch the rest, even though my classes were scheduled at the end of the day during the hours that nobody else wanted. My classes were full. It was not unusual for students to stay after to talk to me about their problems at school or girlfriend troubles. They also really appreciated the fact that I would stop by during their other classes to see how they were doing.

My fellow faculty members had never seen a social studies or business organization teacher act this way. Someone who only taught a couple of hours a week was not expected to behave like this. But how much effort did it take? All it took was a few minutes for me to establish a good rapport for the entire school year.

I was extremely unhappy with my department's policy. I always submitted my grades to the various homeroom teachers but nothing was done with them. Obviously the reasoning was that it would make no difference in terms of whether the students passed.

I had made the unilateral decision that my students were not allowed to get failing grades. If they did, then they had to bring them up; otherwise they would not be allowed to take the final exam. The students faithfully abided my rule.

Even though it was not one of the school's rules, I had made my policy clear at the beginning of the school year. I submitted my grades to the homeroom teachers prior to finals week, indicating which students were eligible to take the exam and which ones were not. Again, nothing was done with this information.

My response was to visit each class during finals week to see whether any of the students with failing grades had managed to sneak in to take the final. Whenever I caught someone I simply asked them nicely to come with me and they humbly obliged. I took my job seriously and I wanted the students to understand that.

I refused to let anyone screw around with me. Of course this was not always appreciated by certain students. Sometimes they got in my face but I refused to let them intimidate me.

Later I found out that students were authorized to take an exam unless they had been refused in advance by an external examiner. It was against the rules to simply pull them out of the room. However, neither I nor the students in question were aware of this. Which was good, because if they had been allowed to take the finals it would have undermined my authority for the subsequent semester. Plus, they most likely would have flunked anyway.

Gay = Sex

"Peter, you just can't show these pictures to the students!" Iris exclaimed.

She and a couple of other teachers were looking at my vacation pictures.

"Although I wasn't intending to share my vacation pictures with the students, I can't help but ask: why wouldn't that be appropriate? You show them yours, don't you?"

"There are men in these."

"Iris, I was in Morocco and I visited family members of my students. Some of these pictures were taken in villages that I visited by myself. The men were really friendly. If I had tried to pose with any women, I wouldn't be sitting here. We're talking about an Islamic culture. Men are allowed to socialize with men. They are not allowed to socialize with women if they are not married to them. You don't know the first thing about their culture, do you? Oh and by the way, none of these pictures are offensive. There aren't any naked men, or sex poses."

"I still think it's best if the students do not see these," Iris said. "I'm only saying this to protect you. The students might make jokes about it."

"I think my students can handle this better than you," I said.

Although I had not been planning on it, of course now I had to show the pictures to my class. Everyone enjoyed looking at them, especially the Moroccan students. They were thrilled that I had visited their country. We discussed the cultural differences with respect to social interaction between men and women. The pictures served as teaching material.

Still, Iris had not properly explained just what exactly the problem was.

A month or so later I was in the car with Daniel on our way to the main building.

"Why does the team always make such a huge fuss about the fact that I'm gay?" I asked.

"Because you are always talking about sex," he answered.

"But I hardly ever talk to you guys about sex! Maybe an innuendo in a joke at most, but I never talk about it explicitly. I can think of another teacher who is way more crude and vulgar."

"Yes, but you are talking about gays. So obviously you are talking about sex."

"But it's not about *sex*! It's a type of relationship. My relationship with my gay friends. Or going out to gay bars. You and the rest just think it's about sex."

Thanks to Daniel I finally got it. He was the first person in all those years to tell me exactly what the problem was. For many heterosexuals, homosexuality was nothing more than sex. In their eyes it had nothing to do with love or affection.

A week later I was in the car with Daniel again.

"My daughter told me to say hello to you," he said. "She asks about you a lot."

"Please, Daniel, do you mind? I just ate. Do you really need to talk about sex right now?"

"About sex?" he asked, stunned. "I'm not talking about sex! I'm talking about my daughter."

"Please, enough, Daniel. I don't want to talk about this. I don't need to know when and where she was conceived. Just stop."

"But I'm not talking about sex!" He was getting angry now. "I'm just talking about my daughter!"

"Oh right," I said. "When I talk about a friend, it's all about sex. When you talk about your daughter or your wife, it has nothing to do with sex."

The car was silent for a few moments. He sat there, thinking.

"I get it now, Peter. It's exactly the same. I'm not talking about sex, and neither are you."

"Finally," I said.

The Islamic Closet

Of course we had gay Islamic students at the school, too. One was in my Salesclerk group. Nizami reminded me of Rico, my former coworker. Short, fat and prone to excessive flitting around and dramatic gesturing. Plus, he never stopped talking. And, like Rico he was determined not to let anyone know he was gay. Even though even the most clueless person in the world would have guessed, it was strictly off-limits to come out and label him gay. The potential consequences were too severe. He would be an outcast in the Turkish community, and there was even a risk of being disowned by his family. That was the worst that could happen. So I had to pretend that I did not know what he was all about. It was up to him to decide whether he wanted to talk to me about it. All I could do was act as someone to identify with.

Judging by the comments from the other Turkish students it seemed pretty clear to me that they knew Nizami was an *ibne*, but they did not openly humiliate or criticize him.

A year later a friend in Amsterdam told me that he had met a Turkish boy who went to my school. He showed me a picture, but I did not recognize the boy. He was definitely not one of my students.

A week later I was standing in the hall talking with Nina, who was the head of my department, when I was approached by a Turkish boy. His mannerisms led me to believe that he was gay.

"Excuse me, are you Peter van Maaren?" he asked.

"Yes," I replied, surprised that he knew my name.

"Do you know Dennis?"

Dennis was the name of my friend in Amsterdam.

"He said to tell you hi."

The boy walked off. He did not look like the guy in the picture that Dennis had showed me, so I assumed that it must have been a friend of a friend.

Not long after the mystery encounter in the hall I attended a Turkish night at the COC. Despite the fact that the event had been organized especially for Turks, most of the guests were Dutch.

I was dancing to the Oriental music when out of the corner of my eye I noticed two Turkish boys make a run for it. Their sudden departure betrayed their intention to slip out unnoticed. I thought I recognized the guy who had told me hello from Dennis.

A half hour later they finally dared to come back inside and they made a beeline towards me. They had come to the club to dance, and it was either come out of hiding or miss out on the fun.

"Aren't you a teacher at our school?" one of the boys asked. I recognized him from the photograph.

"Yes," I said. "But why did you guys duck out?"

"We're scared that you're going to tell everyone. Nobody at school is allowed to find out. Especially the other Turkish guys. Can you please not tell anyone? Otherwise we're going to get in trouble."

I assured them that they had my word, and we were able to carry on dancing and chatting without a care.

About a month later they came up to me in the courtyard after school. They had been waiting for me to show up, and they seemed anxious.

"Mr. Van Maaren, we need to talk to you. A couple of teachers are giving us a rough time, making jokes in class about us being gay. We're angry because nobody is supposed to know about it. There are a lot of Turkish kids in our class and if they start talking we're going to get in a lot of trouble with our parents, our family and our friends."

I could not believe my ears. How could heterosexual teachers be making jokes about something that they did not even know was true? And even if they did know for sure that a student was gay, they should certainly understand that they should keep their mouth shut about it.

I spoke to the teachers in question about the matter. They had no idea their little jokes could have such grave consequences for someone.

The Suicide

Perhaps I was too involved with the students. It could very well be that I went too far. But I believed that my students had already had enough negative experiences in the education system. I wanted them to feel like there was someone on their side. It was time for them to start enjoying school again.

Every morning when I walked through the halls I scanned their faces, I said good morning to them, and I stopped to chat with students. Sometimes students would seek me out to let me know that they were having problems. But I was always sure not to overlook the quiet ones, too, to check whether they were okay. In some cases it was necessary to take a student aside for a private chat in my office right before class. I would arrange to continue the discussion later during the break if we needed more time to discuss the matter at hand.

Despite my alertness and the one-on-one meetings, things went utterly, permanently wrong one time. Merel was a student in the Salesclerk group. The previous school year had been very rough for her after her beloved grandmother became gravely ill. She was very close to her grandmother and was terrified of losing her. There were many times when she would burst into tears and run out of the classroom without any warning.

She was a sweet kid and I felt terrible for her. But she also had a sharp tongue and something wild about her that I deeply admired, too. Merel and I often played a game where we would pretend we were fighting. We would get into these huge play shouting matches. Afterwards, once we had gotten rid of our pent-up energy, we would be back to smiling at each other. But that smile disappeared when her grandmother died. Even though her grandmother's death was not unexpected, it did not make the loss any less profound.

One day I was sitting around talking with a couple of students in the office. Classes were in session and they had a free period. Merel stopped by and announced that her boyfriend had broken up with her. She had gone on vacation with him to Greece but within a matter of days he dumped her and went off with someone else. Lonely and devastated, she had called her parents and luckily they managed to arrange for her to come home early.

Merel sounded calm and collected as she told me the story. Especially considering the fact that she was only 17 years old.

"Anyway," she said, finishing telling me about the breakup, "We agreed that we would still be friends."

"That's revolting," I said. "What kind of a deal is that? He does something low down and dirty like that and you still want to be friends?"

I opened my mouth and motioned with my finger and pretended to vomit. Just kidding around, I thought. This was not the first time I had made the gesture, and she knew it.

"Whatever!" she announced angrily, and stormed out of the room.

I ran after her to tell her that I thought she was overreacting. Right before she reached the classroom I grabbed her by the arm. She managed to pull away and went into class. She took her seat and refused to look at me.

During the break I went outside for a smoke with a couple of the students. She walked past us with a friend and made a show of putting her nose in the air. Again she refused to look at me. It seemed as if she was trying to announce that she was never going to speak to me again.

I figured, just let it blow over, everything will be fine.

The next day I arrived at school to find Iris in a state.

"Listen, everyone," she announced. "I have some terrible news. Merel committed suicide this morning."

I listened, numb. The announcement did not sink in.

"The Victim's Assistance agency called the school," she explained. "Merel threw herself in front of a train. Torn to pieces. Apparently there is nothing left of her that is recognizable."

I listened in shock, still unable to feel any emotion. I was in a haze. A plan was quickly drawn up for addressing the tragedy with our classes. Obviously the students were very upset when they heard the news. The girls especially were crying, and some of them left the room distraught.

In the following days we made cards for Merel's brother Henk and her parents. Two faculty members paid a visit to her parents. They explained that Merel had left a farewell letter that said, "I'm going to grandma now."

Her parents thought that she meant that she was going to visit her grandmother's grave but Henk knew immediately that he had to get to the train tracks. The police met him there. A small comfort to her family was the fact that the initial reports proved unfounded. Her lifeless body was left intact. Only her face had sustained partial damage.

When I heard this, I could put the pieces together rationally, but emotionally I was still numb. I did not feel anything; no sorrow, no grief. It was like my head and my body were no longer functioning as a single entity. Until the funeral.

Together with dozens of students we went to the overcrowded church to pay our last respects to Merel. Her coffin was displayed in the church and surrounded by hundreds of flowers. The other teachers sat together; I chose to sit with the students. I wanted to be there to comfort them if necessary. But during the service I was so overcome with grief that I needed the students to comfort me. I really lost it when the song "Lay your head on my shoulder" by the popular Dutch group Volumia! came on.

After the service everyone had the opportunity to express their condolences to Merel's family at the funeral parlor. I stayed outside with a couple of boys. They did not want to go inside; they could not handle the sorrowful scene.

When Merel's parents and brother walked out I went up to them and introduced myself, and offered my condolences.

"It's nice to meet you," Merel's mother said. "Merel talked about you a lot. She really loved you."

"But obviously I couldn't help her enough; I couldn't get her to choose life instead of death," I said, the tears welling up again.

"You couldn't have prevented this," she said. "She was so unsure of herself. She had been troubled for a very long time. Losing her grandmother was the end of the world to her. We didn't see this coming either. Hopefully she has found peace at last."

A month later I looked up at the sky as I walked out of the building. It was a beautiful sunset, the fading golden orange rays intertwined with bright white clouds. I thought to myself, "Merel, you are with your grandma now. You're okay. It's all over now."

Instantly the tears began to flow again.

I have never managed to get over the fact that despite how closely involved I was with her I was unable to save her. I have tried to remind myself that nobody could have prevented her death, and yet I could not shake that fathomless sense of having failed. And this feeling of utter powerlessness would end up having far greater consequences than I could have imagined at the time.

The Homophobe

I had to travel 30 minutes by train to a different location to teach two Retail groups. Several colleagues had previously taught these kids and had never reported any problems. In fact, by the sound of it they were downright model students. I stepped in the train and headed off to my first day in the classroom with them without any biases or worries.

To my surprise they were plenty biased towards me. They glared at me with contempt and hostility, even though none of them knew me personally. I had never encountered such an unpleasant reception in all my years of teaching. Feeling the insecurity creeping up on me, I introduced myself, called roll and started class.

"Are you gay?" one of the girls asked before the lesson had really gotten underway.

"Why do you want to know that?" I replied.

"Just because. We heard you're…that."

I decided now was not the time to respond to her question in any detail, given the heavy breathing and moaning sounds the boys were making.

"Let's get started with English," I said.

Grudgingly they set to work.

As the class went through the exercises I walked around to see if anyone was having any trouble. The boys in the back had shoved their chairs back against the wall, making it impossible for me to walk behind them.

"Excuse me, boys," I asked in a friendly tone. "May I please get through?"

They acted like I was invisible.

"Move your chairs--NOW!" I shouted at the boy closest to me.

He rubbed his sensitive ears and slid his chair up a few inches. The others followed suit.

But Cobus, a blonde, blue-eyed young man, stayed put, shooting me a dirty look.

It took all the energy I could possibly muster to report to class the next week.

I just knew there would be problems again, and sure enough, there were.

Cobus was the last to arrive. He announced, "I don't want to be taught by some filthy queer!"

"Get out!" I shouted, adding that I wanted to speak to him after class.

"Oh grow up, man," he said. "What's the matter, can't you take a joke?"

"Move it," I said.

He left, but he did not come back after class.

I went up to him the next week in the schoolyard, where he was hanging out with his friends, to have a word with him.

All five of them sneered at me like I was a piece of garbage.

"You better get your act together," I said, "otherwise you are not welcome in my class. Cobus, you did not come back last week. Obviously you are afraid of being alone with me in the classroom. You better shape up or you are out of here."

Later as I was trying to explain something to one of the students during class, Cobus warned him to "stick a cork in your ass. Or better yet, swallow a fork!"

Everyone laughed.

"All of you be quiet. Cobus, get out!"

I had already sent his parents two letters about his homophobic conduct but so far I had not heard anything from them.

The next week, Cobus was the last to arrive in class again. "Are you going to participate in class the way you are supposed to, or are you going to keep up your little act?"

"Aw, shut up, faggot."

"Right, that's the last straw," I said. "I don't want you in class anymore. Your parents will be receiving an invitation for a conference. I do not want to work with you this way anymore."

"Yeah right, like my parents are gonna come," he said, and left.

To my amazement the class fell silent and stayed that way. Everyone proceeded to quietly do their work. Even the boys in the back behaved. Students now even dared to ask questions. I was physically and emotionally devastated, but my angry outburst and Cobus' departure did the class a world of good.

The next day I met with Iris, who was part of the Sexual Intimidation and Discrimination committee. After I finished explaining everything she replied, "Peter, we can't do anything for you. You know that we can only take action on behalf of a student, not a teacher. I am willing to sit in on your conference, but not in my capacity as a committee member."

Although I had a hard time understanding just why this committee had been established in the first place by now, I was happy that she supported me.

Cobus and his father arrived for the conference. Cobus continued to glare at me with contempt.

His father sat there listening to what I had to say. "Excuse me," he said, after I was finished. "May I go outside for a moment? I need a minute to pull myself together. I'm shocked. Shocked."

He got up and left. After a few minutes he returned.

"I would like to apologize for my son's behavior. I have always managed a bar, and our nicest customers were gay. I never had any problems with them. And now I find out that my son is a homophobe?"

He turned to Cobus and said, "You are going to apologize to Mr. Van Maaren. And if you don't, I'm going to pull you out of school and you can find yourself a job. I am not going to pay all this tuition just to have you make your teacher's life miserable."

Cobus offered his "sincere" apologies and promised to never do it again.

He returned to class and did the work. Although we never became friends, I was able to get through the time I had left there.

Multicultural Spitting

You tend to get very spoiled after spending many enjoyable years working with ethnic minority students. The battle with the students over my sexual orientation seemed settled. I got the impression that the Islamic kids I worked with no longer had any problem with me whatsoever. My relaxed openness in combination with the informal gay awareness talks had paid off. Of course, everyone knew me as "the gay teacher." There was no need to sashay around or to announce this in the cafeteria. Everyone simply knew. Even the Turkish students who had been in my Dutch as a Second Language classes would stop by my office with friends and proudly introduce me: "This is my teacher. He's gay!"

One day a group of Turkish girls were sitting on the stairs. Halima, a former student of mine, was among them.

"Hey, teach, how are you?" she asked enthusiastically as I passed them.

"Fine, Halima," I said. "Sorry, I can't stop to talk right now, I'm in a hurry. But you know, right? *Seni sevyorum!*" That was Turkish for "I love you."

The other girls stared at her in shock. I was completely out of line. What I had just said qualified as a mortal sin. It was *haram*.

"No, no, he's *ibne*," she quickly pointed out. "So it's okay."

Her friends were satisfied by the explanation. Giggling, they watched me leave.

It was also fine for me to tell my Moroccan students, boys and girls alike, "*Ana ken hebbek,*" which also means "I love you." Everyone understood how I meant it.

But despite all the good times with my students, I was having a huge problem with the Turkish and Moroccan students in the other departments. Their behavior was irritating and downright threatening.

Every day 10 or so Turkish and Moroccan students would wait outside. As soon as I approached to enter the building they would glare at me and often start spitting on the ground. This was usually followed by utterances of "*ibne*" or "*zemmel*."

Instead of backing down I would walk right up to them and ask, "You guys have a problem with something?"

"Go away, get out of here," was their response.

"Get real," I would tell them. "And knock it off if you don't have any problems with me."

During every break, two guys would always stand in the doorway, blocking my exit. Calmly I would go through the door, throwing them a casual glance. Although I was intrigued by their behavior, at the same time it felt threatening. It was intriguing because it was a new type of power struggle. The threatening part was that I did not feel like I was capable of turning their negative conduct into something positive.

My Turkish students tried to talk to them but their efforts were in vain. Powerless, I began to feel increasingly threatened. I had this strong sense that if I did not take action this could be the end of me. Perhaps I already should have noticed that I was struggling. Where was my fighting spirit? What had happened to the man who was not intimidated easily?

It seemed totally logical to me to ask Carry for help. After all, she was in charge of the school. I told her that I felt threatened on a daily basis by several Turkish and Moroccan students, describing how they spat on the ground when I arrived at school and called me "faggot."

"I can't take it anymore," I told her. "Can you please help me? Let me talk to all of the Muslim students about gay awareness. I have always managed to transform negative behavior into positive behavior by having one of these talks. Give me a large room and I'll do it."

She half-listened to my story and when I was finished informed me: "Peter, you brought this on yourself. You never should have paraded around school on a mission."

I was floored.

Her response made me see red.

"Paraded around? Excuse me, you may have failed to notice, but I am not walking around here in a pink tutu. I look like pretty much any other teacher. The students know about me because they talk to each other, they shared the information. It has been a known fact since 1986. And besides, have you ever given heterosexual teachers this speech, that they aren't supposed to 'parade around'? That they aren't allowed to tell their students that they have a girlfriend, or a boyfriend, or that they are married, or have children? Are they obliged to hand over their wedding ring at the entrance?"

I could feel myself shifting into overdrive, but I was unable to stop, the tidal wave of sheer powerlessness crashing down on me. I was gradually losing my mind.

"Well, Peter," she said, calmly herding me towards the door, "I think this is a good discussion, but I don't have time for it right now. Talk to Esat first. I am not authorizing any awareness assembly."

I stood out in the hall, on the verge of tears. Here I was again, out in the cold. Now what was I supposed to do? Once again, the emancipation group against discrimination would not do anything. Apparently, Article 1 of the Constitution that prohibits discrimination applied everywhere except the school. And obviously it did not apply to gays. I did talk to Esat, but he indicated that he did not think that a gay awareness assembly was a good idea. It would only make waves and cause problems for me and the school. Instead, he asked me for the names of the boys in question, claiming he would discipline them accordingly. By now these elementary school antics had gotten too much for me. Plus, I did not feel that punishment was the only appropriate discipline for this type of problem. Sharing information, or at least a combination of the two, would possibly prove more effective. Unfortunately, nobody except me saw things that way.

Roller Coaster Room

The part-time Retail program was doing better than ever. Enrollment was up and thanks to Jan Pieter's creative management more and more businesses approached us to organize projects. Together with the tourism department, our department raised a considerable amount of extra money for the school by creating business-oriented programs. Happily, there was a little cash left over to spend on team-building, too.

The plan was to go to the Warner Brothers amusement park in Germany for an overnight visit. Daniel was in charge of organizing the trip, and he informed us about the sleeping arrangements during the bus ride to Germany. I was surprised to learn that I would be rooming with Iris and Ines. Sure, they were nice women and fun to be around, but I preferred to be with the men. I checked my clothing, my crotch and my chest and after a brief moment's hesitation concluded that someone had made a mistake.

"Daniel, I think you made a slight mistake. I'm the only man assigned to room with women."

"Is that a problem?"

"Yes. I have roomed with women before, but I want to be with the men this time."

He quickly re-assigned the rooms. My new roommate turned out to be a colleague with whom I regularly clashed. It was not a good idea to put us together unless the idea was to spoil the field trip. Daniel indicated that he would see if he could do anything once we got to the hotel.

The hotel was beautiful and had lots of rustic charm. Out back there was a huge garden with long wooden tables. We sat down and practically everyone ordered beer. I opted for mineral water. During the pleasant drinking session the matter of roommates was once again raised, and now I was assigned to a room with one of the other faculty members. He was a nice guy, I had known him for years and we had always gotten along great. Everything seemed fine.

But when he heard the news he pulled a face and announced, "Even if I have to sit here the whole night guzzling beer there is no way I am sharing a room with him!"

I was perplexed by this intense, negative reaction. Since when had we ever had any problems with each other? To add insult to injury, Iris had the following unsettling announcement to make: "My dear ladies and gentlemen. Daniel has done a fine job arranging a couple of relaxing days for us. However, due to no fault of his, it turns out that all of the even-numbered rooms have a three-quarter bed instead of two single beds."

A three-quarter bed? Was she serious? That was smaller than a standard double bed!

My roommate looked at "our" key and blanched when he saw the even number.

Once pale white, his face quickly turned a sickly grey. He jumped up and ran into the hotel to inspect the room.

Iris burst out laughing. "Ha! Just kidding! The room has two separate beds. Oh man, did you guys see his face?!"

Everyone roared along with her.

I was not laughing. I found the entire incident deeply unsettling and hurtful. I was very insulted. The fact that everyone thought it was so hilarious only made matters worse.

Apparently none of the male faculty members dared to share a room with a gay man. Fear of rectal penetration? In the meantime my roommate was back, and the color had started to return to his face. He laughed sourly.

After this unpleasant incident we adjourned to the dining room for a luxurious meal. Everyone was free to order whatever they wanted from the menu. Despite the delicious food and the pleasant conversation with my colleagues I still had the gnawing feeling that ultimately I was not really part of the gang.

Later that evening I went for a walk with Melita and Daniel. I tried to explain how deeply hurt I felt about the whole sleeping arrangement issue, but my outpouring fell on deaf ears. They told me that nobody had intended any harm, and that I should not let it ruin my fun.

But it was also very difficult to explain just how hurtful it really was. Especially because it was this recurring issue. Every time I thought my homosexuality was no longer a problem I would get slapped in the face again.

The visit to the amusement park the next day provided enough distraction, thankfully. The faculty from the tourism department joined us. They were staying in a different hotel. The Lethal Weapon and Batman roller coasters managed to scramble my brains enough that I was able to start seeing things in perspective again.

During dinner I was back to joking around and socializing with the group. They could have fun with me, just as long as they did not have to share a room with me.

Broken

The school underwent a metamorphosis. It had nothing to do with new construction; it was a series of internal changes. All of the sector heads, department heads, deputy directors and directors were required to take an assessment. Our director had already been suspended for mismanagement. He had made the school out to be wealthier than it actually was. That was how the mergers came about in the first place.

The assessments revealed that many of the administrators were utterly incompetent; they were obliged to find new jobs. This mess caused a great deal of anxiety at school. Nobody knew anymore what the future held in store for us. The school was overrun with interim directors. An official director was hired, too; her official introduction was done in writing. I sat with several other faculty members in the smoking lounge, carefully reading the official letter. "*As of today, Ms. Such-and-Such is the director of this school. She lives with her partner and has two children.*"

"That's nice," I said. "She's a lesbian."

As if on command everyone snapped their necks back and stared at me in shock.

"Where did you get that idea?" someone asked.

"Well," I said, "otherwise they would have said 'husband' or 'boyfriend.' I'm thinking she might be gay. You're thinking she has to be straight. There is room for interpretation that allows each of us to read the letter differently. But anyway, so what? It's not a problem if she's a lesbian, is it?"

Nobody said anything. I suppose by now their opinion should have been obvious.

After five months in the new school I was a total wreck. The acute anxiety attack that I had suffered over the summer should have sent a clear enough signal, but due to some deeply-rooted bizarre Calvinist work ethic I ignored the red flag and simply kept working. "The devil finds work for idle hands," right?

Here, at this remote location, saddled with a difficult group, I could barely make it up the stairs anymore. I had to stop after every four and rest. Normally I would run up the whole flight in one go. Every time I opened the textbook I suddenly had no idea anymore what it was about. Forced to improvise, I sat in a circle with the students and we discussed the subject material. Together we managed to get through it.

One morning I arranged to meet with a new student but an hour later I could remember neither her nor the appointment.

It was late January, early February when it finally hit me. I was supposed to be grading some multiple choice tests. It was utterly impossible to concentrate on the rows of letters. Terrified that I had made dozens of mistakes correcting the tests, I asked my fellow faculty members to re-check them for me. But we were short staffed and there was no time.

I had never experienced a concentration problem of this magnitude in my life. I blamed the pressure at work. I went to see my department head.

"Nina, I'm having trouble concentrating. I'm exhausted and I can't remember faces anymore. I can't even remember what happened an hour ago. What should I do?"

"Let's wait a little bit and see what happens," she said. "Things are very busy here right now. Maybe you'll feel better when it calms down a little."

That was what I expected; after all, I did not seem to have anything physically wrong with me. I was not running a fever. I simply had no energy. And my brain was not functioning properly. It was so bad that sometimes I could not manage to find my house. Once the anxiety attack subsided and I regained my composure somewhere out in the street, I would remember where I was.

I had no idea what had prompted this. Could it be that the death of a close female friend had hit me harder than I thought? Or was it Merel's death, and the feeling of having failed? Or had the endless struggle against the reactions to me being gay finally gotten to me?

After consulting with my regular doctor I decided to see a psychologist.

Within two minutes of arriving at the psychologist's office the dam burst, and I started to bawl. My entire body shook violently. I was engulfed in a flood of tears, snot and saliva. It seemed like it would never stop. Then, 10 minutes later, it was over.

The psychologist said that I would simply need to take it easy for a while. This did not seem necessary to me; after all, I had just cried it all out, right? I had calmed down.

The next day I boarded the train as usual and headed to the energy guzzling site. I had a good group and a not so good group scheduled that day. No sooner had I arrived in the good group's classroom I burst into tears. In between sobs I managed to let them know that my outburst had nothing to do with them and that it was strictly me.

I left the classroom to try to collect myself in the teacher's lounge. But as soon as I got there I went on another crying jag. The other teachers tried to comfort me. None of us, especially me, had ever experienced anything like this. I was usually Mr. Cheerful and seemingly carefree.

As soon as I got myself together I decided to go back to class. I had not even set foot in the room when the waterworks started again. Now I finally got the message. I could not go on like this. I know that I had effectively violated every last boundary. I called Nina to tell her that I was going to be out for a while.

At the time, I figured that I would be fine after a couple of weeks. Ultimately I was condemned to a zombie-like state of suspended animation that would last four years. I was afraid of going outside. I was unable to read. I had trouble speaking. I would sit on the couch for hours. At night I would go out for a walk around the block, shuffling slowly, each step a monumental effort. I tried to take care of any errands early in the morning. Aside from that I basically slept for hours and hours.

I dreamed about my students constantly. There I was, in front of the class, having a great time with them. I juggled three classes simultaneously while my coworkers took a break.

I would have loved to receive get well cards from my students but I never got any, despite begging my former colleagues to help the classes with the project. I wanted to hear how they were doing. They had been the reason for my existence. They had given me energy. They were my pride and joy.

Weeks would go by and the mailman would pass my house but he never had any cards for me. There came a time when I simply gave up hoping. Later I heard that the teachers had instructed the students not to try to get in touch with me.

But guess who actually did come to visit, and to call, to see how I was doing? The Islamic boys from the Dutch as a Second Language class. Even after four years. But my teaching career was over. I was burned out. On 1 October 2001 I finally received my dismissal notice. I was declared 100% unfit to work.

Epilogue

When you spend years swimming against the stream you end up exhausted and you drown. When you always go with the current you might survive.

But what would that really mean, in concrete terms?

It would mean adapting to the greatest common denominator, the heterosexual norm.

I suspect that, in the long run, denying or keeping silent about your personal homosexual orientation would eventually prove just as destructive as swimming against the current.

It would be nice to turn the tide. To be able to function while at the same time maintain your personal identity. But that is impossible for one person to do alone.

This is something that we must solve together as a society.

First of all, the government needs to make sure that Article 1 of the Dutch Constitution, which forbids discrimination on the grounds of religion, gender, cultural background and sexual orientation, is actually enforced. If this is not the case and violations are left unpunished, then the law becomes nothing more than window dressing, and nobody will feel any allegiance to it.

Article 1 led to establishing the Discrimination and Sexual Intimidation committee in the educational system in the Netherlands. I believe that its powers should be expanded. In its current incarnation the committee is tasked exclusively with handling cases involving student allegations against teachers. However, it should also handle cases involving teacher allegations against students, students versus other students, and faculty against faculty. Administrators and faculty need to be aware that students need boundaries. Rules are fine, but they need to be enforced. Rewards and punishment should be given accordingly. This requires actually interacting with the students, and circulating among them. You need to see what students are doing right, and what they are doing wrong. Action must be taken as necessary, in a mature but not necessarily authoritarian way.

Young people understand whether a comment or punishment is justified or unfair. Shouting is not an effective disciplinary technique. When they refuse to do as they are asked, there are other steps that can be taken, and other ways to ask. I have learned from experience that students always want to comply with a request. Regardless of the student in question. Cultural backgrounds have nothing to do with it.

Of course, gender counted for a lot. An ethnic minority student would respond differently to a request coming from me, a man, as opposed to one of my female coworkers. The lack of respect for women played an undeniable role. In these cases a student must be taught that we do not view men and women unequally in the Netherlands. Everyone deserves the same respect.

Also, administrators need to set their fears aside and take care not to assess curricula, classroom interaction, appropriate social conduct or conflict situations through the prism of Islam. Furthermore, they must avoid toning down or changing school rules, curricula or expectations regarding children's behavior in general. Young people want to learn how to function in our society. They want transparency. You should not be afraid of them. When fear is what guides your actions you will be fighting a lost cause.

Administrators must also protect both students and faculty if they need protection. It is wrong to tackle bullying, aggression and discrimination only in cases where a student is the victim. Teachers, too, can be the target. Students should not be led to believe that this is acceptable. Which also means that homosexual teachers, male or female, must not be given a gag order; instead, they must be protected. It may be necessary to organize gay awareness talks in order to do away with prejudices and fears. Not only among the students but also the faculty especially. In my experience this is an effective approach.

The administrators' greatest fear was that Islamic students would leave the school in droves or that their parents would pull them out of school once they found out that a homosexual was teaching. Real-life experience proved that this fear was unjustified. There may be isolated incidents in which this is the case, but some Dutch parents may react similarly due to their particular religious or cultural background. There are always reasons for pulling a student out of school. Societies are constantly in flux, and thus can be changed. Kids absolutely want to be a part of this, but they need guidance, and we must be the ones to offer it to them.

And when I say "we" I mean the parents and the school.

Maybe I was lucky, but I was always able to talk to students about their behavior both at school and outside of school, without ending up with a knife in my ribs. Stories in the news remind me that it could have turned out very differently. But I simply kept trying to avoid letting fear guide me, and it worked every time. When I think about how homosexuality has evolved, I cannot help but notice that many gays retreated into the closet again, either out of fear or due to social pressure.

In theory society seems to have fully accepted them: homosexuals have equal rights, they may not be discriminated against, and they are entitled to get married and adopt children. But we still have a long way to go.

It is good for native Dutch and ethnic minority students alike to learn about the progress that has been made here over the past decades with respect to equal rights for women and homosexuals. When certain behavior threatens this emancipation, it is important to specify boundaries; a task which rests with society, schools and government.

Rewarding the cultural identity of ethnic minorities at the expense of our specific freedoms can have a ruinous effect on the richness of our culture. At the same time, we must not forget that "foreign" cultural expressions can be enriching, too. But these expressions cannot oppress other groups. In spite of everything that happened, the years I spent teaching at the Regional Community College were fantastic. The cultural diversity of my students helped me grow. It was my students that made being a teacher so worthwhile to me. I am sorry that the school refuses to see what I managed to achieve with my students -- regardless of their ethnic background, despite or in fact because of my sexual orientation.

Most of all I am happy that I was able to offer several students the support and encouragement to come out of the closet by their own free will. They felt secure enough around me to take that step. The only way we can change the world and make it a safer place is by working together. The kids have the will to do this. Let us seize the opportunity. The ultimate learning experience is to teach.

Alhamdulillah, thank God.

Peter van Maaren

Acknowledgement

First of all I would like to express my thanks to Siep de Haan at Gay Business Amsterdam for his efforts to help me go public with my story. He informed every media outlet about the dire situation facing homosexual teachers at our nation's schools.

In addition I would also like to thank Stichting Yousuf for encouraging me to put my story on paper. I am grateful to my twin brother Freddie van Maaren, all of my friends and acquaintances for their endless patience in listening to all of my stories. They must be relieved now that everything is finally on paper.

It also took a lot of courage for Wiard, Elina Zonneveld and Fred Bonte to re-live all of these stories. Their hard work and persistence resulted in the book in its final version. Robby Davidson and Jilles van Dam were a great help for the niceties of the English version.

Finally I also thank the government for being more aware and changing the law toward equality for everyone and the gay movement for being watchful on behalf of the LGBTQ community.

Peter van Maaren

Lightning Source UK Ltd.
Milton Keynes UK
UKOW05f1024181115

262995UK00011B/287/P